Australians Don't Take Prisoners

The Great War Diaries of Private Charles Briggs Hardy

Peter Hendy

Connor Court Publishing Pty Ltd

Published in 2021 by Connor Court Publishing Pty Ltd.

Connor Court Publishing Pty Ltd.
PO Box 7257
Redland Bay QLD 4165
sales@connorcourt.com
www.connorcourt.com

ISBN: 9781922449764

Cover Design by Maria Giordano
Cover photograph of Private Charles Briggs Hardy. It was a postcard photograph inscribed on the rear: "To dear Flo and Wal [his sister and her husband] from Charlie, 2nd Coy, 19th Batt, 3rd Contingent, 27 April 1915".

Printed in Australia.

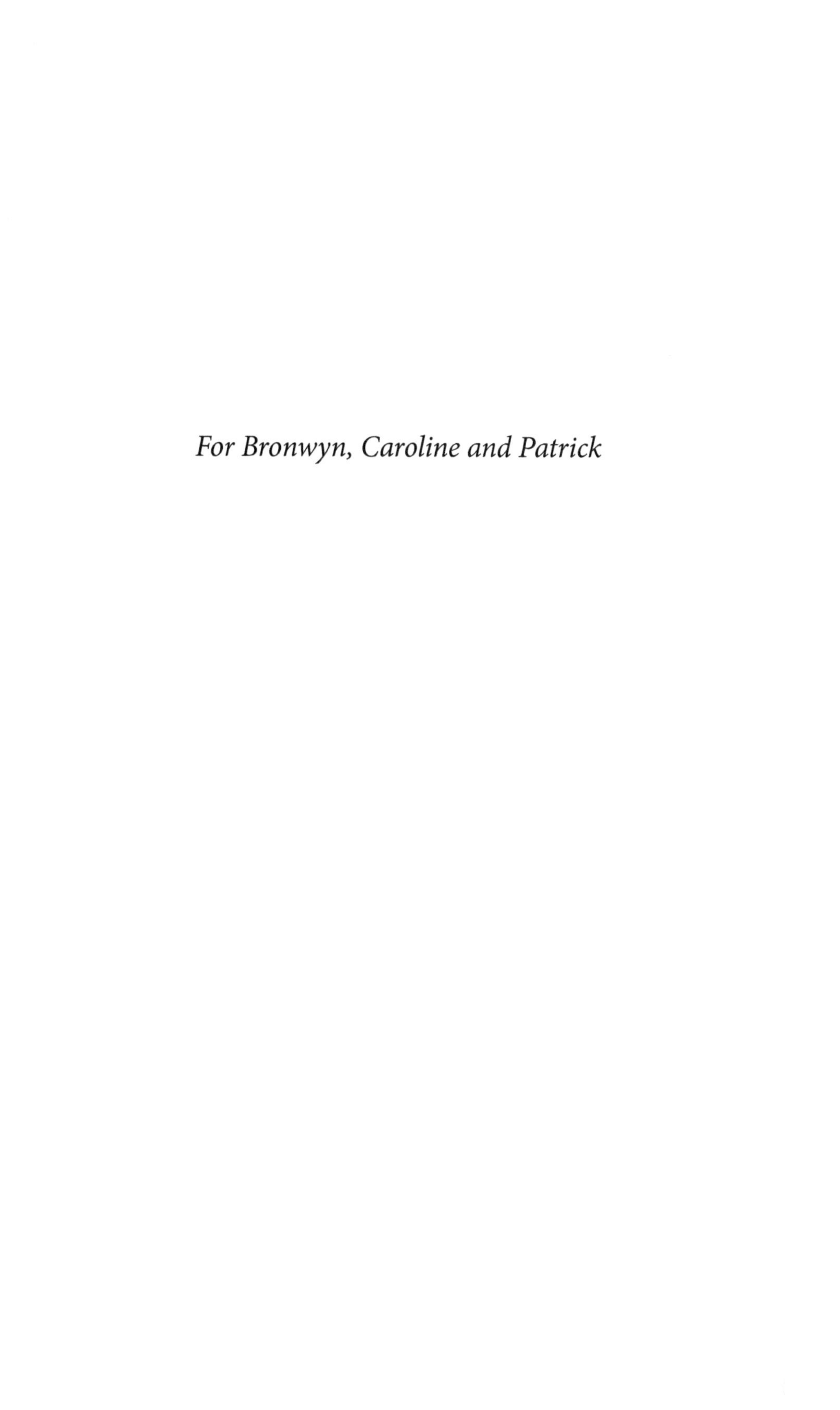

For Bronwyn, Caroline and Patrick

Contents

Foreword

The Hon. Peter Reith AM

Former Australian Minister for Defence

I would like to congratulate Peter Hendy on writing a deftly constructed history of the Great War, that weaves the narrative from a private soldier, fighting in the trenches, into a comprehensive retelling of the War, particularly from the Australian point of view. What he has done is not new. Many authors have, like him, taken the War diaries of former combatants and put them into the context of the wider military campaigns. However, in this case I believe he has done a remarkable job in bringing out the details of a unique, personal story and the accompanying emotional turmoil, set against the backdrop of familiar events.

Charles Hardy, the younger brother of the author's Great Grandfather, fought at Gallipoli and the Battle of Fromelles – two of the most legendary military actions in the annals of Australia's wars. By all accounts, he was a bit of a larrikin but he did his duty. He fought hard, was wounded more than once, and took part in the historic rearguard action at the Battle of Fromelles that saved many – perhaps thousands – of lives. He was surrounded by acknowledged heroes and was along with his mates an unsung hero.

As a former Minister of Defence, I was involved in sending Australian troops into action. These are heavy decisions that weigh on your mind. However, I always knew that our troops would do their duty to their utmost. The book raises the question of the treatment of prisoners of war in the context of the Great War. The author has treated this controversial subject with sensitivity, but also great professional objectivity. While wars have their share of glory, they are brutal, awful things and should always be the last option for a national government. I commend this book and especially hope younger readers can absorb the lessons there are to learn in it – not only about the horrors of war, but also the nobility in self-sacrifice and duty to your country.

Brighton, VIC

Winter 2021

Prologue: August 1915

It was late 1915. The war had already been going for over a year. Not long really. But it was a horrendous year. The toll was already enormous for the young nation of Australia. And young men – really just boys in most cases – had already confronted the worst in human nature. It was only going to get much worse. It was dog-eat-dog fighting and a young man brought up a world away in the friendly surrounds of the beautiful city of Sydney, Australia. was brought to despair and wrote on the first page of his War Diary:

> Allah Allah they yell &
> when they know they are
> beaten they throw down
> their arms and want to
> be taken prisoners but
> Australians don't take
> Prisoners.

Private Charles Briggs Hardy, postcard photograph, 2nd Coy, 19th Batt, 3rd Contingent, 27 April 1915
(reproduced from Hardy Family collection)

1

The Emerald City: 1915

"A sense of humour worth bottling"

Talk to someone whose family arrived in Australia before the post-World War II migrant boom and you will get a story of a father, son or brother who went off to war in 1914-1918 or 1939-1945. Every family was touched – most, if not all, in a devastating manner.

This is the story of Private Charles Briggs Hardy of the First Australian Imperial Force (AIF)[1]. He was mainly called "Charlie" or "Chas" or "Chicka", but sometimes by mates "Snowy", because of his sandy blonde locks. He was my Great Grandfather's younger brother. His granddaughter, Amanda Glen, described him as "a big man with piercing blue eyes and a sense of humour worth bottling. … although he did manage to embellish his stories, if you get my drift".

Charlie was a blacksmith's assistant from Sydney, and was aged 21 when he enlisted as a private in the 19th Battalion in February 1915. He served in Gallipoli and in France. Fortunately for us, he kept a War diary of his time at the front. The diary is moving reading – though some of my great-great-uncle's entries are less than politically correct, as one might imagine from a 21-year-old from over 100 years ago. In the early parts, for example, in August 1915, he is very matter of fact when recording that "Corporal Wilson got his head blown off. He was the first to go down in B Company". And in September, he noted a friend had "died of wounds. Hard luck for Dick". As time passes there are increasingly sad entries, such as: "Today ... I am 22 years old and have never had such a miserable birthday in my life". It is followed by a moving passage from 23 November 1915, where he writes of a nightmare in which he is in the trenches standing next to his younger sister, Rose, whom he then kisses, just before going "over the top" to die.

Private Hardy was wounded at Gallipoli in the Battle for Hill 60 – a "holiday wound", he called it – but returned to the fighting, and took part in continued trench warfare at Pope's Post before the evacuation in December 1915. After convalescence in Cairo and then serving in the Sinai desert, he was shipped to France with B Company of the 55th Battalion. He was wounded again, this time very seriously, at the tragic Battle of Fromelles on the 19 July 1916. Luckily, that was the end of the War for him. He was shipped back to Sydney, married his sweetheart, had four children and lived until 1973. He had a relatively short war but was able to cram into it participation in two of Australia's most legendary military actions.

The book also records the reactions and thoughts of many of his comrades in the 19th Battalion and later the 55th Battalion, who also wrote war diaries and letters at the time or memoirs after the War. They include Private Ernest King in the 19th and Privates Robert Harpley (B Company), George Gill, Herbert Harris, Herbert Allen, Frank Brown and Lieutenant Percy Chapman (B Company) in the 55th; and others like Sergeant John Park the 4th Field Company Engineers, Sapper William Smith of the 14th Field Company Engineers, and Sergeant John Falconer of B Company, 18th Battalion.

Gallipoli was a costly miscalculation and a strategic blunder. Over eight months there were 28,000 casualties. The Battle of Fromelles was that dreadful initiation for the Australians to the Western Front in France. Over 5,500 Australians became casualties, almost 2,000 of them were killed in action or died of wounds and some 400 were captured. This is believed to be the greatest loss by a single Australian Division in 24 hours during the entire First World War. Many consider the Battle of Fromelles the most tragic single event in Australia's history.

My mother was May Hardy, Charlie's great niece, and she spent her childhood in Sydney not far from where Charlie was born and lived. I'm not so sure they knew each other. I can't ask my mother as she has passed on. My mother's younger sister, who is now in her eighties, has no recollection of Charlie although she remembers his younger sister Rose. Indeed, as a young woman, down from the country, Iris lived with Auntie Rose in Sydney. Rose is mentioned many times in Charlie's War diaries. Cousins reckon that Charlie had very little to do with the wider Hardy family in Sydney after World War I. Maybe it was an estrangement caused by some now forgotten family squabble or maybe it was directly related to what we now call post-traumatic stress disorder (PTSD). Certainly, more than one family member has vague memories that this was whispered about in family get-togethers. That would hardly be a rarity. Robert Hardy, a cousin, relates how his father, Alwyn (who was Charlie's nephew and is mentioned in one of Charlie's wartime letters), suffered from his time in the Second AIF in Papua New Guinea in World War II. A manifestation of this was that there was to be "no talk of war" in the household and if ever a war movie appeared on television – a standard fare for decades in post-War Australia – it was immediately switched off.

When the Great War, or World War I, began in 1914 Australia had not even reached a population of five million. Sydney, the largest city on the continent, had a population of around 720,000, or roughly 40 percent of the population of the State of New South Wales, of which it was the capital. At the time the city had for the most part been prospering well since the last downturn around 1906.

Sydney started as a British penal colony, housing convicts who had to be diverted from North America after the British lost its war with the Americans. However, that had been in 1788. Some 126 years later it was a growing town that had electric street lights (but not in domestic homes just yet), railways, and was the principal international port for New South Wales' pastoral products of wool, wheat, meat, and butter. Although, despite all its modernity, it remained a country and economy that was at the mercy of Mother Nature. Due to drought in 1914, the whole wheat harvest from the southern part of the state was lost.[2]

As a proud city in the British Empire, it is not surprising that most of the rural produce was destined for Great Britain. Australians also prided themselves on their sporting prowess and, in 1914, the Australian Norman Brookes won Wimbledon and at home there was keen interest in horse races like the Melbourne Cup, rugby league and Australian Rules Football. They also had a vibrant domestic film industry with a favourite at the time being "Neath Australian Skies" starring Lottie Lyell and produced by Raymond Longford.[3]

However, the War was having an impact on Sydney, even from the earliest days. "From August to December 1914 trade exports were reduced by £6.5 million. The shortage of ships and war time restrictions, combined with the effects of drought, hit home".[4] There were increases in unemployment and without today's generous social welfare safety net too many families were going hungry. To top it all off, these conditions may have sparked recurrence of a smallpox epidemic in Sydney that year.

Before going to Charlie's personal adventure, it is worth summarising the Great War as it played out, and understand some of the key motivations for the actions, over the four years from 1914 to 1918.

The Great War formally began when the Austro-Hungarian Empire declared war on the Republic of Serbia on 28 July 1914 in the wake of the assassination by Serbian sympathisers of the Empire's heir to the crown, Archduke Franz Ferdinand, four week earlier. The Balkans had long been seen as a simmering cauldron of conflict and, indeed, the famous German statesman, Otto von Bismarck, had previously told a younger colleague: "I shall not live to see the great war. But you will see it and it will start in the East".[5]

The next day the Government of Great Britain, sitting in the Empire's capital of London, informed Dominion governments (including the Commonwealth of Australia) that war was imminent. The timing was awful. Australia was in the middle of a national election campaign. In response, the then Prime Minister, Sir Joseph Cook, said in Horsham on 31 July that "all our resources in Australia are in the Empire and for the Empire, and for the preservation and security of the Empire" and the Australian Labor Party Leader (and soon to be the new Prime Minister), Andrew Fisher, famously declared on the same day at a speech in Colac that Australians would defend Britain "to our last man and our last shilling".

Australia began preparing for war and started mobilising the navy and raising a force of 20,000 troops. Things then only accelerated. When Germany invaded Belgium on 4 August, that triggered the involvement of the British Empire. Great Britain had a defence treaty with Belgium, guaranteeing its security, going back to 1839. This was an important geopolitical issue for the British as they depended on Belgian and Dutch ports as their primary access to lucrative European markets. Thus, on 4 August, the British Government declared war on Germany and as a part of the British Empire that meant that, both legally and de facto, Australia was also at war.

Irrespective of the declaration of war, Australian democratic processes continued and the election was held on 5 September 1914. Indeed, not only does it show that the Australians were truly wedded to their democracy by proceeding with the election in the face of this unprecedented emergency, but there was to be a peaceful transition from the Liberal Government of Prime Minister Cook to a new Labor Party Government led by Fisher.

Within days, Australia dispatched a force to capture German New Guinea just across the waters north of the Australian mainland. This occurred over the period 11 September to 8 January 1915. This meant that, on behalf of the British Empire, Australia took part in some of the first military actions of the worldwide conflict. Equally, it is not unimportant to note that the first Australian military action was against the Germans in the Pacific as they were particularly worried about securing their trade routes in their area of the world.

Of crucial significance for Australia's part in the War, the Ottoman Empire in Turkey entered the conflict on 29 October 1914 on the side of the Central Powers, allying itself with the German and Austro-Hungarian empires. This led to deliberations at the highest governmental levels in the British Empire. While Australia had been recruiting men to go to Europe to fight against Germany, it was decided, in consultation with the British Government, that the Australian troops would first go to the Middle East to help secure the all-important Suez Canal. The canal was a trade lifeline between Britain and its Empire in the Asia-Pacific, which included Australia, India, Burma, the Malayan States, New Zealand and more. Thus, the first contingent of the First AIF left Australia on 1 November 1914 to arrive in Egypt on 3 December. Indeed, only a month later, on 26 January 1915, the Ottomans (led by a German officer, Colonel Kress von Kressenstein) raided the Canal with 20,000 troops. This was eventually repelled on 4 February. Further minor skirmishing occurred until the Gallipoli Campaign began.

The landings at Gallipoli occurred on 25 April 1915. Tragically, not long after this, the commander of the AIF, Major General Sir William Bridges, died of wounds at Anzac Cove on 15 May 1915. Furthermore, a famous figure at the landings, Private John Simpson (who used his donkey to stretcher wounded men to safety), was killed on 19 May. On that day, the Turks started a new offensive.

Struggling to defeat the Turks, on 6 August 1915 the British landed more troops at nearby Suvla Bay, with a coordinated attack over the next two days by Australians at Lone Pine and also at the Nek. The Battle for Hill 60, which was effectively a continuation of these battles, occurred later in August. None of this worked and a stalemate occurred with continual trench warfare. By the end of the year, on 19-20 December 1915, all but a few British Empire troops, including the Australians, were withdrawn from the Gallipoli Peninsula. I will have much more to say on the Gallipoli Campaign in Chapter 4.

Over the course of the first six months of 1916 the bulk of the

Australian troops were diverted to the Western Front in France. Meanwhile, back in Australia there had been some major political manoeuvrings and Prime Minister Fisher had resigned on 26 October 1915 to become the High Commissioner (ie Australian Ambassador) in London and William Morris Hughes became Prime Minister. Hughes also left for London on 16 January 1916, arriving there on 3 March, participating in the Imperial War Cabinet and attending the Economic Conference in Paris on 14-17 June. He arrived back in Australia on 31 July 1916, where he remained Prime Minister for the duration of the War. He was particularly absorbed in the struggle to increase AIF recruitment and embroiled in an unsuccessful fight for conscription that will be further referred to in a later chapter.

The Allied nations begin the Battle of the Somme against the Germans, on 1 July 1916, and, as part of this wider offensive on 19-20 July, the Australian 5th Division was committed to an attack at Fromelles. This was an utter failure but was followed up a few days later on 23 July by the Battle of Pozières. This battle lasted on-and-off until 4 August and was followed by the Battle of Mouquet Farm between 10 and 14 August. In the space of less than seven weeks the AIF suffered some 28,000 casualties, more than the total in the entire eight month campaign at Gallipoli.[6] These battles were so devastating to the Australians that for the remainder of 1916 they were not committed to any major battles on the Western Front. They were assigned to so-called quiet sectors. However, they still suffer many casualties in the never ceasing trench warfare. For example, there were 2,754 casualties in September, 1,441 in October, 4,772 in November and 1,694 in December. That makes a total of 10,661 casualties in four months in so-called "quiet" sectors.[7]

As we will see, Charlie's war service had ended by this stage. However, it is worth giving a summary account of the remainder of the Great War to understand the historical context.

The War continued and by early 1917 much had happened. The Russian Czar abdicated on 16 March and on 6 April the United States declared war on Germany. However, while US troops started entering the line in October 1917, it was not until 27 May 1918 before they first entered battle in France or for the Russians to finally surrender to the Germans at Brest Litovsk (on 3 March 1918). Meanwhile, in France the British 3rd Army began an attack at Arras on 9 April 1917; the first Battle of Bullecourt occurred on 11 April; and the Second Battle of Bullecourt began on 3 May. The French Army mutinied on 4 May 1917; the Battle of Messines began on 7 June; the Third Battle of Ypres began on 31 July; the Battle of Menin Road occurred on 20 September; the Battle of Polygon Wood on 26 September; the attack on Broodseinde Ridge on 4 October 1917; and the Battle of Passchendaele began on 12 October 1917. Many of Charlie's mates would die or be seriously wounded in these various battles. Those to whom he refers in his war diaries are remembered in this book.

More was to come. In a last gasp the Germans mounted an offensive at Arras on 21 March 1918, but without any great headway. Australian troops had an historic success when they captured the French town of Hamel on 4 July 1918. The end was now in sight. The British (including the Australians who by now had their own separate Army Corp) launched an offensive at Amiens on 8 August and then proceeded to attack the German "Hindenburg Line" on 18 September. The German Army was brutally pushed back many miles towards their own borders over many months of grinding battle. Finally, an armistice was signed – firstly with the Austro-Hungarians on 3 November and then the Germans on 11 November 1918 – and the horrendous war concluded.

The Great War was, indeed, a horrendous experience for Australia. It accounted for 61,591 Australian deaths. In all its wars, starting with the Sudan conflict in 1885 and including World War II, Korea, and Vietnam, Australia has suffered a total of over 102,000 combatant deaths. So even today the Great War represents some 60 percent of all Australians killed in action. The total number is not as large as that for other Allied combatant countries. For example, Great Britain lost some 744,000 killed in the War. However, in Australia's case deaths as a proportion of active combatants is one of the worst for all countries. The reason for this is that an overwhelming majority of Australian troops ended up in front lines. The myriad administrative and logistics backup jobs for the Australian Army were for the most part provided for them by the British Army. It should be remembered that the Australian Army was simply a component part of this larger force. Therefore, a higher proportion of the Australians were available for active duty facing the enemy in the trenches. Unfortunately, that meant a higher casualty rate. Thus, the overall casualty rate for Australians was 64.98 percent compared to 59.01 percent for New Zealand, 50.71 percent for the British Isles, 49.74 percent for Canada, and 12.77 percent for India.[8]

Australia was only formed as a nation in 1901, when six separate British colonies federated together. For Australians, the crucible of Gallipoli, together with other theatres of conflict in the Great War, is seen as the real start of the national spirit. It was a cathartic event that fostered the culture of mateship and the bringing together of all the people. Charlie Hardy's story is just part of all that.

2

Liverpool Barracks: 1915

"If killed please inform my sister"

When he lined up at Liverpool Barracks on 8 February 1915, all he knew for certain was that he was excited. He didn't really know how he would fit in. Nor did he know much about a lot of things.

Charlie Hardy was well educated for a tradesman. However, he had no grand pretensions to be an office worker or the like. He was a French polisher, having become so after leaving school. His family included solid middle class citizens of the British Empire and their wives. So he had received a good education. Indeed, his father and his father's father before him were quite well-off grocers and merchants, owning much property around Sydney. The Sydney chapter of their lives had started in 1866 with farmland in the French's Forest area of the North Shore of the magnificent Sydney Harbour. If the family had had the foresight not to sell this property at the end of the 1940s (as they actually did) they would have become very rich indeed, as the Sydney property boom went on and on from decade to decade.

The Hardy family had originally come to the Australian continent from the industrial centre of Birmingham in England, via the British Colony of Victoria in 1856. They had joined the famous Gold Rush which made Victoria, for a time, the richest province on Earth. It is not clear that they had any success on the goldfields – almost certainly not. However, they worked hard and eventually lived in the raucous Melbourne suburb of Collingwood until ten years after arriving on the great southern continent the whole extended family upped stumps and move to the emerald city of Sydney. No doubt they were motivated to try to make their fortune there. They had cousins in Adelaide in the Colony of South Australia who included Arthur Hardy the richest man in the colony. That is until a property boom and bust ended the high life. That side of the family included some quite notable people including Arthur's sister Harriet who, back in England, married the enormously influential liberal philosopher, John Stuart Mill. Whether Charlie was ever aware of this is not clear. Certainly, the South Australian Hardys knew of their poorer Eastern cousins. Harriet's brother, Edward, in one of his letters is "scornful about a cousin John [Charlie's grandfather] who had gone to the gold diggings in Victoria 'but has done no good and is now a navvy or something of the sort'".[9]

Charlie stated in his army signing-on papers in 1915 that he was a blacksmith's assistant. Although in years hence, as far as his family knew, he had always been a French polisher – even before the War. He was 21 years old, having been born at Cottage Hospital at Manly, a Sydney suburb.

Charlie was to be eventually assigned the number 569 and allocated to B Company, 19th Battalion of the 5th Brigade of 2nd Division of the AIF. [CBH 1 A, ie sourced from Charles Briggs Hardy diary "1", page "A", see Bibliography]

B Company was initially led by Major Victor Sampson and Captains Francis Coen and Ivan Sherbon. The Battalion commanding officer was Lieutenant Colonel William Mackenzie.[10]

Major Sampson had an imposing list of given names – Victor Horatio Buller Sampson. Prior to joining the 19th, he had served as a lieutenant in the ANMEF in New Guinea in 1914 and since then had rapidly risen to the rank of Major. Before the War he had been a clerk living at Bringelly, NSW, although he had also been a junior officer in the Australian Garrison Artillery.[11] Captain Francis Coen was a barrister from Yass, NSW.[12] Captain Ivan Sherbon was from Forrest Lodge, NSW, and was a wool branch clerk before the War.[13]

Lieutenant Colonel William Kenneth Seaforth Mackenzie was also a barrister from Sydney. He had 14 years' experience in the Citizens Military Force, rising to be the Lieutenant Colonel in charge of, first, the 1st Battalion of the New South Wales Scottish Rifles, and later, the 25th Infantry.[14]

The Battalion was principally made up of men from New South Wales. Charlie joined a Battalion of some distinction, for it harked back to the original regiment created by the then New South Wales colonial government in 1860. This contingent was originally called the 1st Regiment New South Wales Rifle Volunteers (The South Sydney Volunteer Corps). After Australian Federation of the six British Colonies in 1901 it was renamed the 1st Australian Infantry Regiment. However, Australia had adopted strict rules about how their Army could be used and at the start of the Great War, the *Defence Act (1903)* did not provide for sending conscripts overseas. As a result, an all-volunteer force was created – the Australian Imperial Force – which was separate from the domestic defence force and the existing regiments.

There was a rush to recruitment across the country. In 1914 alone some 52,560 young men had volunteered, while, along with Charlie, another 18,590 enlisted in the first two months of 1915.[15] They were the cream of the Australian manhood. During the War, 38.7 percent of all Australian males aged 18 to 44 made up the total enlistments of 416,809. It was 39.8 percent in New South Wales.[16]

Even though the war was only in its early stages, many men of the 19th Battalion had already seen action in German New Guinea in 1914 as part of the original Australian Naval and Military Expeditionary Force (ANMEF).[17] The expedition was a strategic success but there were also reports of widespread looting. Indeed, it was so bad that two weeks after Charlie signed up to the battalion it can be supposed that he and his mates weren't happy to hear that the Federal Government set up a court of inquiry into the events.[18] By March 1915 the ANMEF were back in Australia and the newly minted veterans were distributed amongst the newly created 17th,

18th and 19th Battalions to form an experienced core in each. Upon its establishment the 19th Battalion was allocated to the 5th Brigade, part of the 2nd Division AIF.

The 19th Battalion was formally established on 3 March 1915 in Liverpool. The basic training regime took four months and was principally conducted at the Liverpool Camp, 32 kilometres or 20 miles south west of Sydney. A lot more training would occur in Egypt before they were sent into battle. It does not appear that Charlie began his diary until he embarked on ship for the other side of the world. He records nothing of the training, which could be harsh. In fact, in late 1915, albeit after Charlie had left the camp, a Royal Commission was set up to investigate the poor conditions at the Liverpool Camp. Recruits faced "inadequate accommodation, appalling food, boredom and lack of leave … . They lived in 'bell' tents, sleeping on the bare ground or on palliasses (sacks filed with straw). … The hours of work were from 6.00am until lights out at 10.15pm and all visitors to the camp had to be gone by 8.00pm".[19] A riot took place over conditions involving a large number of soldiers on 26 November 1915 in which a light horse trooper died from a gunshot wound and several soldiers were injured.

The 19th Battalion sailed from Sydney Harbour on 25 June 1915 on His Majesty's Australian Troopship (HMAT) *Ceramic*. The former Steam Ship (S.S.) *Ceramic* was a large cruise ship with the capacity to carry up to 2,800 troops. It was owned by the White Star Line, the same owners of the ill-fated S.S. *Titanic* that sank just three years earlier. Also, like this more famous cousin, the *Ceramic* was built at the same Belfast shipyards. On this occasion the bulk of the passengers were from the 18th and 19th Battalions.

We know from the diary of Sergeant John Falconer,[20] who was in the 18th Battalion and also boarded the ship that day, that the departure was a great celebration involving thousands of cheering crowds lining the streets of Sydney. The troops started with Reveille in the dark at 5.00am, they then marched to the railway station in Liverpool. From there they took the train at 8.00am to Central

Station in Sydney. In front of a delirious crowd, the troops of the two battalions then marched slowly to Woolloomooloo wharf on Sydney Harbour.

According to Private Edward Lynch of the 45th Battalion, who similarly marched through the streets of Sydney the following year:

> Through flag-bedecked streets we go ever onward. The windows and roofs of shops are gay with bright flags and pretty, laughing girls. The crowds line the footpaths happy in the *bon camaraderie* of their farewell to us. … [A] shower of halfpennies lands amongst us, thrown from the roof of a big verandah. We break step and formation as we battle for those halfpennies, for glued to each is the address of a girl. Most of us collect girl's addresses as a hobby these days. We seize the halfpennies, wave to the roof of girls as we fall into step with our mates and forward again as the girls wave and *coo-ee*.[21]

Charlie's battalion eventually boarded the ship at 1.00pm. After they had settled in, the ship steamed out of the Harbour at 5.00pm. That is the last that Charlie would see of his home town for the best part of three years.

What follow are extracts from Charlie's principal War Diary and an accompanying second diary he kept on a pocket note pad. There are also a number of letters that he wrote during and after the War that are quoted in this book. The principal War Diary that Charlie began was A5 in size and leather bound with the words "Where is it" embossed in gold lettering on the cover. He was to have a quirky style of writing. Punctuation was not one of his strong suits and he seemed to capitalise words that would not normally require it. His spelling was often shy of the mark but it was normally clear what places and people he was writing about. In what follows, I have left his style and spelling alone as much as possible so the reader can appreciate what it looked like. However, I have also taken the liberty of editing where required to allow the sentences to make sense. Nonetheless, I have striven to ensure that on no account have

I manipulated the text to change Charlie's original meanings (as I could discern them). He also had a haphazard way of recording his memories. He was no disciple of chronological order and many of his entries are not dated. Sometimes his entries – like when recording the end of the war – are put on pages that are in the middle of the diary entries that are otherwise noting the events of years before. It appears that he literally grabbed the diary, often while sitting in the front line trenches, opened a page and began writing. A lot of my time in compiling this book was spent in ensuring that the events as related were dated accurately or as near to as accurately as possible. Lastly, the two diaries and the letters are almost completely written in pencil and thus often hard to read over 100 years later. That creates its own problems for research. There are some notes written in ink. They, sadly, principally appear to be notations added after the War noting when and where a mate mentioned on any particular page may have died as the War progressed. Very sad, indeed.

So to begin. The diary starts with a somber entry. He recorded in his diary on the first page:

> If Killed
> Please Inform
> My Sister
> Mrs W.A. Lawson
> 96 Bligh St
> Newtown
> Sydney
> NSW
> Australia. [CBH I 1]

From there he embarks on a journey of a lifetime. As Charlie noted in his diary:

> Left Sydney by S.S. Ceramic
> on the 25th of June and
> our first stop was

Melbourne where they left
our first Mail & then
Pushed on. We then struck
the [the Great Australian] Bight where it was very
cold & Rough. Mostly all
the boys were sick [However] all I
was sick of was stewed
Rabbit & Prunes. [CBH I 142]

They sailed firstly to Melbourne, but did not dock, and then came the four to five week trip to the Middle East. The distance was some 9,989 nautical miles.

Charlie was interested in what was occurring around him, as he catalogued what had been happening in the War up until that date:

1914

July 28th Austria against Serbia
Aug 1st Germany [against] Russia
Aug 2nd Germany at war with Belgium
Aug 3rd Germany against France
Aug 4th Great Britain [against] Germany
Aug 10th France against Austria
Aug 12th Great Britain [against] Austria
Aug 23 Japan against Germany
Nov. 5 Great Britain v. Turkey

1915

May 23 Italy against Austria
Oct Bulgaria against England [CBH I 156]

Sergeant John Falconer of the 18th Battalion tells us that the journey was smooth and that they ate well – three full meals a day with three courses each time. They would not be so well fed when they were in the trenches. Falconer says that the journey was dominated by training, adding:

> We quickly fell in to the routine of life on board a troopship and everything went well for some time. Our Regimental band was beautiful to hear of an early morning or an evening, playing all the latest airs, both comic and sentimental. Our routine consisted of early morning parade of physical exercises, then breakfast followed by a parade in the morning of rifle exercises or bayonet fighting. After dinner parades were held daily, with the exception of Saturdays and Sundays, then we had lectures consisting of first aid, military work and life in Egypt. Sunday mornings and evenings were held Church Services, which were welcomed on board.[22]

It is worth noting that there was genuine danger in the transportation of troops by ship. Of course, there was the ever present danger from the weather. However, there was a significant submarine threat. In fact this very ship, the S.S. *Ceramic*, was the subject of a number of attacks during the War, but thankfully was able to survive. In May 1916, on one occasion, it was carrying some 2,500 troops (as it was on this journey that Charlie was undertaking). On the day in question two torpedoes from a German U-Boat narrowly missed the ship. Later, on the 9 June 1917, a similar event occurred in the English

A40 HMAT *Ceramic* boarding troops of First AIF, Melbourne, December 1914 (reproduced from National Anzac Centre extracted at nationalanzaccentre.com.au on 13 August 2020)

Channel and on 21 July 1917, off the Canary Islands, she saw action against a surfaced German U-Boat. On this occasion she fired at the submarine in retaliation and was able to outrun it.[23]

It was not all smooth sailing, for while there were no U-Boat attacks, sickness was ever present. As Charlie noted:

> Had misfortune to bury five
> men at sea. Between Melbourne
> & Port Suez on the
> HMAS Ceramic [CBH I 29]

3

Egypt & Sinai Peninsula: 1915

"No more a toy soldier"

Egypt was a completely alien experience for the boys from Sydney. It was here that they would continue their training under the harsh sun and soaring temperatures. Their initial impressions were in many cases what you would expect for young colonial men living over 100 years ago. Their views on race relations were not what we accept today with their lack of respect for the local Egyptians considered intolerable in our age. However, Charlie's diary is not as scathing and confronting as that of his contemporaries, who were also writing war diaries at the time.

Charlie reports in the diary:

> Left Liverpool [New South Wales] on 25th June 1915 for Egypt. [CBH I 91]

> Our next
> stop was Aden to Receive
> Orders Very Hot & the
> Country is very barren [CBH I 142]

After so many weeks at sea, unfortunately their stay at the Port of Aden on the tip of the Arabian peninsula, in what is now Yemen, was to be only one hour while they received their orders. However, there were some sights to see:

> The natives amused us
> very much no sooner
> had the anchor [gone]

down they went [and]
tied up to the side of our ship
then the fun started.
The boys heaved loaves of
Bread at them
they didn't seem to mind
they all had something to sell us
Silks & sweets feathers Post cards &ct [CBH 142-143]

Nonetheless, Charlie's character assessment of some of the locals was far from flattering:

And Robbers they beat a Path Hollow. [CH 143]

But they still had 1,781 nautical miles to go. Firstly, they reached the Port of Suez in Egypt on the northern extremity of the Gulf of Suez and at the southern entrance to the Suez Canal, at 4.00pm the next day.

Now in Red Sea & its still Hot
Suez was our next stop where we
stayed about 24 Hours. [CBH I 142]

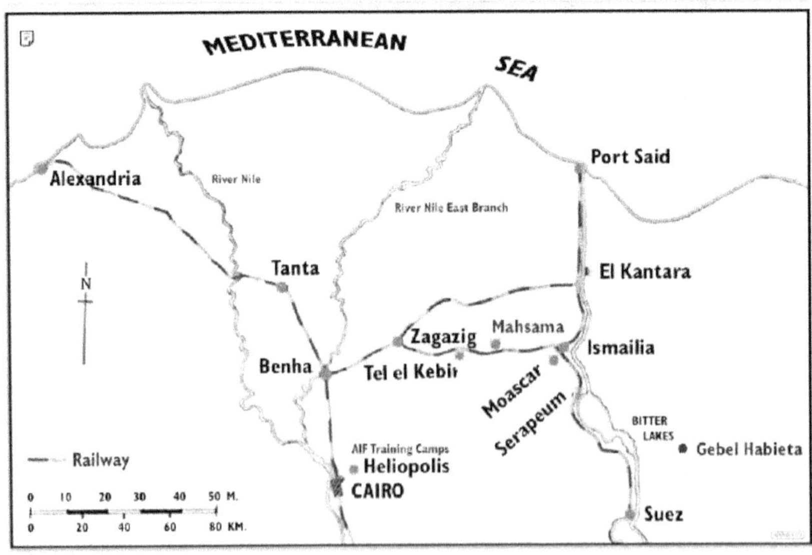

Egypt, 1915-1916
(reproduced from Matthews and Wilson 2010, Research Disk)

They then departed for a four-day sail through the famous Suez Canal.

> We then left for the Suez Canal where it was full of interest to us.
> We passed all sorts of French War vessels
> we both Exchange Cheers I thought we would be heard in Sydney.
> Our next stop was Port Said where the natives coaled our ship
> they opened my eyes so they are the fastest coalers in World. [CH 143]

As he noted:

> They never stop to eat. They keep going all the time yelling & singing some ragtime noise. [CBH 142]

While it was good to have some entertainment the men were still not permitted to disembark and go ashore at Port Said, at the northern entrance of the Suez Canal and on the Mediterranean Sea. However, some men decided to enjoy their first, limited taste of freedom from the confines of the ship. Although, some men went too far:

> Some of the Boys swam ashore and get Pinched.
> I had swim but didn't
> go ashore. [CBH 142]

But maybe the reason Charlie didn't go ashore was less out of goodness. He noted:

> we then had more Rogues trying to Rook us. [CBH 142]

As he was to summarise the journey later:

> Called at Port Suez & stayed a
> Night left for Port Said &
> Stayed about 24 hrs [CBH I 116]

At Port Said he noted:

> Had good swim at Port Said
> Opp[osite] the offices of the Suez Canal [CBH I 116]

And soon after they departed:

> We left there to proceed to Alexandria where we arrived the next day & we meet more thieves & the way the police
> banged the latrines about would make you burst
> your sides laughing at them. [CBH 142]
> Landed in Egypt on 24th of July [CBH I 91]
> Had good swim off ship at Alexandria
> Around about me at present
> there are thousands of captured
> Turks. [CBH I 3]

Alexandria, which was on the western side of the country, is Egypt's main and busiest seaport on the Mediterranean Sea. It was here that a significant event was to occur for the troops of the 19th Battalion. As Charlie notes:

> Ammunition was issued out today.
> No more a toy soldier. [CBH I 3]
>
> we then Entrained for Cairo and was
> in camp 3 weeks before we
> left for Dardanelles. [CBH I 116]

Thus, HMAT *Ceramic* reached its final Egyptian destination at Alexandria on 24 July 1915. The troops were disembarked the next day and by 5.00pm were on a train to Heliopolis, which was a northern district of Cairo. They arrived there on Wednesday 28 July.

The troops were "issued with tropical equipment that included shorts and pith helmets, a welcome break from the heavy khaki uniforms designed for European use".[24]

Charlie continued his narrative, expressing criticism of the Egyptian railways:

> We now [continued]
> & it took Nearly all day
> to get us into the dog Boxes

I mean The Egyptian State Railways they are
equal to our goods [freight] trains
in Australia. [CBH 142]
We arrived at Cairo [after] about
6 Hours run & was shunted
about & We got out of the
Boxes at Zeitoun [a district of Cairo] where we
marched to our camping
Ground Heliopolis where
we first got taste of sand & Discipline [CBH 141]

Heliopolis is about 10 kilometres from the centre of Cairo and was a suburb fashioned out of the Saharan Desert sands at the beginning of the 20th century. At its centre was the luxurious Heliopolis Palace Hotel, which was to become part of the No 1 Australian General Hospital during the Great War. In 1915 troops were encamped nearby at the Heliopolis aerodrome. Nowadays it is the site of Cairo International Airport.

As Charlie described it:

Heliopolis Egypt
8 years old [the district was only a new residential development]

Heliopolis is about six miles
from Cairo and is where
our Brigade the 5th stayed
three weeks before leaving
for front. No doubt its fine
place the Buildings & Mosques
& Churches are Beautiful
The streets are very wide
and smooth and is kept
fairly clean alongside other
places of Egypt The Palace
Hotel now Australian

Hospital is supposed to
be the finest in world &
also the largest. The Turks
built and I think I[t] must
of taken years & years
The Tram Service is very good indeed The Trams [CBH I 11]
Are much better than those
of Australia and travel
much faster. The natives
of Heliopolis are very
dirty. Most of them do
nothing but hang around
the soldiers quarters looking
for food some of them you
see in the streets are filthy
flies all over their eyes &
nose and sleep any where
convenient [on] sides of the Road
or on the desert
[CBH I 12]

Upon arrival Charlie was able to report good news for one of his mates:

Bill Dwyer made Lance Sargent on
28 July 1915 [CBH I 29]

Corporal William Dwyer of B Company, 19th Battalion, was from Randwick, Sydney, and had been a motor driver before the War. He appears to have been a close friend of Charlie's. Dwyer was wounded at Gallipoli and sent to England but was to later rejoin his Battalion. He was often absent without leave and was later "reduced to the ranks", but this in turn was later reversed. He was wounded in action during the Battle of Pozières in France on 26 July 1916 and returned to Australia on 4 May 1917.[25]

Life was now to be absorbed in training and more training. As Sergeant Falconer, who was at Heliopolis the same time as Charlie, reported:

> Owing to the intense heat of that time of the year, troops were not allowed to drill between the hours of 9am and 4pm. Our first parade was 6am to 9am, the next being 4pm to 7pm. Our routine consisted of bayonet fighting, trench digging and rout marches, with the ordinary company drill to fill up time with. We found the dust and heat very objectionable at first, but as the tucker was fairly good, and we had plenty of showers to refresh ourselves with, we were very soon in tip top condition, which resulted in a very small sick parade. The climate is peculiar in Egypt in this way, that however hot it is in the day time and however dusty, it is always followed by a cool bright night.[26]

As Charlie described it:

> The Great Sudan Dessert is
> place where we got discipline
> knocked into us [CBH I 12]

Actually, there is no "Great Sudan desert" and certainly not in this region of Egypt. It was in fact the eastern part of the Sahara Desert. Charlie went on:

> I can
> tell you its no place for
> any white man
> no water
> no trees
> nothing but sand & stones &
> whirlwinds galore. [CBH I 12]

However, when leave came the troops were not always disciplined. Many of the men in Charlie's battalion received leave to travel into Cairo on the following Saturday, 31 July. They had barely been in

Egypt long enough to catch the gastro. Yet soon enough they were warring against people of their own Empire.

While on leave in Cairo that day, Charlie witnessed one of the most disgraceful episodes for the newly minted AIF, when hundreds (possibly thousands) of Australians took part in a riot that saw the deliberate burning down of multiple buildings and the outrageous cutting of fire hoses to prevent the Cairo firefighters from dousing the flames. Eventually officers brought in troops to quell the rioters.

As Charlie recorded:

> Big riot in Cairo 31 July 1915 [CBH 121]
> Battle of Wasser Troops took possession
> of Cairo [CBH 147]
>
> But was not long there before
> the boys got into a riot
> and you talk about
> comic opera but they weren't in [one]
> they started the Ball
> rolling by burning a
> couple of terraces of Houses
> each about 4 storeys high
> Then the fire Engine turned out
> The Arab firemen
> the boys stopped the Engine before it
> got to the fire & went
> joy riding and returned
> after a fly around Cairo [CBH 141]
>
> The Fireman had started their
> hose going but not for
> long as the boys cut
> the hose in about yard
> lengths. The police came but
> to their sorrow they got

> badly knocked about
> I think the riot started
> among a few Arabs
> but ended up [with] about
> 25,000 Australians.
> [Of] Course I was not in it. [CBH 140]

As a consequence of the riot, discipline for a few was to be meted out:

> A Private of B. Co[mpany] got 6 years
> In Jug for Trashing & another
> For Killing native got 8 years [CBH 147]

This incident was more accurately called by historians the "second battle of Wasser" or "Wass'ah". The first "battle" had occurred a few months earlier on Good Friday. The first riot, it has been argued, may possibly be seen as the consequence of a series of unfortunate events. But when it was duplicated so soon after, it was a bad look for the Australians. It was no wonder that they had quickly earned a bad reputation with British senior officers, given instances like these. It was only to be later, by the demonstration of their sheer heroism on the battlefield, that the Australian army was able to redeem its honour.

Having said that, the general views of senior British officers were not all bad. As one historian of the period notes:

> The army, appears to have been at the same time satisfied about the good general level of discipline but also worried about the possibility of it breaking down. Of course, working with a 'mass' army was a new experience for the commanders and bound to be something of a worry. On the other side of [the Secretary of State for War, Field Marshall Herbert] Kitchener's concern, however, was [Chief of British Army on the Western Front, General] Douglas Haig's general, strong satisfaction.[27]

Away from the rarefied heights of supreme command, Charlie pragmatically noted:

> Shortly after we went into
> real thing where you
> could fight as much
> as you liked with the
> Turks [CBH 140]

Even then, in July 1916, the realities of war were not far away for those troops training in Egypt. Charlie noted that the Australian Army had:

> Landed on the Beach at
> Gallipoli on the 27.4.15 [CBH 147]
>
> Anzac. Where the
> Australian & N.Z.
> Troops landed under very Heavy fire
> Meaning of the above place Australia New Zealand Army Corps
> A.N.Z.A.C. [CBH I 2]

It is worth at this point of the narrative to give a detailed account of the war against the Ottoman Empire and the start of the Gallipoli Campaign.

For many decades the Ottomans had been considered by the British as the "sick man of Europe" and would be relatively easy to defeat. The Ottomans or Turks had also won a dubious reputation because of their recent poor performance in the two Balkan Wars in 1912 and 1913; and a war against Italy over Libya in 1911-12. The soon to be appointed commander-in-chief of the Mediterranean Expeditionary Force, General Sir Ian Hamilton, believed the Ottoman troops were second rate. He is reported to have said: "Let me bring my lads face to face with Turks, in the open fields we will beat them every time because British volunteer soldiers are superior individuals to Anatolians, Syrians or Arabs".[28] And it was not just the British who held this view. Chief of the German General Staff, Helmuth von Moltke, opposed the Ottomans as an ally (albeit he was overruled by the German Government). He said that "Turkey is militarily a non-entity. If Turkey was described before as a sick man, it must now be described as a dying man".[29]

Unfortunately, this was, at least during the early years of the Great War, to prove to be incorrect. The Ottomans had an extensive Empire and still had a lot of fight left in them.

The Germans saw Turkey as the leading Islamic country in the world, with its Sultan and the Grand Mufti as the Sheikh-ul-Islam (the leader of the faith). As a result they perceived an opportunity to use Turkey as a means of fomenting revolution amongst the millions of Muslims across the British Empire, especially in India. They had for years assiduously cultivated the Ottoman Government (which was made up of a group called the "Young Turks" who had taken control in 1909 and ironically were not fanatical Muslims) and were helped by the strong Germanophile, the Ottoman Minister for War, Enver Pasha (the effective ruler of the country), who bypassed his own Cabinet and secretly signed a military alliance with Germany on 2 August 1914. This remained confidential for some time.

The British, of course, also tried to bring Turkey into their alliance with the French – the Entente Cordial. However, an incident at the beginning of the war strongly swayed Turkish public opinion against the British, the instigator being Winston Churchill. The British were building two battleships for the Ottoman navy. They were just completed at the beginning of the Great War and were ready for a handover. In fact, the Turkish crews were already in England to take over ownership. The cost of the warships had been partly paid for by public subscription, so there was keen interest in the ships across the Turkish population. Churchill made the unilateral decision to cancel the handover and keep the ships. There were understandable military reasons for this, and some justification in light of the subsequent knowledge about the Ottomans' secret treaty with Germany, but most historians also believe that the Turkish public outrage was the last straw that pushed Turkey fully into the German camp. It didn't hurt the German cause when, on 11 October 1914, they "gave" the Turks their battleship *Göben* and the light cruiser *Breslau* as a token of friendship. These ships proceeded into the Black Sea and under Ottoman flags attacked a number of Russian ports on 29 October. War was now inevitable.

Following the Ottoman entry into the war in October 1914, soon after, on 14 November, the senior religious leader under the Sultan, the Sheikh-ul-Islam, declared Jihad hoping for a general uprising of Muslims in British colonies. However, this was not to occur and, in fact, the Ottomans instead provoked uprisings amongst the Arab peoples that eventually contributed to the end of their vast empire.

As noted above, the Ottomans quickly came into conflict with the Russians on their Eastern borders and the British on their Western borders in the Sinai Peninsula.

The Gallipoli Campaign was initiated in January 1915 by requests from Britain's ally Russia to divert Turkish resources away from their battles occurring in the Caucasus in eastern Turkey and to create a supply route across Ottoman territory to help Russia in its fight against Germany. Russia would receive munitions and in return grain would be sent back to Western Europe. It would also open up the possibility of attacking the Central Powers via the Balkans. While the British Secretary of State for War, Field Marshall Lord Kitchener, had his reservations, the First Sea Lord, Admiral Jackie Fisher (at first) and his political boss the First Lord of the Admiralty, Winston Churchill, backed the idea. Since 1914 Churchill had argued for the creation of another front to relieve pressure from the trench warfare stalemate on the Western Front in France and Belgium. This was the opportunity he was looking for. Not surprisingly, given its backers, it was to be a seaborne operation that would clear the Dardanelles sea-lanes between the Aegean Sea (in the east of the Mediterranean) and the Sea of Marmara and allow the British and French capital ships to break through to the sea of Marmara from where they would reach Constantinople at the eastern extremity of that sea, and shell the Ottomans into submission.

The original naval plan to "force the Dardanelles" did not succeed. Between 19 and 25 February 1915, the combined British and French navies attacked the Ottoman gun emplacements. Also a Royal Marines detachment went ashore on the Gallipoli Peninsula to further destroy what they could. In fact, many of the strategically placed Ottoman coastal forts were destroyed. There was initial success. However, the Ottomans also had mobile gun units and these proved harder to subdue. They needed to be dealt with as they stopped the Allied minesweepers that ran close to the coast. On 18 March, in an endeavour to consolidate any gains, a large Allied naval contingent, comprising 18 major warships and other vessels, essentially bit off more than they could chew. Three battleships were lost and three more were badly damaged. This included the sinking of the British HMS *Irresistible* and HMS *Ocean* which was sent to its rescue. They both hit mines. The French battleship *Bouvet* also struck a mine and sank. HMS *Inflexible* was damaged and had to withdraw as were the French ships *Suffren* and *Gaulois*. Also, not long after, two submarines were lost.

Churchill, noting that the ships were mostly old and outdated, argued that the losses were bearable and so more could be risked. However, Admiral Fisher countered that, while the ships themselves were to some degree expendable, the crews were not, given that over seven hundred seamen died in the encounter. Fisher argued that this was a huge loss and not sustainable for the Allies. The argument became bitter and Fisher was eventually to resign his position in May 1915.

Lord Kitchener and the War Office now argued that the Army should take over from the Navy. In consultation with the French, the British War Cabinet decided to undertake an amphibious landing in force to capture the Gallipoli Peninsula (the north shore of the Dardanelles straits) with the aim of moving overland to take the remaining Ottoman gun installations overlooking the Dardanelles. This would permit the Allied fleet to steam toward their objective of Constantinople. Initially, the force was to consist of one British Division – the 29th – made up of three infantry brigades comprising men from England, Scotland, Wales and Ireland, and assorted artillery brigades. There was also the British Naval Division and Indian artillery. Added to this was the Australian and New Zealand Army Corps (ANZAC) made up of two divisions. One was the 1st Australian division with the 1st, 2nd and 3rd Australian Infantry brigades, comprising twelve battalions numbered from the 1st Battalion through to the 12th Battalion, plus artillery. This was made up of men from all six States of Australia. The second division in the Corps was the New Zealand and Australia Division made up of the New Zealand Infantry Brigade and the 4th Australian Infantry Brigade, comprising the 13th, 14th, 15th and 16th Battalions, plus artillery, of the AIF. Further the French provided a contingent called the Corps Expéditionnaire d'Orient, led by General Albert d'Amade, consisting of one division, made up of French and colonial troops including parts of the French Foreign Legion, plus artillery. In all, there were some 78,000 men in the invasion force.

As mentioned above, the overall commander was General Sir Ian Hamilton, a highly regarded veteran of the Second Anglo-Afghan War in the 1870s, the Gordon Relief Expedition to Khartoum, Sudan in 1885, the First and Second Boer Wars, and service in India. The Australian and New Zealand troops were under the command of an Englishman, Lieutenant General Sir William Birdwood (who by all accounts was remarkably popular). He had extensive experience in the Indian Army, seeing action on the North West Frontier and serving in the Second Boer War. The Australian 1st Division was led by a Scotsman, Major General William Bridges, who had emigrated to the Colony of New South Wales in 1879 and, during a career in the NSW, and then Australian, Armies, had fought in the Second Boer

War and previously been Australia's first Chief of the General Staff. The New Zealand and Australian Division was led by another British veteran, Major General Sir Alexander Godley, who had served in the Second Boer War, taking part in the Siege of Mafeking, and had been appointed Commander of the New Zealand Army in 1910.

The landings occurred on 25 April 1915. In Australia and New Zealand this date would be commemorated each year as Anzac Day. The casualties the two countries were to sustain were nowhere near as large as the British or the French. However, as a proportion of total combatants the colonial troops fared much worse.

After the initial landings in April, the Ottomans were able to hold onto the peninsula. But this was at a great cost and the loss of men and resources on both sides was large. Even though the Allied objectives were not reached, it can be argued that the offensive severely weakened the Ottomans and contributed to their ultimate defeat in 1918.

That was to be a long way off and we will concentrate for now on the events at Gallipoli in 1915.

The principal assault included landings in two geographically separate areas on the west of the peninsula. Overall it was the greatest seaborne invasion in history up to that point. The Allies used the Greek Island of Lemnos as their staging post, some 50 kilometres due west of the peninsula in the Aegean Sea. Interestingly, the Greeks were at this stage neutral in the War but the pro-Allies Greek Prime Minister, Eleftherios Venizelos, made the island available to the British and the French. During the course of early April 1915 the British troops were transferred there from their training grounds in Egypt. Hamilton moved his headquarters to the town of Mudros on Lemnos on 10 April.

The British 29th Division concentrated its attack at Cape Helles with five separate beach landings designated "S", "V", "W", "X" and "Y". Their objective was to push north east directly up the mountainous spine of the peninsula. The Anzac Corps was landed on a beach north of Gaba Tepe on the Aegean Sea. This beach was subsequently renamed Anzac Cove and was a few kilometres north of the southern landings. Their objective was to cut laterally across the peninsula to take the village of Kilitbahir on the Dardanelles coast and form a line to prevent Ottoman reinforcements meeting the troops coming up from Cape Helles. Some 8,000 Australians, New Zealanders and British landed at Anzac Cove. The French mounted a diversionary attack on Besika Bay and made a landing at Kum Kale on the southern or Asian side of the Dardanelles.

The Ottomans were caught unawares on the day but had been expecting some type of attack in the region because of the repeated naval raids. They therefore had many troops in the area. Indeed, their whole 5th Army of some 62,000 men was placed on the peninsula under the command of German General Otto Liman von Sanders. (In fact, there were many German officers in the senior officer corps of the Ottoman Army). The Turks had also spent their time since the naval attacks in March 1915 building fortifications and supply roads. However, the Ottomans were unsure of where their enemies would land so they spread out thinly along the coast and kept the bulk of the troops inland as a reserve. This strategy of flexibility was insisted upon by Liman von Sanders and ultimately proved to be a crucial factor in their success. However, in the early stages of the invasion it was a weakness and is acknowledged that it was the independent action of a single field commander that saved the Ottomans on the first day. But more of that shortly.

The initial landings at Anzac Cove involved the 1st Australian Division coming ashore. It is generally recognised that the site they landed at was incorrect, either due to the strong coastal currents or simply bad management. As a result, rather than an area that gave them room to prepare for an assault up the ridges, they landed at a beach that immediately ran into sharp inclines which were hard to climb. A small unit of Turkish troops, maybe five hundred men (although this increased to over 4,000 by the nightfall), were on hand and were quick into action firing machine guns from their advantageous positions on the ridge line. They inflicted massive casualties in the order of 2,000 men. The Australian 1st Division was then followed by the New Zealand and Australian Division onto the already overcrowded cove.

South at Cape Helles things were no better. Many officers had assumed that there would be little resistance. However, again, while there were not many Turkish troops, those on hand (for example there were some 200 soldiers each at both beaches "V" and "W") set up machine guns and laid down a withering fire on the British and French forces.

The Turkish 19th Division was allotted the task of covering the area that would become the immediate battleground. Its commander was Lieutenant Colonel Mustafa Kemal. On 25 April he was out early personally leading one of his battalions on a route march from the village of Boghali on the eastern side of the peninsula and far away from the landing grounds. He had marched them over the Sari Bair Mountain Ranges that formed the spine of the peninsula and reached Chunuk Bair hill on the west coast when he sighted retreating Turkish troops being pursued by Australian soldiers. He stopped his own troops, formed a defensive line, and brought up his battalion. He famously told his troops: "I don't order you to attack, I order you to die. In the time which passes until we die other troops and commanders can take our places". Further, when later ordered by his superior, Liman von Sanders, to commit only one battalion (as von Sanders believed the landings to be only a feint), he defied these orders after personally seeing the invasion fleet off the coast and committed a whole regiment that consolidated the Ottoman line across all the ridges. Every man in that regiment was to be a casualty. This is the same Kemal who would, only nine years later, become the president of the newly formed nation of Turkey. He was later known as Kemal Atatürk or "Father of the Turks". His reputation was built at Gallipoli and overwhelmingly the memorials there in Turkey today are concentrated on this man's resolute actions.

The terrain was particularly unhelpful for the attackers. It was very hilly and the Ottomans could man the strategically important crests of the hills and send down withering fire on top of the Allies. However, the Allied troops were able to climb the hills through this torrent of death and make some headway. Nonetheless, after the initial push on the first day, a stalemate had been created. The commander of the 3rd Brigade, Colonel Ewen Sinclair-Maclagan, made an early unilateral decision to cease the forward push and consolidate at what became known as the "Second Ridge". He convinced Colonel McCay of the 5th Brigade to do the same. These were controversial decisions, and whether they were correct have been debated by military historians for the last 100 years.[30] Inland from Anzac Cove, the colonial troops occupied a small area of territory that stretched across only two kilometres (or 1.2 miles). The breakthrough across the peninsula had stalled immediately. At the end of that first day, Division commanders Generals Bridges and Godley recommended re-embarkation to Corps commander General Birdwood. Birdwood agreed, but was informed by the navy that this was not possible, and so the order was given to dig trenches and consolidate.

Equally, the same story can be told for Cape Helles. While at Y beach the troops were unopposed and actually moved freely inland to the village of Krithia (a main objective); this was not the experience of their colleagues. On V and W beaches, where the main forces landed, it was a bloodbath. Again there may have only been two companies of Turkish troops, but their machine guns wreaked havoc. Of the first 200 Lancashire Fusiliers who sought to disembark from their ship, only 21 reached the beach. In all the Lancashires lost 600 of 1,000 troops and in the desperate fighting six Victoria Crosses were won. From Ireland the Dublin Fusiliers and the Munster Fusiliers took massive casualties as well. Amazingly, lacking clear instructions, those troops who had reached Krithia abandoned the village and moved back to the beach. The Allies were never able to recapture it. In reality, they had only gained a foothold, capturing towns like

Sedd-el-Bahr, but not making the advances up the peninsula that they planned for.

After the Turks were initially able to hold the line – commanding the ridges above Anzac Cove – the Anzacs then sought to push inland two days later on 27 April, this time with the support of naval gunfire (which was largely ineffective as the shells were mainly armour piercing for ship-to-ship battles rather than the high explosives to cut barbed wire). At Cape Helles, French troops joined the battle on the eastern side of the peninsula. On 28 April, a push was made by the British to capture Krithia and was dubbed the First Battle of Krithia. There were further heavy casualties of some 3,000 men and the attack was unsuccessful.

The Ottomans were pouring in reinforcements and themselves counterattacked on 30 April at Anzac and Cape Helles. The fighting was desperate. The French line waivered at Cape Helles but was saved. At Anzac Cove the 4th Infantry Brigade under Colonel John Monash, the New Zealand Infantry Brigade and Royal Marines attacked Russell's Top and Quinn's Post towards a hill called Baby 700. Unfortunately, they were repulsed suffering around 1,000 casualties.

Monash was the standout Australian leader of the Great War. He was a successful civil engineer, as well as a Colonel in the Citizens Military Force. He was to be rapidly promoted – first to Brigadier in September 1914, to Major General and 3rd Division commander in July 1916, which he led at the Battle of Messines in June 1917, and the Third Battle of Ypres and Battle of Broodeseinde. He was knighted in 1918 and, on 31 May 1918, he was promoted to Lieutenant General and given command of the Australian Corps (which comprised all the Australian Divisions), the largest field army in Australian history, with 166,000 men. He was tasked by Haig with breaking the Hindenburg Line, which his troops did in October 1918.[31]

On 6 May, the Second Battle of Krithia occurred at Cape Helles. Along with the British and the French, this included Australian troops from the 2nd Infantry Brigade and New Zealanders from the

New Zealand Infantry Brigade. The French troops were directed to capture the Gully of Kereves Dere, the British and Australians to capture Krithia and the hill at Achi Baba. Ottoman artillery and machine gun fire stopped the advance. The next day the battle resumed. The Allies gained some 600 metres, but fell short of their targets. Some 1,000 casualties were the result.

The intensity of fighting then eased, although there were continual raids, sniper fire and grenade attacks, let alone artillery bombardments. Some of the opposing trenches were only mere metres away from each other. During this period the commander of the 1st Australian Division, Major General William Bridges, was shot by a sniper while inspecting troops. He was to die shortly after on 18 May. The next day saw a major Ottoman counterattack at Anzac using some 42,000 men. It was their turn to suffer major losses in a failed bid. The Turks had some 13,000 casualties, while the Australians and New Zealanders a comparatively small 630. Shortly after, both sides agreed on a temporary truce to bury the dead bodies that were putrefying under the hot sun.

Towards the end of May the Ottomans also detonated a large mine after tunneling around Quinn's Post and attacked the Australian lines in force. This also failed to make a breakthrough. For their part, on 4 June the Allies launched the Third Battle of Krithia at Cape Helles, again with no success. This was followed by an attack called the Battle for Gully Ravine on 28 June, which gained some minor ground on the western side of Cape Helles. The Ottoman counter attack in this area on 1 to 5 July saw them suffer in the order of 14,000 casualties, without meeting their objectives. Many thousands more casualties on both sides were to occur in fighting in mid-July at Achi Baba Nullah which was also gruesomely called Bloody Valley. Again, any gains for the Allies were small.

Charlie catalogued the key events in his War Diary:

Diary of Operations

April 25th Allied forces landed

" 26th Sedd-el Bahr taken
" 27 Two miles advance
From Point of Peninsula
' 28th Astride the Peninsula
Australians at Sari Bair
May 6th Allies reinforced three
days battle for Krithia begins
7th Achi Baba Heights attacked
8th Battle ends Slight gain of Ground
19th Allied advance in Southern
Peninsular Australians
Inflicted 7000 casualties on Turks
June 4th General attack in Southern
Peninsular renewed
June 5th after night Engagement
At Quinn's Post net gain 50
11th & 12th Advanced Turkish
Trenches taken
19th Turkish Trench Captured
lost and retaken 1,000
Turkish dead [CBH I 6]

He went on:

June 21st After all day Battle
French Harried redoubt & Trenches at Kereves [Dere]
28th Battle of Gully Ravine
British advanced 1,000 on
their left Gurkhas captured
Knoll due west of Krithia
July 2nd Sir Ian Hamilton
estimates Turkish losses
At 5,150 Killed & 1500
wounded in Battle of 4 days

Turkish Attack Beaten
July 4 attack on Naval Div[ision]
and 29th Div[ision] defeated
the Turks Practically
wiped out by the 29th
Aug. 2nd Australians
Stormed the ridge &
improved their
Position. [CBH I 7]

This is a reasonably accurate catalogue of recent events, albeit overstating Allied gains. Charlie was obviously keen to be on top of what was occurring. Interestingly, there is no record of Allied casualties. It can be imagined that amongst the troops back in Egypt, while it was permitted to freely discuss Turkish casualties, this may not have been the case for casualties on their own side. Having said that, Charlie noted in late July 1915:

Wounded are arriving at
Alexandria in thousands [CBH 147]

By this stage "casualties were approximately 25 per cent on both sides; the British lost 4,500 from 20,000 men and the French 2,000 casualties from 10,000 troops. Ottoman losses were 9,000 casualties according to the Turkish Official History and 10,000 according to another account".[32]

And with the wounded arriving back in Egypt others were sent as replacements:

Reinforcements of 19th Batt[alion] left to day
1st August [CBH I 121]

Meanwhile, Charlie and his mates were enjoying their last chance at comparative freedom for a while:

Paid today 5 August 1915 [CBH I 116]
Went to Cairo today 8.8.15
had half Rum but wouldn't take

the lot so I P.O.Q. [ie piss off quickly]
Bill [McFarlane] had go but found big
sponge inside. Buckshee. [ie a prize, a catch, a windfall] [CBH I 21]
Beer gone up half Peastre in Canteen
5 Peastre Bottle gone up one Peastre
Beer dead crook in our own
Canteen hope to walk up to
the Victorian Canteen where
it is near Nile[CBH I 13]

There appears to have been a bit of inflation in the price of beer. Charlie is referring to the local Egyptian currency. One Egyptian pound was equivalent to 100 piastres or 1,000 milliemes. Charlie's spelling is close to the mark.

Then we see an entry where Charlie catalogues letters he received and dispatched. There will be many similar entries in the diary:

Sent Mervyn [Hardy, Charlie's nephew] 30 assorted Japanese Stamps on about the 8/8/15 Besides letter [CBH I 97]

Got letter from Miss Hinemoa Llewelyn [friend]
August 1st 1915 Answered same
Day
Posted letters to
Mervyn 2 Including Stamps

Mrs Latham [friend] 1	Post Cards
A. Latham [friend] 1	Walter [Lawson, brother in law]
Hardy 1	Roy [Hardy, brother]
Alma [sister] 1	Rose [Hardy, sister]
Sam Ostman [friend] 1	

Sent HandKerchief to Jack's baby [Hardy, brother]
I sent Kerchief to Rose, Alma
Roy & [CBH I 91]

> Only received 2 letters in camp at
> Egypt one from Mervyn & one
> from Miss H Llewelyn. Disappointed [CBH I 104]

Letters were from family and friends. Family was mostly his brothers, sisters, nieces and nephews. One of his other correspondents was Hinemoa Llwellyn. She was then a 15-year-old schoolgirl who had been "enlisted", possibly at school, to write to a Digger at the front. It is unclear whether or not she knew Charlie before he departed for the war, but it would appear from conversations with his family that she had not. She is mentioned many times in the diary and, as we shall see, some of Charlie's letters to her are still in existence.

Finally, he noted further training and, eventually, that some of his comrades from the 5th Brigade had already been dispatched to Gallipoli:

> [Route] March, 12.8.15

> Aug. 16 5th Brigade
> Reinforcement Arrived [CBH I 7]

The same day Charlie was to embark for the Peninsula. It was now the turn of B Company of the 19th Battalion, 5th Brigade, to plunge into the cauldron.

4

Gallipoli: August-September 1915

"Only holiday wound"

It was so different from Sydney. Home was always a verdant green. The rain fell frequently and often in deluges that frightened Charlie when he was a child. There was not much he had been afraid of but the crashing thunder and lightning of a summer downpour always made him anxious and uneasy.

At Gallipoli, although green, it was dry. But the thunder was there. It was there almost all the time. It was almost beyond endurance and it never seemed to go away even when it wasn't there. The ominous threat never left you like some awful thing that sat on your shoulders weighing you down but never going away.

Charlie and the battalion were sent to Anzac Cove on 21 August 1915 as part of a wave of reinforcements that were sent to the Peninsula, following the first landing in April. The 5th Brigade initially took part in the Battle of Hill 60.

However, before we proceed with Charlie's story, we need to understand how the Gallipoli Campaign developed through August 1915.

The continuing stalemate and huge losses of men caused the Allies to take stock. As the invading force they had to take the initiative. The Turks, while wanting to expel the invaders, had the advantage that their fallback was simply to defend their lines.

On 6 August 1915, the British landed some five miles (eight

kilometres) to the north of Anzac Cove at Suvla Bay, with thousands of English, Irish and Welsh troops. It was a much more satisfactory landing place and the troops came ashore unopposed. However, eventually this seemingly smart strategic move also failed. The British did not press the attack into the Anarfarta Hills beyond the beach straight away, wasting valuable time and allowing the Ottomans a breathing space to reinforce the ridges. The planned-for flanking attack into the Sari Bair mountains therefore also stalled into a trench warfare stalemate.

These second landings involved a large increase in troops. Besides the battalions the British previously committed to the Peninsula, these landings and further landings in late August, were to add to the existing XI Corps and the VIII Corps under Lieutenant General Sir Francis Davies. Also, the new 2nd Australian Division and the 29th Indian Brigade, including three Gurkha battalions and one Sikh battalion, were to arrive.

The elaborate plan had been for the British to head from Suvla Bay inland to win the Sari Bair Range of hills. At the same time, further south there was to be a feint on Cape Helles that became known as the Battle of Krithia Vineyard and further attacks from the Anzac Cove region, also into the mountainous range in the centre of the Peninsula. In the latter case, the Australian 3rd Light Horse Brigade (obviously dismounted) advanced in the Sari Bair region with an attack on Baby 700 from their trenches at a sector called The Nek. Meanwhile, the New Zealand Infantry Brigade would try to secure the summit of Chunuk Bair. The Australians of the 4th Infantry Brigade and the Gurkhas from the 29th Indian Brigade would attack Hill 971.

The various diversionary battles of early August 1915 in the Anzac region had mixed results. In the Battle of Lone Pine, the Australian 1st Infantry Brigade had some success in capturing Ottoman trenches. The attacks on Chunuk Bair by the New Zealanders, supported by English troops from Wiltshire and North Lancashire, also had some success, but the attack on Hill 971 failed to meet its objective. Even in the case of Chunuk Bair the Turks regained their ground within days.

Thus, overall, the Battles of Sari Bair and Chunuk Bair also ended in failure and, as noted, the British attacks from the north into the Anarfarta hills at Kavak Tepe and Tekke Tepe ground to a halt.

At this point, in mid-August, Sir Ian Hamilton considered the option of an evacuation. However, within days he proceeded instead with another push. This occurred on 21 to 23 August with the Battle of Hill 60 and the Battle of Scimitar Hill, which were further attempts to directly widen and deepen the links between the British lines at Suvla Bay with those at Anzac Cove and then push further inland.

AUGUST 1915

As part of this grand plan Charlie's 19th Battalion embarked on 16 August 1915 at Alexandria on HMT *Saturnia* headed for Lemnos. As Charlie noted:

> Leaving Heliopolis today Sunday
> 15 8.15 all the boys are singing [CBH I 91]
>
> Left Alexandria for the
> Dardanelles on the 16th.8.15
> With Good Spirits, not
> drinking spirits [CBH I 91]

S.S. *Saturnia* (reproduced from Australian War Memorial extracted at www.awm.gov.au on 13 August 2020)

Passed the Grecian archipelago on the 18.8.15
Wine growing and olives on the way to Dardanelles
All the hills are pretty well cultivated
White Gurkha we are called by Turks
I shouldn't wonder why
they call us that [CBH I 53]

Dead stiff not a bean 18/8/15 [CBH I 118]

H.M.S. Saturnia left Alexandria
[W]as conveyed by SS Saturnia for Dardanelles 16.8.15 [CBH I 135]

SS *Saturnia* was described by Sergeant Falconer as "a filthy ship, the food tainted and the accommodation rotten"[33] and by Lieutenant Colonel Mackenzie of the 19th Battalion as "a crowded dirty coal ship".[34]

Private Ernest King of the 19th Battalion described the journey that same night thus:

> Dropped anchor about 5am near Lemnos, moved off again about 10.30am. saw lots of warships, cruisers and destroyers, troopships, hospital ships both French and English, anchored again about 12 o'clock. Received orders at 5pm to fall in on top deck with all equipment including 200 rounds of ammunition and 48 hours rations and stand by for further orders. 20th Aug. Slept on deck fully dressed still waiting. Transhipped into troopship Osmanieh A.O. at 6.30pm and left at 7.15pm where the first landing was made at midnight.[35]

And as Charlie noted:

There are about 400 [war] ships
here [at Lemnos] 18/8/15 [CBH I 104]

Bully Beef is plentiful tonight
Just about to go into firing
line No wonder it is plentiful [CBH I 13]

Dunley went into Hospital 18.8.15

to-day with Gon[orrhoea] We were very
sorry he went He nearly
cried when he was leaving us.
Put it down to hard luck. [CBH I 29]

Private James Dunley of B Company, 19th Battalion was from Marengo, NSW, and was a labourer before the War. He returned to his battalion at Gallipoli in October but within days was wounded with "Gunshot Wound Concussion". He was later sent to hospital in England. After treatment for "shell shock", he returned to Australia on 31 August 1916.[36]

Charlie's diary continues:

19/8/15 Boys are taking things very
well Mostly all Happy
except four who wish they were
Home.
Biscuits are very hard & dry only
12 months old [CBH I 13]

I am just about to go into my
first Battle I wonder
Will I ever see my
Brothers & Sisters again
God Knows. [CBH I 118]

H.M.S. Osmanian left Lemnos [CBH I 152]

Left Lemnos for Dardanelles
SS Osmanieh at 6.30
Arrived at Dardanelles MIDNIGHT [CBH I 104]

H.M.T. *Osmanieh* was a troop transport hired by the Royal Navy. Again, its fate shows the dangers in these sea crossings. It was sunk just over two years later on 31 December 1917 by a mine laid by a German U-Boat at the entrance of Alexandria harbour. Over 200 people were killed.[37]

Charlie's diary continues:

> Landed at ANZAC
>
> 21.8.15 Rear of the firing line [CBH 1].

Sergeant Falconer of the 18th Battalion landed that same night. He records:

> I was wakened from my reverie by the dull sounding of a big gun. Everybody around was standing to, looking, and a good few rumours went around as to what it was. A search light flashed out, way over on the hill and everybody was full of interest. A few minutes later we could hear rifles and machine gun rattling. At last we pulled up and lighters came along side on to which we speedily transhipped and were very soon landing on that famous beach "Anzac".[38]

The Battle for Hill 60 was the last major offensive mounted by the Allies at Gallipoli and was under the command of Major-General Herbert Vaughan Cox. Cox was another British veteran of the Indian Army, having fought in the Second Anglo-Afghan War in 1882, the Third Anglo-Burmese War in 1885 and the Boxer Rebellion in China in 1900. At this time, he was commanding officer of the 29th Indian Brigade and was later to command the 4th Australian Division in the Middle East.[39]

The British goal was to secure a hilltop occupied by the Turks that oversaw Anzac Cove and Suvla Bay. To capture it would solidify the connection between the troops at the Cove with those at the Bay.

A large force was assembled, including troops of the New Zealand Mounted Rifles Brigade led by Brigadier-General Andrew Hamilton Russell, with the primary objective of taking the hilltop. They were to be supported on their left by Irish men from the Connaught Rangers and Gurkhas who were to capture water wells at Kabak Kuyu and Susak Kuyu. To their right, the Australian 4th Brigade, led by Colonel John Monash, and 10th Hampshire Regiment and 4th South Wales Borderers Regiment were to mount a feint to draw Turkish reserves away from the New Zealand assault. The attacks began at 3.30pm on 21 August. It was to have been preceeded by an artillery barrage, but this had not occurred. Initially, the New Zealanders made good progress as the Turks abandoned their first line of trenches, and the Connaughts and Gurkhas captured the wells. The Connaughts and Australians were then directed to support the NZ advance. However, the overall advance was stopped by a Turkish consolidation in their second line of trenches and their ability to concentrate accurate artillery fire on the Allied positions.

The allied casualties were large. In addition, the artillery barrage started a bush fire that killed many of the wounded lying on the battlefield. By about 7.00pm, the advance ground to a halt with the various Allied units still short of the summit and in fact unable to connect up across their splintered front line. The attack resumed on 22 August. This is when fresh troops from the 5th Brigade of the 2nd Australian Division, newly arrived from Lemnos, were committed to their first battle. This was principally the 18th Battalion commanded by Lieutenant Colonel Alfred Chapman with the 19th Battalion in reserve. At around 5.00am, the 18th made a bayonet charge and were ferociously opposed by the Turks. Out of 750 men the Battalion suffered an appalling 383 casualties in their first action.

Here Charlie records the fate of the 18$^{th:}$

> 18 Battalion got cut up on
> 22.8.15[CBH I 4]

There is no better account of what happened than that of Sergeant Falconer:

> We eventually arrived behind a high crestwork long after dawn had broken. The officers had been called out by the Colonel and we were left to our thoughts again. Bullets were whizzing overhead and now and again cheers sounded very close. We wondered time and time again how our comrades were faring. In a few minutes our officers came back, and Lieut Addison told me, that we were going to charge almost immediately. I asked for orders, but was told, that they would be communicated to

> us later. We moved off in single file, and had been marching for about half an hour past Indian & English troops, when the order came down the line to "Fix Bayonets". No sooner had we done this, than another one came down to "Unfix Bayonets" and load magazine with five rounds. We had no time to comply with this order, when another came down to "fix bayonets" again. I had drawn my bayonet from the scabbard when all those in front of me were running like "blazes". Following Lieut Addison and followed by my platoon and fixing our bayonets as we ran, we were met by a thunderous rattle of machine gun and rifle fire. Men were falling in dozens, and still we went on. Looking round and taking in everything I saw I realised that I was separated from my platoon, and was among the very few left standing so down I went. The first sight I saw was Major McPherson, my O.C., throw up his hands and fall down dead. Someone was crawling up to me, and when he was near enough I looked into the face of our Coy Sgt Major Roy. It dawned upon me very soon, that a ghastly mistake had been made, and as we had received no orders, we had to act on our own initiative.[40]

It is not a complete surprise that the commanding officer of the 18th, Lieutenant Colonel Chapman, resigned in September due to ill health and was shipped home to Australia.[41]

The 19th did not suffer the devastation endured by the 18th. However, the men were under constant fire during that day. As Private Ernest King recorded in his diary:

> Left Argyle Gully about 10am and marched around still further to the left towards Suvla. On our way we passed through artillery fire on the double for about 150 yards with no great loss, a few wounded and two men killed. Entered trenches at 1 pm and had to keep low as the trench was only three feet deep and the bullets were whistling over. Moved off again at 10 pm and worked till about 4 am at trenching about ¼ mile away.[42]

By 22 August B Company also lost their corporal:

> Corporal Wilson got his head blown off
> Permanent Light Duties. [CBH I 4]
>
> Salam Johnnie
> Salam [CBH I 4]
>
> Corporal Wilson got his
> Head blown off
> He was the first to go
> down in B Comp[any]. [CBH I 16]

Corporal Frederick Wilson of B Company, 19th Battalion, was actually born in Canada, but was living in Goulburn, NSW, by the time he joined up. He was a gasfitter before the War and was killed in action on 22 August 1915, aged 32.[43] In his entry, for some unaccountable reason, Charlie records the date of Wilson's death as 25 September. This is inaccurate. It was on 22 August, soon after the 19th Battalion's landing at Gallipoli. The extract has therefore been placed in its correct chronological place. Charlie's statement that Wilson was "the first to go down in B Comp[any]" then makes sense. Charlie's diary continues:

> Beachy Bill was very busy
> today 23.8.15 [CBH I 13]

"Beachy Bill" was the name given by the Diggers to the Ottoman artillery that fired down from the ridges into the Anzac Cove sector, including the beaches.[44]

Lieutenant Frank Boyden of C Company, 19th Battalion, also recorded his observations of those first few days when the Battle for Hill 60 was raging:

> By this time [ie morning 22 August] the leading company [of the 19th Battalion] had opened out into extended order, the first couple of lines and were beginning to double out across the open plain, when we heard the shriek of the first shell, as

she came tearing over us. She burst with terrific noise and tore up the ground between the first and second line, then came another one and burst almost over the second line and down went a couple of chaps, the first to fall of the 19th – but our men never wavered. On they went as though they were just doubling across the fields at Liverpool. All this time we were sitting down waiting our turn to come when a stray shell burst about 30 yards to our left, some of the men ducked for cover but my chaps sat perfectly still, quite unconcerned. One of them said 'Alright Mr Boyden, we won't fail you, we'll follow you right through'.

At last our turn came, opening out into extended order away we went – Major Norrie and I side by side – it was certainly a nasty sensation when we heard the shriek of the first shell we knew was aimed at us, she seemed to burst right over our heads. Everyone ducked and then looked round to see if anyone was hit but no one thank God that time, so I breathed a bit more freely – then another came, then another and another, each one bursting just behind us. Running all the time, we at last reached the other side of the plain; where there was cover for us to get behind and there we sat down to get our breath. I had offered up a little prayer, that God would take my platoon across safely and He did, for I didn't lose a man. The other platoons were not so fortunate – poor Mr Killeen's platoon had a whole section wiped out completely, he being one of them. As you no doubt heard, he had one of his legs blown to pieces. After we had an hour's spell, we were led along a communication trench for about a mile and then told to sit down thinking of course that we should soon be led out and told to charge. But instead of that we sat their all day until 1 am the next morning. …

The following night and for several nights after, we had to go out and dig fresh trenches, which was always very trying to the nerves and we lost a few men each night from stray bullets, for

> they were only strays, the Turks never saw us digging, so that we were never deliberately fired on. …
>
> During that 3 days battle we never took part in a charge but I honestly think our work was just as trying for we worked with our blood cool, while those in a charge have their blood up and plenty of excitement to carry them through.[45]

Charlie's initial stay at Gallipoli was quite short. B Company was not at the forefront of the action. However, as Lieutenant Boyden's observations above show, in one sense the whole of the Anzac Cove was the front line. Like thousands of other troops, within days of landing, he was wounded and had to return to Lemnos Island for recuperation. It would appear from what he writes in subsequent diary entries this initial wound was relatively light and soon enough he would be back in the trenches.

As Charlie records it:

> But I didn't last
> long as I got a smack
> in the left knee with
> shrapnel but could not
> get a spell with it [CBH 140]

Despite what he says, he did have a short "spell", as he describes it, being shipped back as a casualty to Lemnos Island after only three days at Gallipoli. Maybe he thought he deserved more time for recuperation. As he recorded:

> 23 August 1915
>
> Returned to Lemnos
> On SS Ceramic Transferred
> To 1st Australian Stationary H[ospital]
> at Mudros [CBH I 104]

And:

> 24 August 1915

> Colours of 19th Battalion Chocolate
> & Green.
>
> Casualties are very heavy in
> our Brigade 24.8.15 [CBH I 21]

As the Australian historian, Alan Moorehead, noted:

> Some 45,000 Allied soldiers had fallen in these August battles, and the hospital service which had never been organised to deal with such an avalanche of wounded, were for a few days in almost as bad a state as anything which Florence Nightingale had found at the Crimea. Even private yachts which had turned up from England were pressed into service as hospital ships.[46]

And a first-hand account of one of the nurses, Lydia King, gives a sense of the awfulness:

> I shall never forget the awful feeling of hopelessness on night duty. It was dreadful. I had two wards downstairs, each over 100 patients and then I had small wards upstairs – altogether about 250 patients to look after, and one orderly and one Indian sweeper. Shall not describe their wounds, they were too awful. One loses sight of all the honour and the glory in the work we are doing.[47]

It wasn't a great time for Charlie personally either:

> 25 August 1915
>
> August. My unlucky
> month it is five years
> today 25th [ie 25 August 1910] since my
> Dear mother died. And
> I am in Hospital at Mudros [Lemnos] near Greece. [CBH I 2]
>
> 18th & 17th [Battalions in] Action before us
> Wounded of the 18th Battalion
> Are with me now
> Mostly wounded in the arms [CBH I 147]

I am in what they call a
Convalescent camp they
send you here after you have day or so in
Hospital and they teach
you to eat Rice with
Pen Knife & Eat [CBH I 13]
With your fingers. Its marvelous
What a man can do when
he tries [CBH I 14]

Sent Flo [elder sister] service card today
25.8.15 [CBH I 117]

Breakfast at 7[am] consists
Slice of bread & Rasher
of fat Bacon & tin of tea
Dinner at 12 [noon] Stew
(Bully Beef) few bad spuds
& rice. Tea at 4[pm]
Bread one slice & Jam
Tin of Tea above meal.
You eat with your Jack
Knife its very funny
to see the boys trying
to carve spoons out
of wood. I have two
chop sticks & try to
manage with them
To-day one of the boys
(English) pinched
50 Packets of cigarettes [CBH I 14]

The Battle for Hill 60 was resumed on 27 August. During the evening, an assault by the 9th and 3rd Light Horse Regiments was mounted. Some further progress was made but the summit was beyond them. The 3rd took particularly heavy casualties, including the death of their commanding officer, Lieutenant Colonel Carew Reynell. Fighting continued until 29 August. While some Turkish trenches on the summit were taken, the Turks retained the strategically important northern face of the hilltop that overlooked Suvla Bay. Nonetheless, there were some gains for the Allies in that they secured the southern face which partly consolidated the links between Suvla Bay and Anzac Cove. Although this was at a significant cost, with over 1,100 casualties.

The Battle of Scimitar Hill, which coincided with the Battle of Hill 60, was no more successful. While the Battle of Hill 60 involved Allied troops pushing inland from Anzac Cove, this attempted advance came from Suvla Bay under the command of Major General Sir Henry de Beauvoir De Lisle. De Lisle had been temporarily promoted to command IX Corps at Suvla Bay after Stopford had just been sacked. He was a veteran of the Egyptian Campaign in 1885 and the Second Boer War, where he commanded the Australian Brigade. He had already fought on the Western Front in France. After Gallipoli he would return there, participating in the Battle of the Somme and serving until the end of the War as a Corps commander.[48]

Scimitar Hill was in the Anafarta Hills and had been an original objective of the landings on 6 August. It had actually been captured by the East Yorkshire Regiment on 8 August, but had been quickly abandoned. The large attack on 21 August consisted of troops from the British 29th and 11th Divisions. Part of the 11th Division, the Royal Inniskilling Fusiliers from Ireland, captured the Scimitar Hill but sustained large casualties and again had to abandon it because the Turks were able to concentrate fire on them from other vantage points on the Anafarta Hills. Later in the day, a further attack was mounted with a large number of dead and wounded. Overall there were some 5,300 casualties in this Battle.

While convalescing at Lemnos Charlie included a series of

drawings across the pages of his diary. The first was a drawing of a cross which has inscribed on it:

> In Memory Of
> My Dear Mother & Father [CBH I 154]

Then there is another drawing of crossed British and Australian flags with transcription above saying "King & Country" and, below, "Your Fallen Pals". The third is a pencil drawing of a man's head in profile with the heading "Cairo Jew". Finally, at the bottom of the page, he has written:

> Some Sketches
> By an
> old soldier
> in the
> Hospital at
> Lemnos Island
> Greece 1915 [CBH I 154]

SEPTEMBER 1915

Nevertheless, within a week and a half, he was up and about:

2 September 1915

> Sept 2nd Mick Woolcott. Young
> chap of 24 from Manly
> & myself went for walk
> to day left camp at
> 8.30 and made for
> the Entrance to Island
> but walked till noon
> & could see the water
> about 5 miles away
> so we gave it up
> & made back to camp

To our surprise we
wandered past 2
villages and found
ourselves the other side
of the island. [CBH I 53]

We came across some
tomatoes and my mate
kept watch while I
filled my helmet with
them. We next found [a]
bonser well & had
drink & washed the
tomatoes & pushed on
we then came to Greek
farmer [and] had another
drink & made him
understand we wanted
food he gave me some
stuff like hard mud
but after soaking
it for 10 minutes in
water we ate it.
It wasn't bad but
by God it was hard
He also gave us some
Cheese & some sort of
Melon
got chased by [CBH I 54]
some Greek woman with
stones & she had big
big stick but we didn't
mind as [we] were pretty

well used to that sort of affair
we arrived back
in camp about 3[pm]
very tired and hungry. [CBH I 55]

Mick Woolcott was in D Company of the 18th Battalion and came over to Egypt on the same ship as Charlie. He was called Mick instead of his actual mouthful of names – Hampton Prout Woolcott. He came from Manly, Sydney, and signed up at the age of 23.[49] There will be another mention of him later in the diary at which point more will be said about this interesting character.

Charlie was to also to enjoy a bit of swimming:

Had another good swim off ship
At Lemnos Island Today [CBH I 104]

Nonetheless, the war was never far away.

After recuperating for about two weeks, he was back to the front line. This was initially to be on the slopes leading up to Hill 60. The 19th Battalion's next stint would be a prolonged one in the trenches at Pope's Post, after they were assigned there on 18 September. As we have seen, the Battles of Scimitar Hill and of Hill 60 had failed.

Pope's Post or Hill was named after Colonel Harold Pope. Pope was born in Middlesex, England, and had emigrated to Western Australia to work as a railway clerk just before the turn of the century. He was a Lieutenant Colonel in the Citizen's Militia before the War. In 1914 he was made commanding officer of the 16th Battalion and was in the first wave of landings at Anzac Cove. It was on that first day that he established control of a strategically valuable hill that was to bear his name.[50] Pope's Post was on the frontline and formed part of the central line of trenches across the Anzac Cove sector, made up of Russell's Top, Pope's Hill, Quinn's Post and Courtney's Post. It was subject to continual sniping and bombardment from the Turks and was one of the points from which tunneling occurred to either lay mines or to go under the Turkish trenches. As Private King of the 19th described it:

Australian troops, Pope's Hill, Gallipoli, 1915
(reproduced from Australian War Memorial extracted at www.awm.gov.au on 13 August 2020)

> The ground is very clayey and when wet is very sticky and is heavy walking. … The place here is lousy and the fleas are very plentiful so that it keeps one scratching and rubbing.[51]

As Charlie noted, trench warfare was very ugly and brutal:

> My God this place is Hell [CBH I 118]
>
> Soldier's life not happy one
> Don't I know it too
> Show no mercy on German
> Officers [CBH I 118]

Charlie lamented the stalemate:

> When will we capture the Narrows [the Dardanelles]
> My God the boys wish the war
> was over it is Hell
> day & night Just the same
> cannons roaring & dead
> mates lay all round you
> why should we take Prisoners

Bayonet wounds amongst the
Australians are very scarce [CBH I 145]

Its hard to get a peaceful sleep
unless you stick your head up
and its good bye
I would willingly give fifty
pounds to be Home in my
little Bed dreaming of the
poor chaps at the Front
Little I thought I would be
one of the boys. [CBH I 69]

My teeth are in bad condition [CBH I 135]

Hell on earth my nerves are
shattered. Destroyers are
blazing for all they are worth
& artillery is also peppering
the Turks trenches. I saw
the wounded of the 17th
& also saw the charred
bodies of the 10th L Horse.
They smell something awful
but they just lay there
& rot. Nobody can get
out to them as the Turks
are dead straight shots.
[CBH I 61]

Turks are getting Particular
Shell[ing] to day [for] 5th Brigade[CBH I 135]

Moreover, it wasn't just the canon-fire that was tormenting the troops. It was the Turkish snipers:

Snipers are very Busy today [CBH I 117]

Sargt Segas of A Comp 19th Batt
Shot sniper the first day
we landed he was in
crevice of Big hill & had
enough provisions to last
him month his carrier
Pigeons are still flying
Around his haunt [CBH I 118]

"Sargt Segas" was actually Sergeant Arthur Richard Seguss from A Company, 19th Battalion. Before the War he had been an engineer from Surry Hills, Sydney, although originally from Kent in England, and was 45 at the time and married. Seguss had served in the Second Boer War with the Australian Coronation Corps. He was to have a relatively short Great War as he came down with dysentery on 23 September 1915 and was eventually shipped to England. Charlie wrote in his diary against Seguss' name (apparently some time later) that "Died of Dysentry 3 months later, 65 aged". [CBH I 118] However, this was incorrect. Seguss, who we have seen, was 20 years younger, and was repatriated to Australia on 11 March 1916 with chronic bronchitis.

Charlie and his mates were also tormented by the vermin:

Lice is pretty plentiful
We have to hunt our
Clothes for them as
often as possible all
always find flock of them [CBH I 104]

And the lack of water:

Water is scarce on the
Gallipoli Peninsula
So is Beer
Westly winds have started
God help us on the Peninsular

When they blow 60 miles [an]
Hour. Sea Ranges 130 ft
Ships won't Guarantee
to get here so we have
to settle Turks by end
of August. [CBH I 147]

And sickness was everywhere:

Lieut. Col. Grant
And what do you do
When you get lice on your shirts. Pick them off. And
what does cat do
dig hole & uses it
Well then If everybody
done that there would
not be any disentry [CBH I 29]

This must be Lieutenant Colonel William Grant of the 9th Light Horse. It is not absolutely clear why Grant would be lecturing men of the 19th Battalion, but his own unit had also been in the Battle for Hill 60 where they suffered 50 per cent casualties. Afterwards, they played a defensive role at Gallipoli. Grant had been a pastoralist from the Darling Downs in Queensland and had risen to the rank of part-time Lieutenant Colonel in the Civilian Militia prior to the War. At Gallipoli he was originally in command of the 11th Light Horse Regiment before moving to the 9th. After Gallipoli, he was again put in command of the 11th Light Horse and fought in the Sinai Campaign where he won a Distinguished Service Order. In late 1917, he was promoted to command the 3rd Light Horse Brigade and then later led the 4th Light Horse Brigade during the Palestine Campaign. It was as the leader of the 4th that he led the famous Light Horse charge at the Battle of Beersheba, one of, if not the last, great cavalry charges of British Army history. It has been described as "perhaps the most dramatic of the war, [it] was decisive. It turned the entire

Turkish position and led to the fall of Jerusalem". He saw out the War and returned home to Australia on 28 April 1918.[52]

Meanwhile, back to late 1915 and the campaign on the Peninsula, the weather soon turned from hot to cold and was to be equally tormenting. As Charlie recorded:

> Very Quiet on Peninsular
> this last few weeks
> Waiting for big charge
> I hope to God we are not
> on Peninsular for Winter
> for I am sure the Colonial
> Troops will Perish [CBH I 5]

The observation in one of the entries above about there being few bayonet wounds is interesting and very valid. In fact, the Great War, with its industrialised killing machines, was the first war for hundreds of years where bayonets had become far less important. Artillery accounted for most of the deaths, followed by bullet wounds and poison gas. The constant artillery bombardments caused most casualties and, even on relatively quiet days, they accounted for hundreds of men dying across the various theatres. Sickness was also to play a dreadful role in many deaths.

Death was an ever-present companion. On 5 September 1915, Charlie noted:

> 5th September
> Had the Sydney Morning Herald
> given to me today
> dated July 28th 1915
> to my surprise saw the photo of Les Pountney
> of Port Macquarie.
> Died of wounds Hard
> Luck for Dick. [CBH I 4]

Private Leslie Raymond Pountney of A squadron, 5th Light Horse

Regiment was from Port Macquarie, NSW. He was a station hand before the War and how Charlie knew him is not clear. He died in a hospital ship from a bullet wound to the right shoulder sustained at Anzac Cove, on 28 June 1915, aged 26. There is a sad letter on his service file from his brother that notes that when notifying of his death the Army referred to an incorrect identification number and that "this now hangs over my parents head as a great suspense". This is because another brother, who was also at Gallipoli, had written a letter that said, "Les slightly wounded in shoulder, not serious, not need to worry, well, 30th June Love Rupert". The first brother wrote: "We all realise that mistakes are made in every business concern and that there are always a certain amount of excuses for them, but this terrible suspension, whilst in doubt, is the hardest part of all" and queries whether Les had actually died. Unfortunately, he had.[53]

Les Pountney's last letter home[54] is full of information:

> Just a few lines to let you know we are leaving for the front tonight (May 15). We go by train to Alexandria, and there embark for the Dardanelles. Rupert left last week with the first Light Horse, but the battalion is dismounted, as we shall be for a few weeks, or until a safe landing for the horses can be effected. The men are all delighted and in great spirits at being given a chance to see what sort of stuff they are made of.
>
> You will find the spirit of courage and daring will be abroad, and that our men will follow the track of our infantry, and die for their country if need be. I am just longing to shake hands with a Turk; I'll make it a severe one too. They are low down beggars. They have committed some terrible atrocities on our fellow-men. Our regiment for one, and possibly the whole of the Australians, vow that no prisoners be taken; quite right too.
>
> My squadron (A) escorted 250 of them out the other day. I missed the chance of going, but saw them passing for the prison. In all about 1000 of them are a few miles from here. They live

well and are treated well. In return, what do our prisoners of war receive? Very bad shift if what we hear is correct. As a matter of fact the British are too good. These Turks simply pray to Allah and eat all day. I believe they couldn't be hunted away.

Was speaking to Dave Baird this morning, and of course he's very pleased to be off to the front. We have discarded our leggings, and are wearing puttees in their place. We all carry a pack, and today we carry 220 rounds of ammunition with us, so we will have a fair weight up. We have been having a good many marches lately in preparation for the task ahead of us.

The First Light Horse went straight into the trenches, and I believe some of their wounded have already returned to Heliopolis. Rupert will be right into it by this, and blazing away at the unspeakable Turk. Thank goodness I shall be close handy to him directly - shoulder to shoulder - and be able to take my share in the defence of our cause.

We shall keep the flag flying though we fall ourselves. I always receive the 'Port News', and hand it on to Stacy. I read my letter, and consider it a compliment for you to pass it for publication.

Stacy tells me he has forwarded you some notes for the paper. (We might here state that many of our readers have complimented us upon the composition and intelligence displayed by the author of the letter referred to.

One instance comes from the late President of the Manning Shire Council, Mr. H. McKinnon, who says: your son's letter was the finest I have ever read of the many that have been published, and the young boy's diary was very good.)

This will be the last letter from Egypt. The next will be from the trenches I hope, and will be precise, something like 'all's well,' or 'doing fine'. Will not be allowed to say much, and business will no doubt be brisk. I think there can only be one issue to this great struggle, and we will win.

Lord Kitchener sent a message to our General (Sir Ian

> Hamilton) in which he said, "Once you set foot on Gallipoli Peninsula you must fight to a finish". Well, we will do that, and do our best. Good-bye, Father, with my best love to you all, and that I be spared to return to you and mother and all friends.
>
> I especially hope little Rupert will pull through, but if not ... we will both return and have a good camping expedition and grand run round in dear old Port Macquarie. Nothing that I have seen so far can come up to it. Good-night.

Charlie further writes:

> Will we have Turkey
>
> No doubt the Turk is great
> Fighter & clean fighter [CBH I 135]

However, despite this one entry of praise, on multiple occasions he records very different sentiments:

> No Turks Prisoner [CBH I 20]
>
> Why should we take Prisoners [CBH I 145]
>
> Show no mercy on German Officers [CBH I 118]

While, at the beginning of the diary, he has expressed the following:

> Allah Allah they yell &
> when they know they are
> beaten they throw down
> their arms and want to
> be taken prisoners but
> Australians don't take
> Prisoners. [CBH I 2]

The preceding passage is pretty stark and grates against the positive image of Australian diggers in the Great War. Did they actually shoot and kill prisoners who had surrendered? Charlie says German officers should receive no mercy. Is this what actually happened? There is definitely evidence that hand-to-hand fighting at Gallipoli was a brutal affair. It would not be unheard of that in the heat of battle some ruthless things happened. When does a fight to the death suddenly change to one where the man who was trying to kill you minutes or even seconds before can surrender and expect total mercy? As Winston Churchill said, the definition of a prisoner of war was "a man who tries to kill you and fails, and then asks you not to kill him".[55] It is very hard to judge from over a hundred years later. Although it should be said that many of the incidents detailed below were unlikely to have occurred in the heat of battle.

This has been very much a taboo subject for discussion for most of the last 100 years. The amount of historical work on British soldiers' actions in this regard has been derisory and is principally encompassed in only a few books, research articles and a PhD thesis – mostly within the last 25 years. As a whole it cannot be denied that to some degree the history of the period has been sanitised.

Particularly, from an Australian perspective, prominent military historian Joan Beaumont has noted:

> Similarly, in the official history of the war Bean tailored his account of the Australian soldier to fit his preconceived notions about the Australian character. Despite his passion for factual accuracy, he has also been criticised for sanitising his account of the war. His official history excluded 'the real and ugly face of battle', omitting some of the less savoury aspects of Australians in conflict, such as the killing of prisoners of war and self-inflicted wounds, even though Bean had himself recorded examples of these practices in the diary he kept in the trenches.[56]

The fact that Allied troops did indeed kill those who were surrendering is clear from the historical record. Why may they have done it? As British historian, Paul Hodges, notes in his comprehensive work on the topic:

> In soldiers' diaries and letters by far the most frequently expressed motivations for perpetrating atrocity were feelings

> of retaliation and revenge. These powerful feelings seem to have been endemic during the war. Soldiers' reactions to these pressures and feelings varied but they could produce incredibly forceful, untypical, unwise and atrocious actions and terrible escalating cycles of violence between the opposing sides. Worth considering in this context is the complicity of various levels of command in promoting revenge feelings and violence cycles, as all the better for the men's 'fighting spirit'. The flood of propaganda utilising atrocity is one of the few aspects of atrocity in the First World War that has received much study, although its actual effect on troops and their actions needs some attention.[57]

Of course, the killing of prisoners and orders of "no quarter be given" were considered morally wrong but they had also been explicitly proscribed in the Hague Convention in regulations 23 (c) & (d). The British had signed the convention in 1907. It is generally recorded that German and other enemy officers were treated comparatively well but the other ranks were subject to varying degrees of harshness. It would also seem from German archives that "incidences of prisoner mistreatment increased steadily throughout the war".[58]

There has been a degree of focus on this topic by a handful of Canadian authors like Tim Cook at the Canadian War Museum.[59] He cites many contemporaneous references from the war years that noted that the Canadians were considered particularly brutal and often did not take prisoners. For example, one Canadian soldier, Fred Hamilton, who was captured by the Germans in 1918, retold how he himself received a beating because, as the German Colonel told him: "I don't care for the English, Scotch, French, Australians or Belgians, but damn you Canadians, you take no prisoners and you kill our wounded".[60]

In one journal article in 2006, Cook relates details of at least 40 cases of executions of German prisoners by Canadian troops. These are all gleaned from soldiers' personal war diaries and/or letters home to loved ones. He notes that there was mostly no shame recorded:

> Perhaps the millions and millions of dead had inured all sense of loss, or perhaps it was just a common, ruthless reality of the battlefield, as it has been throughout human history. Whatever the case, these executions were not secrets to be buried in shallow graves with executed prisoners.[61]

It is not surprising to find out that particular enemy behaviour that led to killings related to revenge and retaliation for snipers, flame thrower operators, those who used saw-toothed bayonets and, in very many cases, the fear of "fake surrender" (ie where the so-called surrendering enemy soldiers turned their weapons on their capturers and killed them).

Cook goes on to note that when the Canadian Broadcast Corporation interviewed over 600 veterans for a radio series entitled *Flanders' Fields* in the 1960s, dozens of those interviewed relate accounts of executing German prisoners. Notably none of these stories made the final broadcast.[62] In fact, from the late 1920s on, official and non-official histories seldom referred to these accounts. Cook summarised:

> The politics of memory had begun to change, and what was acceptable during and immediately after the war seems, by the late 1920s, to have resulted in a stronger rebuke from Canadian generals, who believed they had to fight vigilantly against those attempting to denigrate the memory of the [Canadian Expeditionary Force]. And while veterans of the CEF were willing to depict these battlefield executions during the 1960s, military historians have followed the lead of generals rather than the men who carried out the acts, by burying this harsh reality of the Western Front war-fighting.[63]

Importantly, he concludes that: "The lack of control by officers on the battlefield may be a reason for some of the killings, but there appear to be no cases of [Canadian] soldiers being sanctioned or court-martialed for excessive cruelty".[64] In the Australian case, General Sir John Monash wrote in his memoirs in 1923 that: "Australian soldiers are nothing if not sportsmen, and no case ever came under my notice of brutality or inhumanity to prisoners".[65]

Nevertheless, other studies have noted that "Soldiers often commented that entire national forces were eager to massacre opponents: Australians, Canadians and Scottish Highlanders were the most frequently mentioned in this context".[66]

For example, in a contemporaneous note by a French officer at Gallipoli in 1915, Jean Giraudoux, said that "the Australians massacre all the Turks. One Australian told me that the Turks are their national enemy".[67]

In fact, as pointed out by Hodges, the clearest and first recorded written order from World War I, directing British troops to only take a limited number of prisoners, was an Anzac one. In the *Official History*, Bean relates a raid made by 75 men of the 3rd New Zealand Infantry Brigade on 25 June 1916 on German lines near Armentiéres, east of Pont Ballot. This would have been one of the first actions of these troops who had newly arrived on the Western Front. As Bean states:

> The German trenches were found full of the enemy (including some of his working party), who offered practically no resistance. A large number were shot down or bombed (in accordance with the definite orders for this raid, which limited the number of prisoners to be taken).[68]

The *Official History* notes that 29 Germans of the 133rd Regiment were killed, but "the number of dead does not include those who may have been killed by the bombing of dugouts". Bean comments on this report in a footnote where he states:

> An instruction to take only three prisoners, though rarely issued in a written order, was on several occasions virtually

> given to troops. This was not in accordance with the spirit of the rules of war, nor with the general practice of British, Australian, or New Zealand commanders or troops.[69]

Interestingly, Bean cryptically notes that such orders were given on "several occasions" in a "virtual" rather than written way.

He also reports, without further comment, on a raid by 312 volunteers of the 6th Australian Infantry Brigade (variously from the 21st, 22nd, 23rd and 24th Battalions) a few nights later on 29/30 June 1916, south west of the Armentiéres – Wavrin railway where:

> The operation really comprised three simultaneous raids on separate points, and all parties met with opposition. … The bombing parties entered the trench and turned right and left, bombing the enemy. Some of these were in their dugouts, where one of them who showed fight was killed. … One prisoner was taken, but he appears to have escaped or been killed.[70]

In all, five prisoners were taken and 112 casualties from the 231st Reserve Infantry Regiment.

There is no doubt that trench warfare could be brutal. For example, Sapper Edward Leslie Hughes, watching the 4th Australian Division attack on the Oosttaverne Line on 7 June 1917, stated:

> it was a magnificent, though dreadful sight to witness... As usual the 'Ossies' made a clean sweep... To watch the Huns run out of their trenches towards us – and to see the way the 'Ossies' harpooned them one after another, it was a sight that I shall always recall.[71]

However, this does not in fact talk of killing surrendering prisoners, just the viciousness of war. As to the former there are two examples from Gallipoli recorded by eyewitnesses.

A British Second Lieutenant, Reginald Savory, wrote in his memoir that at the Cape Helles in mid-1915, the men's discussions were: [Hodges 2006, 74]

> not that of demoralized, so much as that of very angry and

> puzzled men. The snipers were the worst. There was one who had been found in a tree, behind our lines, and had picked out the officers. He was found and shot, in cold blood, a very gallant man. Feeling was running high. Some Turkish , who had been bought down to the beach, were said to have been lined up under the cliff and executed. What truth there was in this, I do not know, but it was widely believed, and the name of the officer who ordered it was freely mentioned.[72]

Also, at Cape Helles, Hodges quotes a Chief Petty Officer G.V. Sharkey of the Royal Navy Armoured Car Division, attached to the 29th Division who recorded that:

> Our Red Cross attendants Charlesworth and Kelly worked like heros [sic], they carried the wounded down to the dressing station and returned to the firing line with boxes of ammunition on the stretcher... It was a strong point of his [Charlesworth] never to allow a German to live. He soon made short work of them as he had seen enough of them in Belgium.[73]

Further, Starkey records that on the road back to the landing beach at Cape Helles:

> stands a Serj Major who examines all stretchers as the wounded are being carried down and if the being be a German or a Turk the order rings our 'Drop it and Stand Clear!', immediately there is a sharp report and the wounded man is a dead one. It is some game upon my word. I took his place for a couple of hours till he got a rest and after the things I saw I am quite clear in my mind. One has only to think what these Huns did to the Belgians and I say, that when you catch one kill him slowly but make sure you are doing away with him.[74]

At the Gallipoli Landings on 25 April 1915, the *Official History* recorded (without comment) that Major I. Jackson's company of the 9th Australian Battalion moved towards Little Ari Burnu and:

A desultory rifle fire was coming from the slopes ahead of it. As the company moved down the back of Little Ari Burnu into the valley, it found a small stone hut, in which were half a dozen Turks and a small fire with a pot of coffee on it. The Turks were bayonetted.[75]

On 29 April 1915 Bean wrote in his diary, four days after the landing, that he had been told by Australian soldiers:

That they had orders from their subordinate officers in some cases to take no prisoners, in the first rush at any rate, and whilst things were bad. … I don't believe this either, though it may be true.[76]

During the Battle of Pozières, Private Percy Smythe of the 3rd Australian Battalion says that at one stage on 23 July 1916:

At this time [the platoon] were digging themselves in, connecting up shell-craters, so Bert fell to with an entrenching tool. A few Germans would occasionally appear in front, but did not give them much trouble. A batch of about a dozen Fritzes came towards them, apparently with the intention of surrendering, but some of the boys fired on them, and they ran for shelter to the remains of an old cottage.[77]

On 5 November 1916, men of the 3rd Australian Battalion raided trenches on the Somme sector. It was a brutal affair and a number of Germans were taken prisoner. Sergeant A.E. Matthews wrote in his diary:

Orders came through from Brigade for us to evacuate our position and to leave no live Germans behind. Guessing that there would be dirty work for somebody killing the wounded prisoners, I and a Lance Corporal volunteered to escort the two unwounded prisoners back to Battn Hqrs and we had just got away when we heard the awful screams of the men who were slaughtered through military necessity.[78]

An Australian soldier later related that, during trench fighting in France in August 1917, they took two German prisoners, one wounded, and then:

> The German asked [our officer] to give his comrade a drink. 'Yes', our officer said, 'I'll give the [so and so] a drink, take this' and he emptied his revolver on the two of them. This is the only way to treat a Hun. What we enlisted for was to kill Huns, those baby-killing [so and so's].[79]

During the Battle of the Menin Road, at Polygon Wood on 20 September 1917, Private Walter Bradby of 8th Australian Battalion came across a wounded Australian on a stretcher surrounded by Australian troops and a German prisoner:

> It transpired that he could speak English, and Paddy was pleading with him, cajoling him, threatening him to take hold of the fourth arm of the stretcher – all to no avail. The German, standing at attention and drawing himself up to his full height, stated that as an officer he would not help to carry the stretcher. This went on for a while until Paddy, losing patience, took a few paces forward, drawing a revolver (which he had no right to be carrying), shot the German officer.[80]

In the same battle, military historian Les Carlyon reports on a number of incidents, without any additional commentary. The first related to men of the 2nd Australian Division attacking a line of German pillboxes (ie fortified concrete bunkers).

> Some Germans inside wanted to surrender and others didn't, a common point of confusion. One came out with his hands up. Another fired between the first man's legs and wounded an Australian sergeant. 'Get out of the way, sergeant', a Lewis gunner yelled. 'I'll see to the bastards.' He fired three or four bursts into the entrance and killed or wounded most of those inside.[81]

Equally 1st Division soldiers under the command of Lieutenant Ivon Murdoch were also raiding pillboxes:

> [Murdoch] was passing a pillbox that he assumed the battalions

in front of him had dealt with. A bomb suddenly went off at his feet. Murdoch told his men to fire at the loophole. Another lieutenant worked around to the entrance of the pillbox and took nine prisoners. Murdoch's men were unaware these men had surrendered and shot them all.[82]

Reporting on another nearby incident, Lieutenant Colonel Maurice Wilder-Neligan of the 10th Battalion noted that when a lieutenant was shot in the head:

> the men "went mad". Germans tried to surrender and Australians pelted them with bombs.[83]

Again during the same battle Bean reports in the *Official History* that after Captain F. L. Moore of the 5th Battalion was shot by a German who had grabbed a rifle after already having surrendered:

> The Victorians [of the 5th Battalion] at once killed this man and others, and only interposition by their officers stopped them from exterminating the whole garrison.[84]

In yet another incident, the *Official History* relates the story of Lieutenant W. D. Joynt of the 8th Battalion:

> He states that during this attack he came upon a wide circle of troops of his brigade surrounding a two-storied pillbox, and firing at a loophole in the upper story, from which shots were coming. One man, coolly standing close below and firing up at it, fell back killed, but the Germans in the lower chamber soon afterwards surrendered. The circle of Australians at once assumed easy attitudes, and the prisoners were coming out when a shot was fired, killing an Australian. The shot came from the upper story, whose inmates knew nothing of the surrender of the men below; but the surrounding troops were much too heated to realise this. To them the deed appeared to be the vilest treachery, and they forthwith bayonetted the prisoners. One Victorian, about to bayonet a German, found that his own bayonet was not on his rifle. While the wretched

prisoners implored him for mercy, he grimly fixed it and then bayonetted the man.[85]

The *Official History* concludes:

> The Germans in this case were entirely innocent, but such incidents are inevitable in the heat of battle, and any blame for them lies with those who make wars, not those who fight them.[86]

British military historian, John Keegan, criticised Bean and the *Official History* for essentially condoning this "improper violence".[87]

Lieutenant Percy Lay, also of the 8th Battalion, recounted how at the Battle of Broodseinde on 4 October 1917, he and his men had captured a German headquarters:

> We then started on a machine gun position and shot the crews of the two guns with the exception of one man and we made him turn his gun on his own men but our people thought we were Huns and opened fire on us. So we had to shoot the Hun and get the guns back.[88]

It should be noted that none of this evidence is corroborated, as no disciplinary hearings are known to have occurred. And it should be noted that none of this discussion has dealt with any potential war crimes committed by German or Turkish troops of which there were many accusations through the course of the War. Indeed, there is "evidence that Germans carried out orders to take no prisoners as early as August 1914 at the expense of both British and French soldiers".[89] As British historian Richard Holmes estimated, whatever side they were on, a prisoner of war's chances of surviving and getting to the rear, given attacking troops and artillery bombardments, was no more than 50 percent.[90]

Australian historian, Dale Blair, recounts numerous other cases of Australians killing prisoners on the Western Front. He summarised the issue:

> While questions of ethics and morality are undoubtedly un-

dermined in war, and particularly in the heat of battle, men did not surrender reason or their understandings of right and wrong to it – and, indeed, most did not. Nor did citizens supporting the war have to mutely acquiesce when confronted by knowledge of some of war's brutality.[91]

Certainly, there were also many other cases made against the British troops by the Germans on the Western Front. The German authorities accused the British of ordering the killing and mistreatment of German soldiers. Both during and after the War the German Kriegsministerium (War Ministry) operated a Militäruntersuchungsstelle für Verletzungen des Kriegrechts (Military Bureau for the Investigation of Violations of Laws of War). They collated a number of instances including the murder of as many as 80 unarmed soldiers near Messines in November 1914, the murder of 20-30 surrendering soldiers by Scottish troops at Loos in September 1915, the murder of five soldiers near Fricourt and another 30 nearby on the first day of the Battle of the Somme, the shooting of a prisoner in July 1917, seven soldiers who were murdered by having their throats slit during the 100 Day Offensive in October 1918 and around the same time, near Cambrai, the murder of wounded and medical personnel by English and Canadian troops.[92] None of these were fully investigated by British authorities. Equally, after the War a former German army doctor, August Gallinger, published an account called *Countercharge* that detailed large number of prisoner killing incidents by French troops.[93]

Feltman records that at least two senior British officers acknowledged that prisoner killing was condoned. He quotes Brigadier Frank Maxwell, who was commanding the 12th Battalion of the Middlesex regiment, writing to his wife in September 1916 about a recent battle saying:

> The ground was, of course, the limit itself, and progress over it like nothing imaginable, the enemy quite determined to keep us out, as they had so many before. And I must say that they

> fought stubbornly and bravely, and probably not more than 300 to 500 put their hands up. They took it out of us badly, but we did ditto; and I have no shame in saying so, as every German should, in my opinion, be exterminated, I don't know that we took one. I have not seen a man or officer yet who did, anyway.[94]

The second General is Hubert Gough:

> General Charles Broad admitted that the killing of prisoners "was apt to be encouraged by some high commanders", and singled out the commander of the 5th Army, Hubert Gough, as having set "a bad example in the way he declared in favour of chucking bombs down dug-outs even when the occupants wanted to surrender". Not only was prisoner killing tolerated in Gough's army; efforts to promote mercy met with resistance. If Broad is to be believed, when one of Gough's brigadiers attempted to dissuade troops from simply tossing bombs into dugouts containing men ready to surrender "Gough upbraided him for being too merciful, and insisted that the troops were right".[95]

Also worth noting, Lieutenant General Sir Launcelot Kiggell, who was Field Marshall Haig's chief of staff, issued an order on 28 June 1916, which included the following:

> It is the duty of all ranks to continue to use their weapons against the enemy's fighting troops, unless and until it is beyond all doubt that those have not only ceased all resistance, but that, whether through having voluntarily thrown down their weapons and otherwise, they have definitely and finally abandoned all hope or intention of resisting further. In the case of apparent surrender, it lies with the enemy to prove his intention beyond the possibility of misunderstanding, before the surrender can be accepted as genuine.[96]

This would appear to be an eminently sensible statement and yet some historians have claimed it gave a licence to some troops to act wrongfully.

The eminent historian Niall Ferguson has also written on the topic. He records various incidents gleaned from diaries and letters of British soldiers. For example, he quotes A. Ashurst Moris who wrote in his diary on 16 June 1915:

> At this point, I saw a Hun, fairly young, running down the trench, hands in air, looking terrified, yelling for mercy. I promptly shot him. It was a heavenly sight to see him fall forward. A Lincoln officer was furious with me, but the scores we owe wash out anything else.[97]

He also notes a Private Frank Richards of the Royal Welch Fusiliers who:

> Recalled seeing another man in his regiment walk off down the Menin Road with six prisoners only to return some minutes later having "done the trick" with "two bombs". Richards attributed his action to the fact that "the loss of a pal had upset him very much".[98]

Another case was recorded by Henri Gaudier-Brzeska, a soldier in the French Army, who noted in a letter from the Western Front to a friend in May 1915:

> We also had a handful of prisoners – 10 - & as we had just learnt the loss of the "Lusitania" [ie a passenger ship sunk by a German U Boat] they were executed with the [rifle] butts after a 10 minutes dissertation among the NCO and the men.[99]

As to the officer corps he has further anecdotes:

> In his notes 'from recent fighting' by II Corps, dated 17 August 1916, General Sir Claud Jacob urged that no prisoners should be taken as they hindered 'mopping up'.[100]

And further:

> As Brigadier General F. P. Crozier observed: 'The British soldier is a kindly fellow and it is safe to say, despite the dope [propaganda], seldom oversteps the mark of propriety in

> France, save occasionally to kill prisoners he cannot be bothered to escort back to his lines.[101]

And, finally:

> At Gallipoli in May 1915 Captain Guy Warneford Nightingale of the Royal Munster Fusiliers and his men "took 300 prisoners and could have taken 3000 but preferred shooting them".[102]

In summary there were many instances of Allied (let alone Central Powers) troops taking matters into their own hands and killing prisoners. In fact one could say it was a somewhat common occurrence. However, to put this in perspective, towards the end of the War the Allies on the Western Front had taken more than 360,000 German prisoners in 1918 alone. The proportionate killings were numerically insignificant when compared with the wholesale slaughter of prisoners carried out by Germans, Japanese and Soviet troops in World War II. The Fascist and Communist ideologies of the authorities in the later conflict turbo-charged the massacre of surrendering soldiers. To an extent, it provoked some British and American troops to reciprocate, particularly in the Pacific theatre of war.

Ferguson considers that the killing of prisoners was a tragic outcome of the bitter fighting, particularly on the Western Front, where combatants often came to believe that death awaited those who surrendered and thus a tit-for-tat series of killings escalated. As he has stated:

> [In World War II] forces continued to fight tenaciously long after any realistic chance of victory had disappeared. Part of the explanation lies in the extremely violent battlefield culture that developed … which deterred soldiers from surrendering, even when they found themselves in hopeless situations. This culture had its origins on the Western Front during the First World War.[103]

Ferguson goes on to note that the tragic irony of this is that getting your enemy to surrender as prisoners is actually the way to end wars and so the encouragement of surrendering is in the combatant countries' best interests. As he notes: "It was a common misconception of the age of total war that victory went to the side that killed the most of the enemy in battle. … But if killing the enemy had been the key to victory, the Central Powers would have won the First World War and the Axis Powers the Second". He then quotes German 19th Century military strategist Carl von Clausewitz who noted: "[Captured] artillery and prisoners are therefore at all times regarded as the true trophies of victory, as well as its measure, because through these things its extent is declared beyond a doubt". Thus, in conclusion, Ferguson states: "A logical inference from this is that enemy troops should be encouraged to surrender – or, at least, not discouraged from doing so".[104]

On the other hand, to balance the ledger, below are two cases where Australian troops took a different course and convinced their colleagues not to execute prisoners. The first is reported by Private Smythe, again from the Battle of Pozières on 25 July 1916:

> A German prisoner was brought in, and his thin drawn face was white and haggard. He looked, indeed, an object for pity. He sank down on the ground by the hedge just out of the communication trench, and they left him there. [A sergeant] wanted to go out and kill him, but we all cried him down, for in our own affliction we could well sympathise with a fellow-sufferer, even though he was one of our enemy.[105]

While, in the official citation awarding Private Jorgen Jensen of the 50th Battalion with a Victoria Cross during trench warfare at Noreuil, France, it is noted:

> Jensen sent a prisoner to a nearby post of Germans, instructing them to surrender too. Ignorant of their surrender, Australian troops began firing on the second group of Germans until Jensen, at great risk, stood on the barricade waving his helmet until the firing stopped.[106]

Lastly, when discussing the potential murder of prisoners of war it is worth recalling the celebrated case of "Breaker" Morant.

Australian readers will be familiar with the story of Harry "Breaker" Morant. In a case that related to the Second Boer War, Morant, who it would appear contributed to his own myth-making, was executed by the British Army for killing in cold blood, not only Boer prisoners of war but also unarmed civilians. He was born in England and migrated to Australia as a young man and embellished his life story by claiming to be the son of a British admiral whereas his parents ran a workhouse in Somerset. Nonetheless, he was a dashing bushman who rode a horse well (hence the nickname "the Breaker") and wrote poems for the influential, radical magazine, *The Bulletin*. He went to the South African conflict to find fame and fortune and was made a lieutenant in a British irregular mounted force known as the Bushveldt Carbineers. In July 1901, after the death of his unit's captain, he led his troops on a killing spree that included women and children and (probably) a Christian missionary, as well as surrendering Boer troops. He was tried by the British authorities, found guilty and executed by firing squad in 1902 along with his direct subordinate, Australian Lieutenant Peter Handcock. Another subordinate from Australia Lieutenant Witton received a life sentence.

Their unsuccessful defence against prosecution was that there were different ethical considerations in time of war and that, in addition, General Herbert Kitchener, the British commanding officer, had condoned the killings when he ordered his troops to drive the population into concentration camps and, in the wake of this scorched earth policy, to "leave no living thing". Morant argued: "We were out fighting the Boers, not sitting comfortably behind barb-wire entanglements; we got them and shot them under Rule 303" [ie the 303 rifle bullet] and Witton argued that it was unfair "to judge the participants by the hard and fast rules of citizen life or the strict moral codes of peace". The courtmartial did not accept that this directive was a direct order to murder prisoners and so they failed.[107]

The case had some notoriety in Australia immediately after the events and there were serious question marks raised about the legal procedures. Subsequently, Witton was released from prison in 1904 (although not pardoned). However, it is unclear whether Charlie Hardy or his mates would have heard of the case. There is a reasonable chance that they had. Years later it became a popular legend in the 1980s with the release of a film that lauded Morant as a martyr of British injustice. His victims' families probably had a different view. Nonetheless, today the story of Morant remains a celebrated one amongst large numbers of Australians and there have even been recent calls for the three men to be formally pardoned for their crimes.[108] So it is should not be a surprise, and maybe it is unremarkable, to read a passage in Charlie Hardy's diary that says "Australians don't take Prisoners".

5

Gallipoli: September-December 1915

"I kissed and thought it was my last"

It was not long before Charlie got into the routine of trench warfare at Gallipoli. There is much that he records in his diary. Some of it humorous, some deadly serious. As the pages pass by it is clear that the young man from Sydney, who had obviously started his adventure in a wide-eyed fashion, was having darker thoughts.

After the failure of the big push in late August 1915, Hamilton requested more troops – in fact 95,000. However, he only received some 20,000. The grand strategic picture was changing. On 14 October 1915, Bulgaria entered the war on the Central Powers' side. This threatened Greece and Serbia. Also, and probably more importantly, the French had requested a concentration of forces on the Western Front. Increasingly, British troops were being diverted to Greece and to France.

The Gallipoli campaign, however, continued. Troops died every day. Not just from artillery shells and bullets, but also from sickness, mainly dysentery. This scourge was boosted by the ongoing summer heat, the flies attracted by the bloated corpses of the dead, and the general unsanitary conditions in the trenches, exacerbated by the shortage of water.

Following the failure of the Battle at Hill 60 to punch through the Ottoman defences the 19th Battalion was mainly employed in the defence of Pope's Post. Eventually, it was to be evacuated from the Gallipoli Peninsula along with all other forces on 19 December 1915.

The men did not stay in the front trenches the whole time they were there. There was an elaborate series of rotations. First, a unit might spend up to a week in the front line. They would then rotate to trenches in a second line of defence for another week or two. They would then be sent even further back from the front line for relief and fatigues. Although at Gallipoli nowhere was out of Turkish artillery range and the fatigues they had to undertake could be backbreaking work.

SEPTEMBER 1915

With these rotations Charlie obviously had a chance on occasion to even get off shore to the ships that were anchored in support.

> Had wash to day on
> the S.S. Ceramic. First one
> in fortnight. [CBH I 61]

Further, he could meet up with other troops.

> The French Troops are
> very funny the[y] don't
> get any jam Issued
> to them so they come
> up to us and say
> Jam Johnnie Jam
> Well the usual
> thing for tin of jam is Bottle of Vino
> (wine) I don't care for it
> gives me Pains
> in my incinerator [CBH I 5]

> Had a chat with an
> Indian officer today
> and he said the war
> would last all 1915 [CBH I 18]

Charlie considered himself a bit of a poet and tried his hand as such on more than one occasion whilst whiling away the hours in the trenches. The poems express his unhappiness with trench warfare and also with those men back in Australia who failed to enlist.

The Heroes of the Dardanelles
------"---------"--------"----------

Where shell & shrapnel screaming
fly in Turkey's hostile land,
Where comrades round him drop
and die.
Our brave lads takes his stand.
He takes his stand against
the Turk -----
the vassal of the Hun;
With Bayonet jolts he gets to work,
And yelling scoundrels run.
He fights not for the love of fight;
Nor Battle Crimsons lust;
He fights fights for liberty &
right for all that's good & just.
He fights for freedom
from the thrall
that German rule would bring
upon the world for one and all
For peasant & the King [CBH I 103]

He promptly answered Britain's call
"to Arms, to arms, ye Brave".
And risks not should he fall over
So that our flags still wave.
Eh what is that He's wounded oh
Its but the Battle Brand

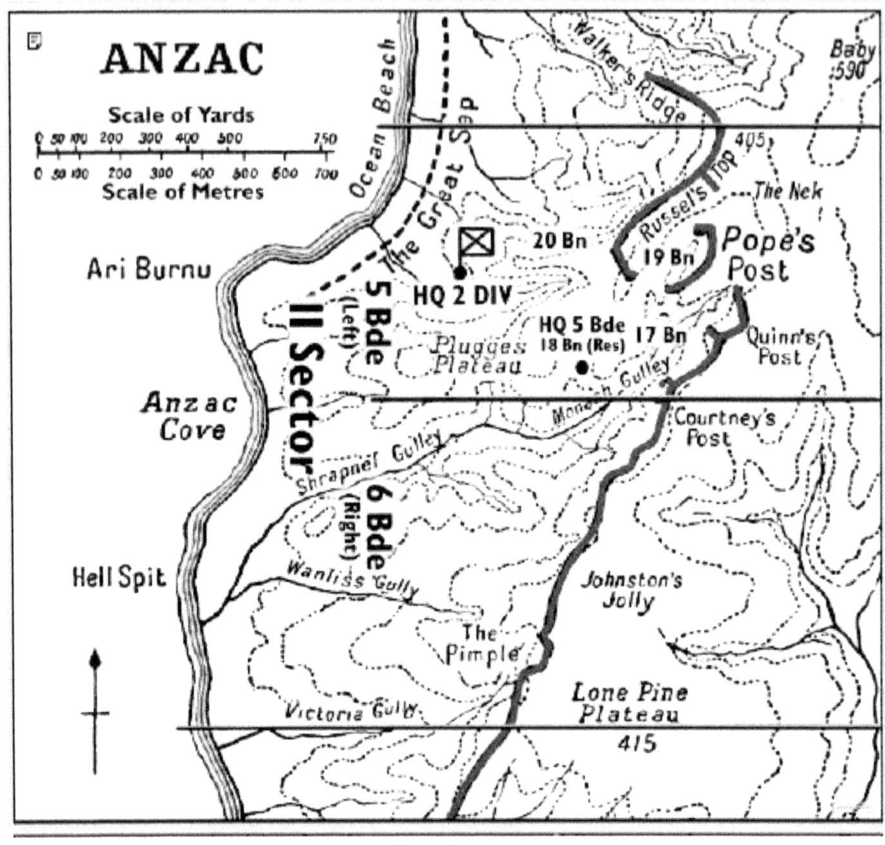

Gallipoli, 1915
(reproduced from Matthews and Wilson 2010, Research Disk)

And soon again he'll meet the fox
In combat hand to hand
And make the swarthy Turk turn pale
And run in dire dismay
And make the Sauerkraut Huns turn red
And flee in haste away
Oh Lord protect our gallant lad
And all his comrades too
Oh make our anxious bosoms glad
And cheer our souls anew
My journey safe return to those

Who left us for thy sake
To fight the "Overbearing" foes
Who would the world
remake

Charles B Hardy
B. Coy 19th Batt [CBH I 112]

As months passed, the problems associated with the heat became problems with the cold. Thousands suffered from frostbite, not least because their uniforms (of shorts and light shirts in many cases) were designed for desert warfare not winter. Things only worsened as time moved on.

For Charlie life at the front continued:

We do our general rounds
of morning looking for
Cigarette Butts & when
we find enough we make
whole ones [CBH I 15]

Sent Flo [sister] service card on 2.9.15 [CBH I 117]

Sept 7 Had very bad night
Dysentry & pains in Head [CBH I 117]

Sept 8 Pretty right again [but]
teeth are giving me Hell. [CBH I 117]

Greeks are kicking up
the devil because
they are going to war
soon. They say
Turkey Finis But I
Think they talk too
Much. Women
snipers are pretty good. They collect
The Discs off the men they snipe also their

cash which they are
very fond of. [CBH I 15]

Poor old Mick I lost to day
how stiff 19.9.15 [CBH I 116]

It is not certain who Mick is, although it is known that besides Private Clyde Compton, the other member of B Company, 19th Battalion, to be killed in action on that day was Private Norman Arthur-Mason, aged 19. He was from Petersham, Sydney, although born in England, and had been a dairyman before the war.[109]

Charlie continues:

22/9/15 Met Sanders – fighting Turks [CBH I 15]

Meet young Sanders the carrier's
son left me to day to have
scrap at Turks. 22.9.15 [CBH I 111]

Again, it is not clear who Sanders definitely was, although it is highly likely it was Private Thomas Sanders of the 18th Battalion who had been on the same troopship as Charlie coming over to the Middle East. He was a saddler before the War from Tamworth, NSW. He was aged 19 at the time of this meeting. Sanders was wounded in France and also had a case of shell shock, most likely acquired during the Battle of Pozières on 31 July 1916, and returned to Australia 4 May 1917.[110]

Charlie continues:

Caught sniper
He was painted Green
all over and had
plenty of ammunition
& water to last him
four weeks[CBH I 16]

That prompted another poem from Charlie:

Gallopoli Penninsular

August. 15

No Smoking

A flash and the sudden
Whistle of a cordite driven
ball.

A sob in the clinging
darkness and privates dead
that's all

From spur of that distant
Mountain for an instant
Gleamed a spark.
From the lips of a Turkish
Rifle a Lightning Stab in dark.

Yes a pipe needs a match to
Light it.
And match is a beacon light
To eyes of Turkish marksman
As he snipes the camp at night.

Though death for smokes expensive yet who was there to say.
[CBH I 17]

That a darned Turkish
Sniper was out on his murdering lay. [CBH I 18]

He also records the movement of the 10th Division:

Troops of the 10th Div[ision] left
Penninsular to go up to
Salonica but when
they got there they
had to turn back
they say the Greeks
didn't want them
they might later on [CBH I 16]

The British 10th (Irish) Division was made up principally of Irish troops but also units from Hampshire in England. It landed at Suvla Bay in early August 1915 but, given the stalemate, in September it was moved to Salonika in Greece to cover the Allied flank due to the impending entry of Bulgaria into the War. Charlie's information must have been trench scuttlebut and was only half incorrect. The Greeks were in a state of turmoil about which side to support in the War. Their King Constantine had German relatives and sympathies (indeed, he was married to the Kaiser's sister) and he was steering the country to join the Central Powers or at best stay neutral. In the ensuing argument he was deposed and forced to abdicate (although he did return to the throne later) and the Greeks joined the Allies‘ Entente. However, despite the original reluctance of the Greeks to welcome the British (and French) troops, the Allies forced the issue. The 10th Division stayed at Salonika for another two years and were not turned around. Importantly, they fought in the successful Battle of Kosturino against the Bulgarians in early December 1915. The Division would later return to the Middle East to participate in the Sinai and Palestine Campaign.

OCTOBER 1915

Public opinion was turning against the Gallipoli Campaign, stoked by highly critical reporting from Australian journalists such as Keith Murdoch, and from criticism by officers such as General Sir Frederick Stopford, who had been in charge of the Suvla Bay landings of IX Corps but had been sacked by General Hamilton on 15 August 1915 and sent home to England.

Hamilton himself was relieved of duty and replaced by Lieutenant General Sir Charles Monro on 16 October 1915. Part of Monro's initial job on taking command was to assess whether an evacuation was warranted. Taking into account the lack of success so far and the fact that Bulgaria's entry into the war allowed Germany free access to resupply the Ottomans with armaments, including planes and heavy artillery, he recommended evacuation.

Meanwhile, the war in the trenches went on. The 19th Battalion continued to man the trenches at Pope's Post at the top of Monash Valley. Charlie recorded:

> The Turks today are very cheeky
> We threw some bully beef
> and they returned it full
> of slops out of their trench
> and one big Turk shook
> his fist over the parapet at
> us. Sent out on patrol today
> to bury Australian dead
> one grave numbered 78.
> No sooner it was finished
> they shelled the graveyard
> and the bodies were all
> blown up again.
> Shooting Turks is fun to
> the boys but its death
> and sorrow on the Turks
> side. Today Thursday
> the Turks made big
> attack but failed.
> They attacked us again
> but also failed. They
> came at us three times in
> all. There were thousands
> of them killed. [CBH I 19]
>
> No Turks Prisoner [CBH I 20]
>
> Shells are too Bad
> to continue
> CBH [CBH I 8]

Anzac [Cove] shows [it] art land of pests
for Turks and hills and the rest
Sandflies & Hornets just bad there
Nearly drive fellow mad
Even round mosquitoes [they, ie the sandflies]
reveal in fact they are
the very devil. [CBH I 8]

During this period, the 19th Battalion war diary records heavy shelling by the enemy on 8 and 11 October. On the later occasion, it is noted that the guns were directed by German officers. Some 30 shells were recorded and, on 16 October, some nine "stick bombs" were fired by the enemy, wounding nine men. There was a 20 shell barrage on 20 October and more stick bombs on 26 and 29 October.[111] Stick bombs "resembled a large skyrocket and [were] constructed of a simple mortar tube that fired an explosive charge with a wooden stick added for stability in flight".[112]

NOVEMBER 1915

October passed into November and Charlie was still diligently recording events great and small in his diary:

2 November 1915

Nov 2nd Very sick Vomiting
No sleep my god I was bad
I think it's the Tucker
they gave us will I ever
forget what we get to eat
Slice of sour Doughy Bread
& slice of fat bacon it's
Impossible to get lean [meat] for
Dinner Pint of Soup & piece
Of meat [they give us] well I sooner have
Biscuit & water than it

Tea Pint of Tea Slice of
Bread & jam This compares [with]
a Tommies camp and they
eat up every piece
They never had feed till
they come out here
my Honest opinion of them
is they are lot pigs
& they hate us Australians
Because we get a lot & they
get all they're worth [and] no more
Wrote this lying on my bed in the dirt [CBH I 26]

There is quite a bit of bile against the "Tommies" (a nickname used by Australians for English soldiers) in this passage. The reference to "they hate Australians because we get a lot" may not just be about the amount of food they each received. The Australians troops were also paid a lot more than the English. At six shillings a day they were paid more than three times the wages of English troops.[113]

However, Charlie displayed much greater friendliness for the Indian troops.

5 November 1915

Today 5th Nov. 15
Visited the Indian camp
And was Welcomed by
Sergeant of 26th Mountain
Battery had some chap
Patty and curry also
Fruit Higarethes [?] They
Think Terrible lot of the
Australian Soldier [CBH I 8]

26th Mountain Battery

Anzac
Gallopoli 15
(Indian) [CBH I 20]

The 19th Battalion war diary records that there was very heavy firing from the enemy at Pope's Post on 4 November and again on 8, 9 and 10 November. It records that:

8 Nov 0700 After daylight and throughout day enemy's fire heavier than usual.

8 Nov 1800 Enemy's fire heavy, chiefly machine guns cutting sandbags.

9 Nov Rifle grenades fired by enemy during afternoon and night.

9 Nov 1900 Enemy opened heavy fire. Rifle and machine gun. Big use of rifle fire. Catapult bombs & Garland Mortar. Enemy's fire reduced by 2100.

10 Nov Enemy used rifle grenades – enemy fire heavy until 2300. [114]

Charlie's diary continues:

10 November 1915

Today 10th Nov 15
Roy's [brother] Birthday (18 years)
Drank his health out
of my waterbottle. [CBH I 20]

Ha Ha
No shave to day
Hee Hee no bloomin
Razor [CBH I 9]

Meet Red Cross Officer
Today 10/11/15
And to my surprise

Had book of missing
Australians and
Mick Woolcott's name
Was amongst them [CBH I 9]

The news about Mick Woolcott would have been interesting to Charlie. According to Woolcott's service record, he was not missing in action but seems to have completely disappeared. On this day, 10 November, Charlie was interviewed by the authorities as someone who had previously met Woolcott at the convalescent camp on Lemnos in September. It seems that Woolcott could not be located and had never reported back to duty. Oddly enough, the authorities were alerted to this by inquiries from Woolcott's father asking where his son was and why he never received any letters from him. His file even notes that the commanding officer of his battalion – the 18th – "states this man did not actually reach Gallipoli Penin." The service record is not easy to follow and it would seem that after the Gallipoli Campaign ended Woolcott went to England where he was charged multiple times with the offence of absent without leave (AWOL), striking a superior officer and insubordination, spending many months in jail as a consequence. However, it is also records that he survived the War, eventually returned home to Australia and received his three obligatory war medals.[115]

The same day Charlie records:

Turks make advance
at Anzac today
& was Repulsed
with very Heavy
losses Nov 10th [CBH I 10]

A few days later Charlie records an important historical event:

13 November 1915

Lord Kitchener Visited us
Today [13]/11/15 [CBH I 10]

The Secretary of State for War, Lord Kitchener, the hero of Khartoum and the dominant British war leader despite his political rather than military office, visited the Gallipoli Peninsula in person on 13 November 1915. His conclusion was to recommend evacuation of the Peninsula to the British War Cabinet.

Kitchener's visit was recorded by Sergeant John Park, who was formerly of D Company, 19th Battalion, but had been transferred to the 4th Field Company Engineers:

> Upon entering the sap, K became very interested in a digger pounding away with an entrenching tool handle in a small case. "What is that man doing?" Kitchener asked. I explained that he was making a fritter by pounding a biscuit to flour, to which would be added some snow collected from the cemetery as well as some condensed milk, and a little fat from a bully beef tin. … Arriving at mines C1 and C2, Lord Kitchener went down a short distance before enquiring: "How far do they go?" I told him that we were under Abdul's trench. He inspects the concealed firing line, but does not comment. Back in the trench General Birdwood asks one of the troops for the loan of his periscope. "Birdie" holds it above the trench, when "bang", a bullet comes right through the glass. The digger remarks to "Birdie": "That chap can shoot the eye out of a mosquito", and proceeds to raise his hat on the end of a rifle, but receives no response from the Turk. Then to Lord Kitchener he says "If I had my head in it he would drill a hole in it!" The Digger next pulls back a slide in a loophole plate and asks "Kitch" to have a "screw" through it. "Kitch" has a look and, before passing down the trench to C3, remarks: "Thank you very much, we can find our way now, thanks."[116]

Around the same time Charlie recorded a tragic event that had occurred two months earlier:

> What-ho the 6th Brigade
> got torpedoed

near Gallipoli
about 60 drowned
and the Brigadier
was buried at
Mudros East Sept 15 [CBH I 10]

The transport ship H.T. *Southland* was torpedoed by a German U-Boat about 30 miles off Lemnos on 2 September 1915. Amongst the drowned were men of the Australian 6th Infantry Brigade and their officer commanding, a Scotsman named Colonel Richard Linton. Linton's lifeboat capsized and he insisted on being the last man back into the rescue boat. As a result he died of hypothermia from being in the cold waters for too long.[117]

In the trenches Charlie was adding even well-known poems to his diary:

Roaming in the Gloaming

Roaming in Gloaming
On wee Banks of Clyde
I am Roamin in Gloaming
With Lassie by your side
When the sun has gone to rest
That's the time we love best
For I am Roaming in
the Gloamin ….. [CBH 1 9]

"Roamin' in the Gloamin" was a popular song by Sir Harry Lauder written in 1911. From Scotland to the other end of the Empire, Charlie then records meeting up again with the Indian troops.

The 19th Battalion war diary records that there was heavy shelling from the enemy on 16 November and that during a heavy rainstorm on the afternoon of 17 November there was another bout of heavy fire from rifle grenades, stick bombs, rifle and machine guns.

The next event was to be something that could be described as rather uncomfortable to the casual observer:

16 November 1915

> Today Nov 16-15
> I secured Mervyn's
> Request. I waited for
> about 10 minutes
> before I fired at an
> old Turk
> to make sure of him I took
> deliberate aim and
> then Bang over he
> went and never moved
> I sneaked
> out at night time
> and cut one of
> his Turkish buttons
> off. [CBH I 22]
> and now it is safely
> fastened on to my
> Belt and if I am spared when [the] War
> is over Mervyn
> shall get his prize. [CBH I 23]

The Mervyn referred to above was Mervyn Hardy, Charlie's nephew, who was about 10 years younger than him.[118] There is no button in the family's keeping and in fact it's not clear whether the button ever made it back to Australia. Many years later, Mervyn's daughter Iris thought it was a particularly gruesome story when she heard of it. The souveniring of buttons, medals and photographs was a common practice through the War, although it was explicitly prohibited by the *British Field Service Regulations* of 1909 and its Australian equivalent.[119] As historian Brian Feltman has noted:

> Trophy collecting has a deeper significance than the obvious financial windfall of selling valuables recovered from a kill or

> capture. In the Great War, trophies confirmed that a soldier had seen action at the front and "proved himself on the field of battle". Souvenirs taken from prisoners implied that a soldier had forced the his enemy to submit and then confirmed his authority by stripping the prisoner of his valuables, military decorations, or reminders of civilian life.[120]

Charlie's diary continues:

21 November 1915

> Today had good time with
> The Indians.
> Siekhs I find them to be
> more friendly
> than the Mo[ha]mmadans [ie Muslims]. The
> Siekhs say Mo[ha]mmadans [are]
> India's Turks [CBH I 21]
> Each one of them wanted me
> to have some tea after
> having about 4 Quarts
> and 5 or 6 Chopattes [ie chapati, an unleavened Indian flatbread].
> I Didn't feel bit hungry
> No doubt they are far
> better than good few of
> the Englishman 21st [November] [CBH I 22]

However, the fun came to an end:

> 26th Mountain Battery
> Finished their Rest
> to-day. No more chop patty and
> Chai [CBH I 23]

In Charlie's diary this was followed up with his record of a bad dream:

23 November 1915

> Last night had very funny
> dream. I dreamt that Rose was in firing line
> with me and I was just
> about to go in charge. I
> kissed and thought it
> was my last. 23rd Nov[CBH I 24]

24 November 1915

> As it happened there was
> great charge the same day
> and didn't hear anything
> about it until the 24th
> More Australians cut up. [CBH I 24]

The Rose referred to here was Charlie's younger sister. It is a poignant entry amongst the records of the various horrors in the trenches. It is not clear as to what action Charlie is referring although there was a charge by the Turks at the Pinnacle inland of Anzac Cove on the night of 22 November, but it was beaten off.[121]

Charlie's birthday could have also been better:

24 November 1915

> Today 24th Nov 15 Wednesday
> I am 22 years old and have
> never had such miserable
> birthday in my life.
> It is terrible cold and
> windy and I am told
> that the winter is about to start
> its no pleasure to
> be on active service. [CBH I 24]

And some more poetry on fighting in the trenches:

My Little Grey Home in West

I've a neat little Home in Trench
Which the rainstorms reasonably drench
There's dead Turk close by
With his feet to sky
And he gives off beautiful Stench

Underneath in the place of floor
There's mass of hard rock, Perhaps some straw
And the Jack Johnstons tear
Through the steel laden air
O'er my neat little Home in the trench

There's sniper who keeps on the go
So you must pop your napsack down low
And their Star shells at night
Make deuce of light
Which cause the language to flow
The Bully and Biscuits we chew
For its days since we tasted stew
But with shells dropping there
There is nothing to compare
With my neat little Home
In Trench [CBH I 25]

"Jack Johnstons" was a slang term for a large German low-velocity artillery shell that gave off a dense black smoke, and is believed to be named after a famous American boxer named Jack Johnson whose nickname was "The Big Smoke".[122]

And Charlie also made an attempt at a humorous short story:

Spare Time in Trenches

At Quinn's Post

Our doctor after tearing up all his
clothes for dressings finally

grabbing up a rifle Brilliantly
led Bayonet charge clad
only in his boots and Identification
disc it was Dr Keen of 19th Batt
and we were at Quinns Post on
the day of Aug 21st 15 General
Bolicks had given an order to
Colonel Knut [?] and Capt Coz[?]
and Lieut Stars led the 19th
Dr Keen [?] was with us and I can
swear he had no boots because
he had used them for making
beef tea for sick Private
when the charge sounded
Dr Keen seized the laces
and 17 Boxes of ammunition
and rushed for the trenches
He lowered the munition [CBH I 34]
Over the parapet with the Boot laces
and then jumping in after
the Boxes regained the laces
and strangled 16 Turks &
Germans who had attacked
him with fixed Bayonets
Hastily constructing shelter
with his identification disc
he lay down amidst Hail
of Bullets when Colonel
Knut led the 19th into trench
seven hours later he assisted
to render first aid to the
strangled Turks Dr Hun then

went back to dressing station
after operating for 7 days &
nights without meals or sleep
he took command of M. G. [ie machine gun] section
He was holding advanced position
when sent for to mend
my legs both had been
blown off with shrapnel [CBH I 35]

But were sent back by the
Turkish Commander in Chief
He made good job of it
merely removing one toe
which he thought overlapped
sufficiently to make it
doubtful whether I would
be accepted for further
service Lt Hun is now
at Lone Pine where he and
Colonel are leading charge [CBH I 38]

It takes Soldier to
spin them [CBH I 38]

Not classic literature, but worth noting for the references to famous battlefronts like Quinn's Post and Lone Pine.

It was around about this time, in late November 1915, that Charlie was shipped out to hospital at Mudros on Lemnos:

Sunday Very Bad pains in my
head. Returned to Mudros
for treatment.
[CBH I 117]

Pains in small of back left side
Coughing very bad and

Comes on between 2 & 3 in Morning
about same time Each morning
cannot move or stretch out
dry cough
OK [CBH I 136]

As Charlie summarised it later:

I had to continual
disentry shortly
after and lots more of
flying shrapnel witch
got me a spell on a small
island called Lemnos Island
in the Greek village named
Mudros but it was no more
than a dozen Anzacs to
a sick man although I
had some fun with the Greeks
Rested there some 3 weeks or so
& was then jumped across to the other
side of the Island among
more Greeks but there
found plenty of my own
countrymen which made
things more lively
but after a short spell
there was sent back
to Anzac [Cove] for a
Few more months [CBH 139]

Not long after arriving in Mudros, he noted:

Major Waller
Is going to send

All A.I.F. BB
To Turks Head [CBH I 23]

Turks Head was a peninsula across the bay from the town of Mudros that was used by the Allies for various military camps. It is not clear what the classification "B.B." meant. It may have meant "fit for light duty only".

24 November 1915

How stiff some of our boys
Went through Medical Board
at Turks Head and were
marked "C" Invalided Home
to Australia & [to] come to details
Rest camp, [then] to get
shipped & whilst waiting
they were sent for another
Board and was marked
"A" fit for Duty
they were all prepared
for Home too Nov 24th 15[CBH I 27]

Your King [and] Your Country
needs you
& this is how they treat
you [CBH I 27]

Oi Oi vot a Game
Vot a game it is
Oi Oi [CBH I 27]

As we will see in future entries, Charlie seems to have had a on-again-off-again desire to go back home. Sometimes he regrets those who have been assigned to go home, while on other occasions it is the opposite.

There was a huge rainstorm on 26 November that lasted three

days with men drowning in their narrow trenches during the deluge. As Charles Bean reported:

> At Anzac this storm caused many cases of frost-bite, and filled with water seven feet in depth the easternmost communications trench to Hill 60. At Suvla, where the troops were more exposed, its ravages were in many ways as severe as those of a great battle. The first rush of rain-water from the hills filled some of the trenches with a torrent, and drowned a number of men. Parts of the front line had to be for a time abandoned or held only by means of patrols. The enemy did not take advantage of this; indeed, the bodies of dead Turks and of mules washed down one of the creek-beds through the British lines proved that he was suffering in the same way.[123]

The losses due to freezing conditions were, as Bean says, "alarming". Between 30 November and 8 December, 15,791 were evacuated from the Peninsula. Of this there were 4,795 cases of "trench feet", a crippling disease caused by continually damp feet – there were 205 deaths.[124]

This was to be repeated and followed by snow blizzards in early December, killing more men.

DECEMBER 1915

Charlie noted the deadly consequences of the weather:

> Dec 1st Rain Cloud Burst
> about 7 am [?] and
> there was six feet of
> water in trenches most
> of the men in Firing
> Line were either Frozen or drowned
> Turks undermined
> Lone Pine and blew
> up the Boys. Casualties.
> many lost [CBH I 32]

A Gunner Roy McLarty of the 8th Field Artillery noted of the same event:

> Yesterday, the Turks tackled "Lone Pine" but were repulsed. Our casualties were fairly heavy. I saw about 20 poor fellows put in one grave.[125]

Charlie's diary continues:

4 December 1915

> Left Mudros East on
> Monday 4th Dec 15
> For Turks Head where we
> will be amongst our own
> men & will be able to get
> some pay [CBH I 28]
>
> Meet Les Hastwell to day 4th
> Wounded in Shoulder and
> He had good trip all round
> England. What-O for a
> Sydney Boy. [CBH I 28]

Les Hastwell was Lance Corporal Leslie Ambler Hastwell of B company, 19th Battalion. He was from Balmain, Sydney, and had been a sugar boiler before the War. Hastwell fought through the War, having been transferred to the 18th Battalion, served in France, and returned to Australia on 5 April 1919.

Charlie's diary continues:

5 December 1915

> Put on as well picquet
> On 5th what a cushey
> Job plenty of grub
> and only 3 men
> and corporal and the

best of it they are all
Australians. [CBH I 28]

I am on Guard near one
of Great Churches they
are very pretty inside
all old Paintings of
Religious people at the
back of Church there is
stone Room full of skulls
and bones of Greeks who
were killed here in last
Balkans War. Lord only
Knows why they keep them
here. [CBH I 32]

Went and had look
at graveyard at
Lemnos Island and
was surprised to see
so many poor chaps
buried without any names
nobody knows
who they are. Mostly
all Australians and I
think it is one of
the prettiest little
graveyards I ever
looked through [CBH I 18]

Reinforcements in Galore
on this Island [CBH I 28]

To see the reinforcements and [an]
old Soldier ready to go to
Penninsular its funny

its Just like Monte Carlo

Talk about Two Up
there's hundreds of them
spinning the coins and
the Crown & Anchor Boards [gambling game played with dice]
are going for all their worth
There [are] officers and all
playing and the Pommies
can't make us out at
all They only wish they
were Australians
The cold weather is playing
hell with the Poms and
I think there is hardly
any of our boys
down with the frost bite
All the Poms are down
They are beauts at
Swinging the lead [ie shirking their duties] [CBH I 31]

Five Pommies got pinched
for spinning the coins
2 of them got two months
apiece. No Australians
got pinched yet they are
the ring leaders. They
Know better to try and
Pinch an Australian
[Be]cause the Police are Poms. [CBH I 36]

8 December 1915

No 1 A Hospital left [for]

The Penninsular to-day
8.12.15 [CBH I 36]

Because of the level of ongoing casualties, No 1 Australian Stationary Hospital was moved to the Gallipoli Peninsula in November 1915. It is about the same time that Charlie reported back to duty there himself. Soon back on the front line he was again involved in trench warfare:

Drove Turks out of their Trenches
and one officer remained
German and put up good fight but was killed
by one of our lads and I grabbed his Automatic
Revolver and it's a beaut [CBH I 49]

Number of Revolver
is 942 [CBH I 99]

The automatic revolver would have most likely been a standard issue 7.65mm Luger P.08 Parabellum pistol.[126] As with the button taken off the Turkish soldier, the British *Field Service Regulations* clearly stated that "the personal effects of prisoners and of the dead [were] to be strictly preserved" (ie not to be taken).[127] These rules were replicated in the Australian Military Regulations and Orders of 1904.

According to the 19th Battalion war diary, during the whole period from 1 December until 12 December there was continual heavy fire, including dozens of shrapnel shells, from the Turks.

And there was also the more mundane:

My Word will I ever forget these
Russian Winds they Remind
me of Home Sweet Home [CBH I 37]

Flies are very thick they are worse
than Shrapnel at present [CBH I 45]

[A] chum [asked] what will [you] take

For your Kangaroo's
Feathers (Dinkum) [CBH I 40]

How Rum was
Served out at Gallipoli
Soldier about 3 spoons
full at most
officers ¾ Bottle (1 Gallon)
You'll be on watch
And someone will
come along side of
you and say
hic everything alright Boy
hic more of the Turks are surrendering [CBH I 40]
Hic my word this weather Kills the flies don't it
Eh hic
and he's hiccupping and coughing
up Rum and he's got
hide to say he wouldn't
mind drop Rum to
warm him up and he's
full up to the eyes and
you are shivering
with cold Oh soldiers
life what happy one
would sooner sell
peanuts than be a
soldier again
once bitten twice shy
no letters
no pay
very little sleep and
very little tucker [CBH I 41]

This latest extract is quite an attack on one of his unnamed company officers for being drunk on duty. We will never know to whom he was referring.

Rumours were rife of a pending departure. Around this time he noted in his diary:

> Not many killed.
>
> I believe the
> Peninsular will be
> Evacuated
> I hope I am not in
> for the Rear guard
> action as I don't
> think it would be very nice as those
> Turks know thing
> or two. [CBH I 36]

In fact, evacuation had been decided in-principle by the British War Office on 22 November. The War Cabinet's final decision was on 8 December. Although Kitchener was optimistic of minimal casualties in such a withdrawal, the consensus view was that there would be many thousands. No wonder the rumours kept coming:

> I Heard today that all
> Australians are to be
> moved off peninsular
> and all going to
> Egypt for winter [CBH I 37]
>
> Later [in] Latrine [heard]
> That the Turks were
> playing hell in Egypt
> and the natives
> had taken arms
> up against us [CBH I 37]

> Official from
> No 1 Dug out [CBH I 37]

Nevertheless, it should not be thought that fighting had ceased. Even up until the last day, bombardments and sniping were killing and wounding men. For example, the total number of AIF casualties in November 1915 were 1,451 including 585 deaths.[128] A Turkish officer, Lieutenant Mehmed Fasih (in the front line opposite Pope's Post), reported a day before the evacuation:

> 08.00 hrs – Our mortars are about to open fire. I'm to observe. Shelling starts. Enemy trenches at the end of the gully which is source of Central Stream, where front lines used to be, are the target. Our gunners have the range. Help them to adjust their fire by reporting where each of the first four shells land and how each one behaves. Tell them to aim a little further to left and just a little shorter. Now our rounds are hitting the central peak. The explosions are spectacular.
>
> 26 shells are fired. 19 explode. 3 shells hit to the rear of targets. Now our howitzers open fire. They are concentrating on Kirmizisirt (Pope's Hill) and Gultepe (Rose Hill). Can spot the shells as they drop from the sky. They are black, high explosive rounds. The explosions are terrific and release billowing black smoke.
>
> One round fails to explode. See it ricochet. After that shot, another one does not explode. It tumbles downhill, doing somersaults. Advise Battalion about the results of the shelling. Around noon, our field-guns start to make themselves heard. This was how the day went.[129]

Elaborate efforts were made to ensure that the Turks were unaware in the lead up to the departure. Various strategies, related to when and where artillery or other bombing and shooting would occur, were implemented over the course of days to confuse the Turks into not picking up the signs of what was actually occurring. Also, innovations such as self-firing rifles were designed using dripping water into pans tied via string to triggers. Thus, even after trenches were abandoned, firing would be coming from the Allied side. Charlie recorded:

> 19 December 1915
>
> 5th Brigade Left Gallipoli
> Penninsular today
> No shells very peaceful
> 19th December 15 [CBH I 38]

Troops began evacuating on 7 December and the final departure at Anzac Cove occurred on 20 December. Remarkably, the Australians lost no men, while across the board casualties were minimal. Some Turkish reports indicate that in the final phase the Turks were aware that the Allies were departing and decided that it was in their best interests to let them do so without further violence. Charlie noted:

> Capt Sherbon stayed
> Back to fight Rear
> Guard action [CBH I 41]

Ivan Sherbon was a captain in Charlie's B Company, 19th Battalion. He was later promoted to Major and will be referred to again later.

The general impression given, and repeated by Charlie, is that during the lead up to the evacuation everything was quiet is not accurate. As the 19th Battalions war diary records, enemy shelling continued, even on the day of departure. But, by then these were "normal conditions":

> 18 December 1730 [ie 5.30pm] Part of the Battalion leaves Pope's Post, embarked at ANZAC for LEMNOS, strength 430 all ranks, 187 all ranks to hold POPE'S POST, remainder of night normal conditions, improving trenches.
>
> 19 December 0900 [9.00am] Enemy shelled RUSSELL'S TOP – COURTNEYS – Fired shrapnel on Popes – Navy and our artillery shelled enemy's positions including the NEK.

> Heavy firing by Navy direction of HELLES. Otherwise normal conditions during the day.
>
> 19 December Final preparations for evacuation made – remaining surplus stores removed – surplus ammunition, bombs, grenades buried –
>
> 1740 [ie 5.40pm] "A" party 98 all ranks left POPE'S POST to embark. Normal conditions.
>
> 2330 [ie 11.30pm] "B" party 10 all ranks left POPE'S POST to embark.
>
> 0200 [ie 2.00am 20 Dec] "C1" party 10 all ranks left POPE'S POST.
>
> 0235 [ie 2.35am 20 Dec] "C2" party 10 all ranks left POPE'S POST.
>
> 0255 [ie 2.55am 20 Dec] "C3" party 10 all ranks left POPE'S POST to embark. Final party completing evacuation. Capt [Keith] Heritage OC Party "C3". No casualties.[130]

Nonetheless, not all the Peninsula was evacuated immediately. Charlie also noted:

> Cape Helles the Troops
> Are still Holding
> Mostly French are there [CBH I 38]

This is half right. The final troops at the Cape were from Lancashire, Newfoundland and the Royal Marines. The very last remained for 21 more days at Cape Helles and, during the extended departure between 7 and 9 January 1916, they faced an attack from the Ottoman forces. Given the wholesale carnage during the campaign, the casualties from this final evacuation could be described as light. Of course, across the Peninsula tons of equipment were destroyed, or left behind, and were captured by the Turks. Moreover, it wasn't just military equipment that was disposed of:

> On 14 December, Birdwood issued an order that all subsequent embarkations would be conducted in complete silence.

There would be no smoking or drinking. Several instances of drunken, boisterous behaviour enroute to the beach threatened the security of the entire operation. Discipline must be countenanced by all. Rum rations and other alcoholic beverages, less those used by hospital personnel, were ordered destroyed. Liquor had a way of loosening the tongue, an effect Birdwood would not chance.

This probably explains the following entry by Charlie:

500 G[allon]s of Rum was
emptied in to sea
One Pommy said
what [a] lot of Australians
there will [be] drowned [CBH I 40]

However, in more somber tones Charlie narrates the outcome from his point of view:

Australians are all from
Anzac [Cove]. the Rear Guard
got away without any Troubles
after all the
thousands of men Killed
we have to leave it to the Turks.
Where the Hell we go
next God only knows
I don't
Sargent Taylor
got Killed few days
before we left
Hard luck He wasn't
bad sort although
he was Pommy he
showed more pluck
than any of Kitchener's

> Army its pity they
> let boys leave school
> so early for I think
> Kitchener Army was
> meant for Boy Scouts
> work. [CBH I 39]

As Charlie particularly notes:

> after all the
> thousands of men Killed
> we have to leave it to the Turks

Lance Sergeant Jesse Taylor of B company, 19th Battalion was killed in action on 15 December 1915, barely days before the evacuation, aged 35. He was married, living at Kogarah, NSW, and was listed as a polisher before the War.[131] He had in fact been a regular soldier, born in Birmingham, England, and having served in the Royal Warwickshire Regiment, seeing action in the Second Boer War.[132]

The reference to "Kitchener's Army" was the massive recruitment drive that Lord Kitchener had planned and implemented from the start of the War in 1914. It was a direct appeal to the patriotism of the English citizens and was very successful. They were all voluntary at this stage of the War and in the first month alone 300,000 enlisted compared to the target of 200,000. By the start of conscription in 1916, just under 2.5 million had volunteered.[133] There is no doubt that many were particularly young, straight out of school.[134]

At Gallipoli the British lost 21,255 dead, the French 9,874, the Australians 8,709, the Indians 7,594 and the New Zealanders 2,701. The Turkish dead were said to number 86,692.

The landings on the shores of the Gallipoli Peninsula was Australia's most significant commemorative event. By the end of the eight-month campaign, more than 8,700 lay dead. The Anzac spirit – the qualities of courage, mateship and sacrifice – was born.

6

Greece & Egypt: January-April 1916

"Got three days confined to barracks"

The return to Egypt was to be eventful for Charlie. It would appear that he and many of his mates were simply delirious to be away from the trenches and horrors of Gallipoli, while it seems they could not help themselves from getting into mischief. Further, the long term effects of exposure to the weather in the trenches at Gallipoli came back to haunt him.

However, before heading to Egypt, the troops spent Christmas/ New Year at Lemnos Island in Greece. As Charlie noted the next moves:

> [At] Anzac [Cove] for a
> Few more months and left
> in Dec 19 15 [on]
> The [S.S.] Eramine
> went from there back to
> Lemnos Island for our
> Christmas which we had
> a most beautiful dinner
> of stew & pudding that
> came from Australia in
> tins. [CBH 148]

25 December 1915, Saturday

> Today Christmas day

and had my dinner on
one of the old Balkan
Battlefields had Bonser
dinner

Poor Father's Birthday [his father died in 1913]

Received Billy full of
Good things
very good of
The Australian people
I thought we were forgotten
my tin come from Victoria

Bill Dwyer left Anzac
for England now in
London Hospital Good
luck to Bill[CBH I 42]

Received Buckshee
Shirt and socks
senders name was pinned on shirt
H. Colley Neutral Bay
Sydney 26.7.15 [CBH I 42]

It is not clear what is the place referred to as the "Balkan Battlefieds". There were two battles associated with the island of Lemnos during the First Balkan War. However, they were both sea battles between the Greek and Turkish navies. The first was the Battle of Elli (or sometimes called the Battle of the Dardenelles) on 16 December 1912, which resulted in Greece acquiring Lemnos and other Aegean islands from Ottoman control. The second was a repeat performance, a few weeks later, with the Battle of Lemnos on 18 January 1913. It started with Turkish ships entering Moudros Harbour and bombarding the town. In the ensuing naval battle, Greece again won.[135] It is most likely Charlie is referring to the graveyard associated with the deaths from this second battle.

Charlie's diary continues:

28 December 1915, Tuesday

Strengthened our Guard today
28/12/15 2 N. Zealanders
& one Irishman from West
[He is as] bad as Paddy
Gets plenty of Buckshees [CBH I 43]

Sent all the Gypos Back
One transport and
About 5,000 on board and
They were yelling at us
Cairo vera good
vera nice
plenty of Beer [CBH I 43]

The reference here to "Gypos" may relate to the shipping back to their home country of Egyptians who had been brought to Lemnos to help build roads and other infrastructure for the war effort at places like Turks Head.

31 December 1915, Friday

New Years Eve
Got relieved off The well piquet
had a go at
The two striper Buckshee
Stripes put back into the
B.X. Lines [CBH I 43]

Advance Guard of 5th [Brigade] has gone
To unknown Place. [CBH I 43]

What "two striper buckshee" means is not clear. Generally speaking a two striper was an army corporal.

1 January 1916, Saturday

New Years Day

Went to Greek village
Called Kondi [ie probably Kontias]
and I think the Kids of the
village are as bad as the Gypos.
If they see your mouth
moving they run after
you saying buckshee
And they won't leave
you be you hand
out something and
if you give one of
them anything you
have mob after you
I bought 1 pound
of walnuts and one
had about six of
them I was handing
out all the time to Greeks
again. [CBH I 44]

Had bit of Sing Song
On News Years Eve
but it was more
Of child's turnout [CBH I 46]

2 January 1916, Sunday

Darkey Hoare got
pinched by Red Caps [military police]
to day for playing
two-up 2.1.16
brought up before Col[onel].
and was remanded

Later Got Discharged [CBH I 46]

Darkey Hoare is most likely Private Reginal Rupert Hoare of D Company, 17th Battalion. He was a farm labourer before the War and came from Lindfield, Sydney, signing up at the age of 23. Hoare returned to Australia on 22 July 1917 after being wounded in the chest, fighting in the Somme sector of France in June 1917.[136]

4 January 1916, Tuesday

Drew first [duty] to-day
At Lemnos Island
4.1.16[CBH I 46]

6 January 1916, Thursday

Leaving for Egypt
Thursday 6.1.16[CBH I 46]

The ship made port in Alexandria on 10 January 1916. It was a new year and the end of the war was nowhere in sight (despite the prediction from the Indian Army officer we read about in the last chapter). The 19th Battalion returned to Egypt and was involved in the defence of the Suez Canal zone in the early months of 1916. However, as we shall see, Charlie did not stay with his comrades for very long.

Left Mudros East
On 6.1.16
Good enough trip [?]
Landed at Alexandria
sneaked off ship
and was put in clink [Egyptian jail]
about 11.30 that night
What night it was
Room about 20 x 30 and
about 50 men in it
stone floor no Blankets

> my God it was cold
> Got returned next day
> and was taken to
> Mustaffa [ie Egyptian authorities] and put in clink
> there not so bad as other [CBH I 48]

His rush of blood to the head had another unfortunate consequence:

> Lost all my kit now I am stiff
> No clothes & Lousey
> Still in Clink but going
> Up before the Major today
> Got three days C.B. [Confined to barracks] [CBH I 49]

And this is all confirmed in Charlie's Statement of Service which notes:

> "Punishment, Offence: (1) Absent without leave from 5pm till 11-45pm 9.1.16 (11) Out of bounds. Award – 3 days CB 14.1.16"

The loss of the kit may explain why a number of the hard-won souvenirs never apparently made it back to Australia, including the German officer's pistol and the button (for his nephew Mervyn) cut off the greatcoat of the Turkish soldier he had shot at Gallipoli. It is in fact a wonder that his War Diary did not also disappear. It was either returned or he had entrusted it to a friend who saved it from being pilfered. Maybe it was the latter case. Maybe the diary had become his most valued possession.

These events were obviously important for Charlie, as he describes it more than once in his diary:

> After being there
> for a while we left for
> Egypt. When we landed
> in Alexandria we all
> took French leave [absent without leave] &

I with mate was arrested
whilst going back to the
ship at 12.30am.
and was dumped in a
Clink on a charge
but after being there for a few
days they gave us
a little to eat as well. [CBH 148]
though we may be hungry
[and] thirst[y] after being there
about 4 days we were
shifted to a camp on
the coast where we
had plenty of sand &
barb wire to amuse ourselves
then we went before a
court & tried but I
put such a good tale up
that they send me
to Cairo where I got
3 days C.B. (confined to
Barracks) but that was
Good oh
I drew my Pay two days after
£7 odd & talk about
a good time for 3 months
pay [for] every week
I got full of a good
time & I volunteered
to go out into the
Desert [CBH 134]

He also recorded:

> Went to Cairo to day first
> Time for nearly six months
> Most of the women were
> gone and I think they
> are following the troops
> the 5th Brigade go into
> trenches next week
> 30 miles from Tele Ke bar [CBH I 49]

However, while Charlie "volunteered to go out into the desert", he was not to go there with his 19th Battalion, part of 5th Brigade. His service records are not clear, and he is not explicit about it in his diary entries. He seems to have been hospitalised in Cairo with heart problems, most likely exacerbated by the poor conditions he endured at Gallipoli. Between 19 January and 31 March 1916, he received his pay at Ghezireh. Ghezireh was a Red Cross Hospital in Cairo, formally called the 2nd Australian General Hospital. It was set up to take casualties arriving from Gallipoli and had some 1,500 beds.

For its part the Diary of the 19th Battalion shows that it arrived at Alexandria on 7 January 1916 and by 8 January had arrived at Tel-el-Kebir. The Diary notes that they were without tents for a number of days. Nevertheless, they were able to "pitch camp" on 10 January. On 11 January "training commenced", while on 24 January they entrained for the Suez Canal via the town of Ismailia, and were in the front line on 26 January at Hill 353 ("Australia Hill"). By 1 February they were in defensive line at "Katoomba" for the remainder of the month. Unfortunately, the Battalion diaries for March through to July 1916 have not survived and so the narrative must stop there for the moment.[137]

Charlie kept tabs on his mates back in the Battalion:

> Australians are the 3rd
> Line of defence in Egypt [CBH I 51]

Meanwhile, he was in the Cairo region this whole time, convalescing, sight-seeing and meeting up with colleagues:

Coptic Churches at old Cairo
District in Egypt 1916

Abou Serges
St Barbara
St Georges
St Mitchael
St Tadros
St John
Abou Kir Lane
Babyone Church [CBH I 65]

Met Tom Shurey to day
and he has suffering
with Dysentry and is
pretty bad 10.1.16

Camped on banks of
Nile the River is about
1 mile across
Sailing boats are sailing
up and down all day

[there a pencil drawing of a boat]

Cairo is about 6 miles away
and its only 2 Milliemes
fare in tram about
2 farthing in English [CBH I 50]

For my first time I saw
Some crocodiles yesterday
Also Giraffes Zebras Hippos
Rhinos and several
Other Ferocious looking Beasts [CBH I 51]

Private Thomas Hansen Shurey was also from B Company, 19th Battalion. Before the War he was a labourer from Marrickville,

Sydney. He was convalescing like Charlie, but his condition was much more serious. He returned to Australia on 11 April 1916 due to complications after surgery for an abdominal adhesion, aged 22.[138]

After these various expeditions Charlie returned to more mundane tasks:

> 4 February 1916, Friday
>
> Sent Flo Registered
> parcel silk scarfs
> & souvenirs from
> Anzac [CBH II 4/2/16]

And:

> 5 February 1916, Saturday
>
> Had my Photo taken
> to-day with Paddy
> & Pea
> They turned out
> Rotten [CBH II 5/2/16]

In retrospect, this is a sad picture (reproduced in this book). Charlie's two mates, Paddy Dwyer and Norman Peacock, were both to be killed in action five months later at the Battle of Pozières in France. "Paddy" was Private Patrick Ignatius Dwyer of the 19th Battalion. Before the War he had been a hairdresser from Yarrbandai, NSW. He had been transferred to the 2nd Battalion and was later killed in action sometime between 22 and 25 July 1916, aged 23. "Pea" was Norman Peacock of the 19th Battalion who had been a farmer from Morpeth, NSW. He was later transferred to the 17th battalion and was killed in action on 28 July 1916, aged 21.

Here, a tone of melancholy can be noted in one of the songs Charlie noted in his diary:

11 February 1916, Friday

Sung at my
Dug out

There's tiny spark of
Love still burning
Yearning deep down
in my heart for you
there's longing there
for your returning
I want you I do
To come come to my
Heart again come
Come let that love
Aflame for there's
Little spark burning
Still burning and yearning for you [CBH II 11/2/16]

Even further, a real tone of bitterness had been developing now and again in Charlie's diary entries. Obviously, he, and (we can conjecture) also his colleagues, were questioning whether people back at the Home Front appreciated the awful time that they had been having. The following is a poem he wrote while in the trenches, either at Gallipoli or shortly afterwards in Egypt.

14-22 February 1916

Written in my Dug out

My Brother that
Stayed at 'ome

I'm pulling off me colours
I've chucked me web away
I'm going back to Cairo
Ter draw one blooming pay

I'm fed up with being a soldier
So 'elp me bob I am
Chewing mouldy biscuits
An' eatin bread and jam
I'm ere fighting Mr Turk
Out on me blooming own
When I think of im in Stralia
Me brother that stayed at home

E's walking up ther street
Is chest puffed out with pride
And skiting to his blooming cobbers
Of ow ee saved is ide
And eres me in the blimey trench
Where I can't even straight[en] me head
For fear of bally sniper
I'll plug it up with lead
But e olds is ead up igh enough
When up the street ell roam
But there aint no bullets out there
Me brother who stayed at home.

E reads the morning erald [ie Sydney Morning Herald]
And sees ther Turks is on ther run
Then e brags about Australia
And what er boys ave done
E shines before the barmaid
E's good at beery skiting
But round the corner of street
Is where e does is fighting
Is dugout's in ther taproom
Ther bar is firing zone
And ther billiard cue ther rifle
Of me brother who stayed at home

Es not a bad shot in ther field
When e gets on bunny's track
And ther aint no blooming danger
Cos bunny can't shoot back
But its different ere with Mr Turk
For Johnnie e aint arf slick
He gets is peepers on yer first
My oath ell make yer sick
But e wont risk is blooming ide
Why is earts a frigid zone
And his feet are blooming
Icebergs me brother who stayed at home

I'm pulling off me colours
Ive chucked me web away
An I'm laying down me rifle
I don't care what they say
If e can shirk is duty
Ses e won't go ter drill
Well two can play the same game
Then in comes Kaiser Bill
I'm not afraid of bullets
I'd ave died without a groan
But e's put the Kybosh on it
All me brothers who stayed

Now when I goes to mother
I've volunteered to fight
She ses Gawd bless you soldier
An bring yer back alright
But in e called me chocolate soldier
And blooming six bob tourist
E ses y'ill never see the blooming firing line
Nor ever get view

E ses y'ill have fine trip
Across te ocean foam
But still e wouldn't come imself
Me brothers who stayed

E's playing golf or football
An many another game
A cries me drippin fer the blooming flag
Ter keep Australia's name
While he waltzes round ball room
For e thinks e used to it
But when the war is over
E'll reap just what es sown
And we'll brand him bleedinn coward
Me Brother who stayed
At home.

I'd like to ave im over ere
Just to show im ow things are
For taint all beer and skittles
And ther aint no blooming bar
We're in these bloody trenches
Eight days out of ten
We can't get blooming spells
Cos we aint got the men
For Mr Turk is wiley
& aint no lazy drone
An es twenty times as
Brave as me brother [who stayed at home]

Ive picked up me Lee Enfield
And I've buckled on web about
For I'm only a blooming Pte [private]
And we got to see it out
And though e shames is manhood

An stains is pedigree
Thank god there's some of us old uns left
And we'll fight until we're free
But should ther foe o'er power us
And we gits overthrown
The he'll know e elped to
Kill me me brother who stayed at home. [CBH II 14-22/2/16]

It is worth noting that the AIF was a completely volunteer force. As previously mentioned in chapter 2, the *Defence Act* did not allow for conscripted forces to serve overseas. On 6 January 1916, the British Parliament had introduced conscription for their armed forces. This was for the first time ever. By 30 August, Australian Prime Minister Hughes announced his intention to hold a referendum on conscription. He was promptly expelled from his own state branch of the Australian Labor Party but continued on in government. The referendum was held on 28 October 1916, but failed to get a majority. On 14 November, Hughes and his supporters left the ALP and formed a new party called the National Labor Party and he continued as Prime Minister. He then negotiated with the Commonwealth Liberal Party, who were the Parliamentary Opposition, and created a merged party called the Nationalist Party on 9 January 1917. They continued to pursue the matter of conscription. Nonetheless, a second referendum on 20 December 1917 also failed.

Charlie's Diary entries for the period 19 February to 2 March 1916 were used for vocabulary for French language training. Later he noted:

3 March 1916, Friday

Meet Bill Dwyer
to-day. Just back
from the old dart
he's looking good [CBH II 3/3/16]

10 March 1916, Friday

Sent Flo [ie sister]
Turk Identification disc
And cross made out
of driving band of
French 75 [ie French standard field cannon]
From Anzac 1915 [CBH II 10/3/16]

12 March 1916, Sunday

Got eight letters to-day
how pleased I am [CBH II 12/3/16]

15 March 1916, Wednesday

5th Brigade left Ishmalia
for Alexandria
En route for
new theatre of war
Unknown yet to us
Rumoured France
Sent Flo Easter Card
The Brigade sent
back all men
With bad teeth
and any way crook
Whats doing eh [CBH II 15/3/16]

Charlie's 19th Battalion family was part of the 5th Infantry Brigade referred to in the above extract. On 5 March 1916, the Brigade was informed that it was moving. That began on 6 March, after first being relieved at the Sinai front by the Auckland Mounted Rifle Regiment from New Zealand. They entrained to Moascar at which stage they were finally informed on 15 March that they were definitely headed for France.[139] The 19th arrived in France on 23 March 1916 via H.M.T. *Arcadian*. But, as we have seen, Charlie's heart murmur prevented him from joining them. He was still convalescing in Cairo and this will principally explain his missing out on this earlier departure.

The 19th Battalion moved to the Armentières area of the Western Front. It missed the carnage at the Battle of Fromelles but, days later, in late July 1916, it took part in the equally awful Battle of Pozières. While Charlie was to be wounded at Fromelles, only the Fates know whether if he had stayed with the 19th he might have died with a number of his friends at the Battle of Pozières. They included Private Paddy Dwyer, Private Norm Peacock and Lieutenant Frank Coen. His good mate Corporal Bill Dwyer and Private Thomas Sanders were wounded. In all, the Australians suffered some 22,900 casualties during that battle between 23 July and 3 September 1916.

In November 1916, the Battalion moved to Belgium. While there it took part in the attack on the German trench system known as "the Maze" near Flers, as part of the larger Battle of the Somme. This was another dreadful battle that has been described as the "worst ever encountered by the AIF".[140] During 1917 it took part in the battles of Second Bullecourt, Menin Road and Poelcappelle in Belgium and the attack on Hindenburg Line. In 1918, the battalion helped to stop the German Spring Offensive. Also, in late 1918, it was involved in the fighting around Amiens, Mont St Quentin and at the "Beaurevoir Line" at Estrees on 3-4 October 1918. Finally, on 10 October 1918, the 19th Battalion was disbanded in order to reinforce other battalions. Sadly, during the war, the battalion suffered 2,903 casualties, 874 killed in action. Of note is that Lieutenant Percy Storkey earned a Victoria Cross at Hangard Wood on 7 April 1918.[141]

That was all in the future. In March 1916, Charlie and his mates were still waiting upon word as to whether they were rejoining their Battalion.

16 March 1916, Thursday

Cairo [written at top of page, possible later]

Peacock has

Joined the soldiers
And is going to
Alexandria how
stiff Poor Pea

Have tried
hard but was no Good [CBH II 16/3/16]

From these entries it would seem that, while he sought to rejoin his battalion – the 19th – before its departure from Egypt, he didn't succeed. As he says, "Have tried hard but was no Good". It seems his friend Norman Peacock also tried but did succeed.

17 March 1916, Friday

Still camped at Eizah
on banks Nile
Pay day drew
30/- and went
out with Bill
McFarlane in night
to Pictures but
got the toothache
and came out
but had few
Beers Eh what [CBH II 17/3/16]

Bill McFarlane was Private William John MacFarlane of the 16th Battalion, who had been a builder from Stirling, South Australia. He served at Gallipoli and went to France with his battalion in 1916. Charlie has added a note in the margin of the Diary that "Bill Mac Killed [in] 1st Battle in France". [CBH II 22/3/16] However, that was not quite correct. He was involved in a number of battles and was killed in action by shell fire in the Flers area of the Somme sector on 6 February 1917, aged 20.[142]

18 March 1916, Saturday

Nothing doing. Windy
plenty of dust
put in for pass to Cairo
had sleep instead
Details left to-day
for Alexandria
Pea was amongst
Them how stiff
had a burst 2 drops
of rain and
plenty of dust. [CBH II 18/3/16]

19 March 1916, Sunday

My word what Beautiful
night we had
rained all night but it
didn't shift us
wrote to Miss Alma [ie sister]
to-day
expect to have more rain
to-night at present
coming over very
black Saeed [CBH II 19/3/16]

20 March 1916, Monday

Cairo

Better luck to-day
received two letters
& one P.C. [ie post card] From
Hinemoa Llewelyn
and one letter
from Alma Latham

Rumoured to-day
that the 7th Brigade
has landed in
France [CBH II 20/3/16]

The 7th Infantry Brigade of the AIF, made up of the 25th, 26th, 27th and 28th Battalions, left Egypt on 14 March on the H.M.T. *Minneapolis*. It was described in the Brigade Diary as "Ship dirty but soon cleaned up. Also rather overcrowded. The usual precautions were taken. Lewis guns mounted, life belts worn, etc. A very comfortable ship and the men well found."[143]

21 March 1916, Tuesday

Dan Ryan volunteered
for duty and
is learning to [prepare]
for his unit
Bill Dwyer five
days up.
No leave after
8 Clock how
Stiff
[CBH II 21/3/16]

Dan Ryan was Private Daniel Joseph Ryan of B Company, 19th Battalion. Before the War he had been a stoker from Botany, Sydney. He had been wounded in the thigh by a bomb at Gallipoli. He rejoined his Battalion and whilst serving in France suffered an accidental gun shot wound to the stomach and died on 5 November 1916, aged 34.[144] Charlie wrote against Dwyer's name, obviously after the original entry: "Since killed".

22 March 1916, Wednesday

Nothing doing so
far. Put in for

pass and got it
from 4pm till 10
Going to social
to night with
Bill MacFarlane
Musical chairs
drink of tea and
Slice of cake
Emchi Home
[CBH II 22/3/16]

23 March 1916, Thursday

Nothing doing
To-day
Wrote letter to
Alma Latham
and also read
one of Marie
Corelli's Books
Entitled Boy
not so bad but
very deep [CBH II 23/3/16]

Marie Corelli was a hugely successful novelist at the turn of the last century but is largely forgotten today. Charlie is obviously referring to her 1900 book, *Boy.*[145]

24 March 1916, Friday

Pay day
but not for me
Bill paid me back
25 PT and Paddy
couldn't get change
Very hot & stuffy

Russians still
Advancing they now
Occupy Ispahan
Rumoured that the
5th Bgde Landed at
Alexandria [CBH II 24/3/16]

The reference to the Russians occupying Ispahan (Isfahan) relates to a part of the Great War that is little known in the English-speaking world. Even before the War the Russians occupied the north western part of Persia (today's Iran) in 1911. This area was to become a major conflict zone with the Turks. In addition, during the War the Russians were suspicious of the German sympathies of the otherwise neutral Persian Government and so invaded the country. The taking of Isfahan occurred around the early part of 1916. The British also occupied parts of the country to secure the oilfields that supplied the Royal Navy. It was a humiliating time for Persia and it is reported that it suffered losses both military and civilian in the order of two million people, principally due to famine and disease.[146]

The reference to the 5th Infantry Brigade arriving in Alexandria is in fact incorrect. The Brigade had by then already arrived in France.

25 March 1916, Saturday

Put in for pass and
got it to 10pm
went to Cairo
Sent Alma 24 assorted
post cards also sent
Moa post card and
letters. Met Bill Dwyer
and stayed with him
till nearly 10 and

then went home in
a Garry (cab) [CBH II 25/3/16]

26 March 1916, Sunday

Abbas the arab.
[The] Fatigue man got the
sack this morning.
[Because] Paddy does his work
and [Abbas also] gets half his pay
from Hassien (Arab)
Went to bed
about 5 clock.
(Sick) [CBH II 26/3/16]

This passage seems to refer to an Egyptian servant being dismissed for not properly fulfilling his duties. There is a suggestion that there may have been some rorting occurring.

27 March 1916, Monday

Nothing doing
Very crook last
night I thought my
heart was going
to stop but no
it kept going
Terrible Hot to
day met Bob
Brown Also saw
Lieut Bastian
Later [had been] Sargt [CBH II 27/3/16]

The passage confirms that Charlie was suffering heart problems at this time.

Bob Brown was Corporal Robert Brown of B Company, 19th

Battalion, from Orange, NSW, where he was a railway man. He was wounded by a bomb at Gallipoli in December 1915, just before the evacuation. He also had all his teeth extracted. Dental problems were very common at Gallipoli, including in Charlie's case. In 1916 Brown was transferred to the 5th Light Trench Mortar Battery and promoted to Sergeant. He served the rest of the War in France and was discharged on 27 July 1919.[147] His service file shows he volunteered for the North Russian Relief Force to assist the Czarist White Russian Army fight the Bolsheviks. But, while being accepted, he did not actually join, although around 100 Australians served in this contingent.[148]

"Lieut Bastian" was actually Lieutenant William Tom Bastin of B Company, 19th Battalion. At enlistment he was a Private but was quickly promoted to Lance Sergeant and promoted again to Lieutenant on 28 October 1915 while at Gallipoli. Before the War he had been a traveller originally from Norwich, England, although he was living in Australia at the time of enlistment at the age of 24. He came down with diphtheria whilst at Gallipoli and was hospitalised in Egypt. Afterwards, he was initially assigned to a training battalion in England but rejoined the 19th in Belgium in November 1917, and later also served in France. Interestingly, his record notes that at the end of the War he caught Spanish Flu in November 1918. Fortunately, he survived to return Australia on 13 July 1919.[149]

Charlie was also to meet other soldiers:

> Jack Ryan
> Winton
> Queensland

Jack Ryan will be Private John Shepherd Ryan from Winton in Queensland. He had been a stockman before he enlisted. He was initially part of the 11th Light Horse Regiment but, after that unit suffered high casualties at Gallipoli and was disbanded, he joined the 5th Light Horse. He himself was wounded at Gallipoli but later rejoined his unit. Back in Egypt, he was again admitted to hospital in early 1916 (where he probably met Charlie). He was later brought back to the 11th Light Horse when it was reformed. But was moved to the Anzac Provost Corps (the Military Police) in November 1916 and was part of the Palestine Campaign, including the occupation of Jerusalem. He returned to Australia on 20 July 1919.[150]

And:

> Pte 101 Elmer, H
> B Coy
> 18 Batt
> 5th Brigade

Private Hartley Elmer was from B Company, 18th Battalion. He was originally a labourer from Surry Hills, Sydney, and came to the Middle East on the same troopship as Charlie. He served with the 18th Battalion at Gallipoli, where he suffered a gunshot wound to the finger in the Battle of Hill 60. After hospitalisation in Mudros, he rejoined his unit. Following the evacuation, he was also in hospital in Cairo before returning to the Battalion and heading to France in March 1916. He served with the Battalion throughout the remainder of the War. At the end of hostilities, he married an English woman and did not return to Australia until 8 October 1920.[151]

And:

> Les Geddes
> 6th Batt
> Liverpool St
> Paddington

Private Leopold Joseph Geddes was an engineer from Paddington, Sydney. He initially served with the 6th Battalion at Gallipoli where he was wounded. He went with his Battalion to France in March 1916 and was in the fighting there. Geddes was wounded in action on 19 November 1916, again on 3 May 1917 at the Second Battle of Bullecourt, and again on 4 October 1917 at the Battle of Broodseinde Ridge near Ypres in Belgium. Towards the end of the War he was transferred to the 1st Divisional Signal Company as a sapper on 3 January 1918. Geddes returned to Australia on 12 April 1919.[152]

28 March 1916, Tuesday

Word came round
that all G.O.C. men
were to be classified
at 11 o'clock as we
fell in and went
before the Doctor
and he said my
heart was bad so he marked me "C"
which meant Australia
"A" meant A[ctive] service
But like a goat
Volunteered for A.S. [Active Service] [CBH II 28/3/16]

The reference to "all G.O.C. men" is perhaps a designation of all men unassigned to units but generally under the orders of the General Officer Commanding, due to their convalescing in hospital. The extract shows that, despite being rated "C", and thus assigned back to Australia, Charlie volunteered again "like a goat". But, simply volunteering again does not appear to have decided the matter. As the next entry seems to imply, Charlie had another series of tests the next day

29 March 1916, Wednesday

Nothing doing
very hot Warned
to fall in at the
mess shed at 11
o'clock for another
test. Whether I am
fit for active service
or not

If its "C" again I got good
chance of going
home [CBH II 29/3/16]

The medical testing seems to have continued for another day. There is a sense from the next entry that Charlie may have come to regret his hasty decision to volunteer again for active service. He seems to be hoping for another C rating.

30 March 1916, Thursday

Still uncertain went
before the doctor
again was told by
the Sarg[ean]t that I was
for the Boat but
I think I am marked
"A" never mind
Keep on smiling
at present we are
experiencing a
Heat Wave [CBH II 30/3/16]

31 March 1916, Friday

A.H. Darley
27th A.A.O.C.
attchd 4 Train
ASC Ghazireh
had six months
& two weeks
on Gallipoli sick
in the back had trip
to Malta [CBH II 31/3/16]

Private Arthur Henry Darley – a first cousin of Charlie's – was originally part of the 7th Company, Australian Army Service Corps. He was from Rushcutters Bay, Sydney, and had been a horse driver before the War. His mother, Ann, was the younger sister of Charlie's father. He was wounded at Gallipoli in July 1915 and in March 1916 was transferred to the 27th Company of the AASC with which he served in France. Darley returned to Australia on 1 November 1918. This was earlier than most men because he had enlisted in 1914.[153]

Charlie probably was unaware of the fact that he had another cousin serving in the Dardanelles. He was Lieutenant Commander (later Captain) Noel Hardy of the Royal Navy. He was a grandson of Alfred Hardy, one of the South Australian branch of the family who had returned to England towards the end of the 19th century. Hardy was in charge of a flotilla inside the Dardanelles Straits in 1915 and commanded the Minesweeper H.M.S. *Folkestone* and later the Destroyer H.M.S. *Racoon*. Later still, he won a Distinguished Service Order for his command of the Light Cruiser H.M.S. *Sirius* in the raids on Zeebrugge and Ostend in April and May 1918. This was a famous action where the Royal Navy sought to blockade these Belgian ports, being used as bases for German U-Boats and other ships, by sinking "blockships" to close the channel. The *Sirius* was one of the chosen blockships deliberately sunk at Ostend. The raid was ultimately unsuccessful in completely thwarting the Germans. Hardy also fought in World War II and rose to the rank of Commodore on Atlantic Ocean convoys in 1944.[154]

Back to Charlie:

1 April 1916, Saturday

> Went to Sporting Club hospital
> but was turned
> down by the major
> Never mind
> Keep smiling [CBH II 1/4/16]

Charlie's service file notes that he was moved on this date:

1/04/16 Sick Heliopolis (No 3 Auxiliary Hospital).
Aortic Reginitamon Adm

It would appear that there were a number of hospitals in the Heliopolis area, one being at the Sporting Club which was associated with the Heliopolis complex of hospitals. It seems that Charlie may still have been undergoing tests regarding his reclassification for his fitness for duty. But, at this stage, it is not known for sure what his preferred outcome was, although his service record shows that he was ill between 1 April and 17 April 1916 with "Aortic Reginitamon Adm".

2 April 1916, Sunday

Paddy Dwyer
Dick & Stuart
are well set
they passed the Major
[with] flying [colours]
met Arthur
Darley out at
[Gi]zah Camp [CBH II 2/4/16]

Paddy Dwyer has been referred to previously. Dick was probably Private Errol Cappie Nepean Devlin of the 18th Battalion. He was also from Manly, Sydney, and was a clerk before the War. He was killed in action on 30 May 1916 in the Armentières sector in France, aged 25.[155] It is not clear who Stuart was. Giza Camp was a training camp situated adjacent to the famous pyramids and the Sphinx.

3 April 1916, Monday

Still in the Hospital
I wish the Hell
they would
send me out as
I am just about
Full of it

Dick Paddy
& Stuart are for
the board to day [CBH II 3/4/16]

4 April 1916, Tuesday

Letters to-day
about dozen
that's not bad [CBH II 4/4/16]

6 April 1916, Thursday

Colours of 55th Battn
Same as 19th Battn
Chocolate & Green [CBH II 6/4/16]

This would appear to indicate that it was around this date that Charlie was notified that he was going to be joining the 55th Battalion and so must have been finally classified "A" and fit for active service. In fact, only a few days later, he transcribed the words from a famous song under the heading "Going in Trenches".

10 April 1916, Monday

Going in Trenches

When Irish Eyes
are Smiling

When Irish eyes are smiling
Sure its like morn in spring
In the lilt of Irish laughter
You can hear the angels sing
When Irish hearts are happy
All the world seems happy bright and gay
And when Irish eyes are smiling
Sure they steal
Your heart away [CBH II 10/4/16]

“When Irish Eyes are smiling” was an American song, first published in 1912, and particularly popular during the Great War, not least due to the recording by the Irish Tenor John McCormack.

Charlie appears to have had one last fling in Cairo:

12 April 1916, Wednesday

Drunk [CBH II 12/4/16]

But faced the consequences of it:

14 April 1916, Friday

Sick [CBH II 14/4/16]

He was to be discharged from hospital on 17 April 1916 and sent on to Tel-el-Kebir to join his new unit.

7

Egypt: April-June 1916

"Landed at the trenches and just about dead"

After the disaster at Gallipoli the AIF regrouped. The British and its Allies made strategic changes. At this stage it was decided that, given the continuing stalemate on the Western Front in France, more troops were needed to concentrate on beating the principal enemy – Germany. In response the Australian Government agreed to send a large contingent of their rapidly expanding army to Europe to help on the Western Front, while some of the Army would stay in the Middle East for the duration of the War. The latter were put under the overall command of British General Archibald Murray, later General Edmund Allenby, and directly under the command of the Australian Lieutenant General Harry Chauvel. These Australian soldiers would take part in the defeat of the Ottoman forces in the Middle East. They eventually conquered Baghdad on 11 March 1917 and Jerusalem on 9 December 1917, marching into Constantinople on 13 December 1918 and otherwise took part in desperate fights like the famous Battle of Beersheba in Palestine on 31 October 1917.

Charlie, though, was not destined to stay in the Middle East, being reassigned to a new 55th Battalion and after months of training heading off to the killing fields of France.

The 55th Battalion was established on 12 February 1916 at Tel-el-Kebir in Egypt.[156] Sensibly, in reorganising the army, new recruits were merged with veteran units. Initially, about half of the 55th Battalion's men came from the old 3rd Battalion that had been fighting in Gallipoli. The bulk of the other half were men recruited principally from the rural south of New South Wales, including the Monaro plains and the Snowy Mountains region. Over the coming months, to ensure a full complement, reinforcements previously slated for the 17th and 19th Battalions were redirected to the 55th. In the end, about a quarter of the strength had served at Gallipoli.

The Battalion was assigned to the 14th Brigade of the newly formed 5th Australian Division. Major David McConaghy commanded the 55th, Brigadier Godfrey Irving was appointed the officer in command of the 14th Brigade, and the commander of the 5th Division was soon to be Major General James McCay.

Major David McFie McConaghy, later to be Lieutenant Colonel, hailed from Sydney and was an accountant before the War. At the start of the conflict he had initially been with the 3rd Battalion at Gallipoli where he was wounded in action in August and September 1915. He was put in charge of the 55th with the restructure of the Army.[157] Brigadier Godfrey George Howy Irving from Melbourne was a career soldier and had briefly participated in the Second Boer War. In early 1915 he was appointed Chief of the General Staff but was later that year assigned to active service in the Middle East, at which stage he first took command of the 15th Brigade and then of the 14th Brigade in March 1916.[158] Major General James Whiteside McCay was also from Melbourne where he had been a barrister and a politician. He had served in both the Victorian and Federal Parliaments and had been Minister for Defence in Sir George Reid's Government between 1904 and 1905. Prior to this, he had been a part-time officer in the Citizen's Militia and after he lost his seat in Parliament in 1906 he joined full time and became Director of Military Intelligence. As was previously mentioned, at Gallipoli he commanded the 2nd Infantry Brigade at the Anzac landings. He was later wounded at the Second Battle of Krithia but returned to the Front. On the formation of the 2nd Division in mid 1915 he was given command but, due to a flare up of his wounds and other matters requiring him to return to Australia, this did not proceed. Instead, he was later given command of the newly created 5th Division.[159] More will be said about all these men below.

Charlie was allocated to B Company, commanded by Captain Norman Gibbins. Gibbins, who was born in Ararat, Victoria, grew up in Ipswich, Queensland, and had just left his position as a relieving manager in the Bank of NSW to move to NSW to begin farming. Even though he had a part-time commission in the Darling Downs Regiment, he only accepted a corporal's rank on enlistment. At Gallipoli he was wounded a number of times, once severely in the shoulder. Nevertheless, he returned quickly to his unit and was rapidly promoted, winning a commission and a mention in dispatches for conspicuous gallantry. He took command of A Company, 3rd Battalion. After the evacuation, Gibbins was transferred to the 55th Battalion. More will be said about him later in regards to the Battle of Fromelles.[160]

The 55th Battalion was assigned to the front lines in the Sinai Desert where Charlie and his mates were tormented by flies and other biting insects, with the heat verging on the unbearable. A boy from Sydney had never faced such harsh conditions.

To repeat what Charlie previously wrote about the Sahara desert:

> I can
> tell you its no place for
> any white man
> no water
> no trees
> nothing but sand & stones &
> whirlwinds galore. [CBH I 12]

The Battalion was assigned to defensive duties along the Suez Canal, the front line against any possible attacks by the Turks across the Sinai Peninsula. They were initially stationed at Tel-el-Kebir, which was a railway settlement about 57 kilometres west of the famous Canal. It was adjacent to the Sweet Water Canal, which carried fresh water eastward across the desert from the Nile River near Cairo to Ismailia near the Suez Canal. It was here that they carried out basic training, remembering half the complement were raw recruits direct from Australia.

On 20 March 1916, Brigadier Irving, as acting commander of the 5th Division, decided that instead of entraining the 14th and 15th Brigades to Moascar, the terminus near the Suez Canal (which was seven kilometres short of their ultimate destination of Ferry Post), he would get the men to undertake a forced march across desert. The 15th Brigade had it comparatively easy, marching on the hard sand next to the Sweet Water Canal. Unfortunately, Brigadier Irving made a serious error and the 14th Brigade, including the 55th Battalion, had to slog through soft desert sand with full pack, rifle and 120 rounds of ammunition. All up, around a 45 kilogram weight.

They started out on 27 March 1916. In the summer heat temperatures went up to 45c or 110F. The march was a torment for the men. As the Australian Defence Force Academy's historical online *AIF Report* notes:

> A combination of recent typhoid inoculations, lack of physical condition, unsuitable clothing, new boots and high temperatures made the march a trying one for many of the troops. On 28 March, the second day of the march, when the brigade halted for the midday break at 11am some of the men began to wander in search of water. Perhaps for this reason, Irving decided to recommence the march shortly after midday. On the recommendation of 5th Division headquarters, Irving made a detour away from some difficult sand hills towards a desert ridge which was supposed to afford a firmer surface. After an hour's marching in the noonday sun, the brigade reached the ridge where a halt was called in a state of utter exhaustion and many men collapsed of thirst and exhaustion. The brigade dissolved into a rabble and eventually staggered into camp at Moascar.[161]

The 55th Battalions War Diary has the anodyne entry:

> Throughout the day the conditions were much the same as the previous day and Moascar reached at 1830. During the day 4 men fell out, making a total of 11 missing.[162]

One soldier, Private Robert Harpley of B Company, 55th Battalion, has a very critical memory of the event. For example he noted:

> We camped for dinner [lunch] now minus 700-800 men who were already knocked up. We had no extra water or tea for dinner so we had to drink out our little supply in the bottle. Many poor fellows who went a little rash with their water had none left at dinner time. The reason for a lot of this is that our Brigadier General told us we only had 3 more miles to do but we found we had 8 miles to do and the heat was intense at least 110 degrees.[163]

Harpley in fact alleged that "the Brigade's death toll [was] two officers, two NCOs and seven enlisted men, with some 200 hospitalised".[164] However, an inquiry by Lieutenant Colonel Arthur Shepherd, commanding officer of the 8th Field Ambulance, found no evidence that anyone died on the march, although he was nonetheless critical of superior officers actions.[165]

The day after the march ended, the men were reviewed by the Prince of Wales (the future King Edward VIII). While the men cheered the prince, Brigadier Irving only received embarrassing jeers.

Major General McCay, who had in the meantime arrived from

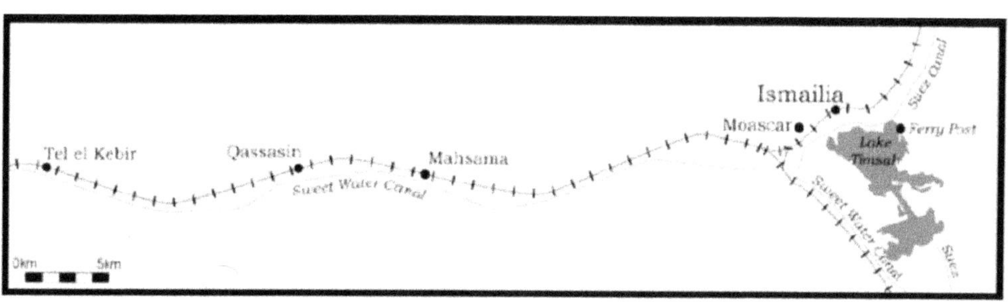

Tel el Kebir to Suez Canal, Egypt, 1916
(reproduced from Cook 2014, 19)

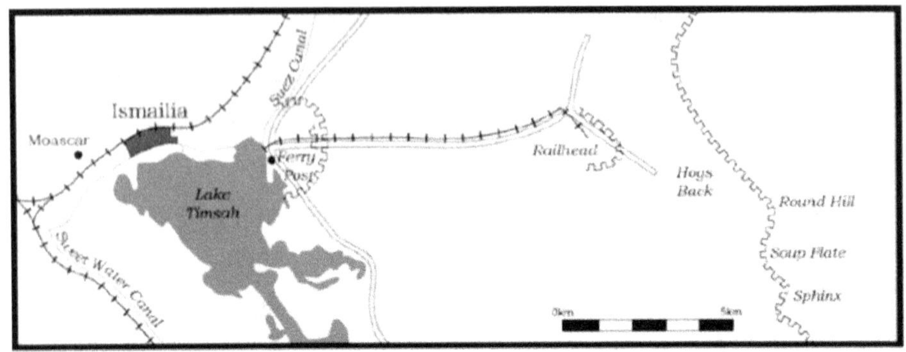

Ismailia to Sphinx (trenches), Sinai Peninsula, Egypt, 1916
(reproduced from Cook 2014, 26)

Australia and taken command of the Division, chastised the men of the Brigade for their behaviour during and after the forced march. However, McCay sacked Irving on 1 May and Colonel Harold Pope was put in charge of the brigade. He was the same Pope after whom Pope's Post at Gallipoli was named. Despite his heroics at Gallipoli, which earned him the prestigious award of the Companion of the Bath, Pope was, like Irving, himself to face the music at another far more serious disaster at Fromelles.[166]

After the Gallipoli Campaign, the focus of the British Army in Egypt was initially to secure the defences along the Suez Canal. As we have seen, the Turks had already been active in probing these defences. The British defensive line was firstly on the western bank, but it was then decided that the trenches should be dug a few kilometers east of the Canal. The British IX Corps were in charge of the southern defences between Suez and Kabrit, the 1st Anzac Corps between Kabrit and Ferdan (with their Headquarters in Ismailia), and the northern defences between Ferdan and Port Said in charge of the British XV Corps.

On 11 to 15 April 1916, Australian troops from the 3rd Light Horse Brigade were involved in a successful raid against the Turks in the Sinai Peninsula at Jifjafa, capturing numerous prisoners. There was also a major engagements involving the 1st Light Horse Brigade during April and May when the Turkish forces raided the Romani region. Turkish aircraft flew over the Suez Canal and dropped bombs on Port Said in May. So while relatively quiet there was active fighting on the Front and the troops manning the trenches were still in a war zone.

To return to Charlie's diary:

17 April 1916, Monday

Discharged from No 3
Aux Hospital and
left for Tel-el-Kebir
where we found
it very crook
put us in with the
10th reinforcements to 19th Battn
and the officers
Oh those mugs
Lucky not too
Bad [CBH II 17/4/16]

18 April 1916, Tuesday

had no sleep last
night got up at
5 am got roared
at for not shaving
two men got
crimed by
the mug O[fficer] C[ommanding]
and got 2 day field Punishment
Been sick
Cold feet I think. [CBH II 18/4/16]

"Crimed" was to be charged with a military offence.[167]

20 April 1916, Thursday

Very tired and
Stiff after last night
Unit marched off at 5am for
Ferry Post which
We landed at
9 o'clock stiff [CBH II 20/4/16]

Hache [ie "Chopped" in French]
put in B Coy 55 Battn
14th Brigade
Rather large group
from the 19th Battn [CBH II 20/4/16]

Charlie's service record says:

19/04/16 Into unit Tel-El-Kebir

20/04/16 Ferry Post – 55th Battalion – "taken on strength"/ Trans. 55th Batt

Ferry Post 20/4/16

The 55th Battalion diary for 21 April 1916 states:

"266 reinforcements marched in (15th/3rd. etc)" [168]

By Easter 1916 Charlie was ensconced at Ferry Post.

21 April 1916, Friday

Good Friday at Ferry Post
had Bacon & Jam for breakfast
Went to Church Parade
and we got days
holiday Went down
the canal suez and had swim
Swam from Arabian desert
to Africa
swim about 190 yds [CBH II 21/4/16]

That day he wrote a letter home to Hinemoa Llwellyn, which still survives. It will be recalled that she was the 15-year-old schoolgirl who had been "enlisted" to write to a Digger at the front. From the content of the letter it would appear she was in contact with Charlie's sisters as he asks her to rouse them up and send him some letters. He wrote:

Good Friday [21 April 1916] 1916

Dear Moa

This is about the fourth letter I have
had the pleasure of writing to you this last
fortnight. I have changed my address
so when you write to me again address them
to 569 B [company] 55th [Battalion] AIF and they
will find me. I met Oscar at Tel-El-Kebir on
Monday night and it took him some time
before he could make me out. But the next
night I went down to see him he had gone to
the hospital with his eyes. I think that he will
get sent home. He told me that you had been
receiving my letters alright and also told me
that my sisters had left Newtown. I am pleased
to hear that as I don't care about Newtown.
I haven't had any letters for some time now
[from my sisters] and they were very [odd].
Cause Miss Moa's letters were amongst the last
batch of letters I think there were 2 from you.
When you see
my sisters shake them up and tell them to
get busy with the pen and ink. I have only had
one letter from Rose, one from Alma. So
please shake them up and also tell them my
new address. I am at present in best of health
and I hope that you all at home are the same

I have no more news to tell you today only
that I went for swim and swam across the
Suez Canal about 200 yards across where we went
swimming. Well my dear I will close now
With Kindest to your Mother and Sister
Your Sincere Friend
Charlie

22 April 1916, Saturday

Routine 0630 to 1100
Route march full marching order [CBH II 22/4/16]

Get up at 5am now
Fell in and went
For route march
Only small one 12 Miles
Sent letters to
Harry, Flo, Hinemoa
Llewelyn & Rosie
Latham [CBH II 22/4/16]

On the same day, he regrets that he has missed going to France with the 19th Battalion.

I am sorry
I missed my Battn [CBH II 22/4/16]

Ferry Post was close enough for troops to go back to Cairo for a bit of entertainment.

23 April 1916, Sunday

Sunday 23rd

Egan, Murphy
Corsie & myself
went to Cairo on
French leave had

> Nine 9 £ & spent it in
> 3 days. Had a good
> time & a good bed. But when we
> got Corsie & myself
> got back easy but
> were fined 15/-
> Murphy & Egan came
> back under an armed
> guard. They got caught
> fined 25/- [CBH I 56-57]

As he repeated in his diary:

> had nine quid and spent
> it in 3 days
> had good [time]
> best of all we
> had good bed [CBH II 23/4/16]

"French leave" described above was actually "absent without leave". As he notes, he and his mates were fined for this little adventure.

Private James Michael Egan of the 55th Battalion was a carter from Glebe, Sydney. Unfortunately, his behaviour deteriorated when the Battalion moved to France. On 7 August 1916, while at Fleurbaix, he was charged with absence without leave, drunkenness, and threatening a superior officer. Unusually his file gives more than the usual scant information. He was convicted for pointing a rifle at Lieutenant Cecil Agassiz of the 55th Battalion and saying, "Let me get at Agassiz, the bastard. I'll blow his bloody head off". Egan was sentenced to four years penal servitude in a Military Prison in Le Havre, France. This was commuted to two years hard labour and he was released early. Egan rejoined his Battalion on 20 June 1918 and only 10 days later was wounded in action, dying from his wounds not much more than a week later on 9 July 1918 at Morlancourt in the Somme sector, aged 23.[169] Private Edward Peter Murphy of the 55th Battalion was a labourer from Kerraville near Wollongong. He was killed in action on 20 July 1916 at the Battle of Fleurbaix, aged 26.[170] In fact, Charlie noted some time after the original entry, "(both dead)".

Lastly, Private Phillip Clarence Corsie of the 55th Battalion was a shearer from Cobar, NSW. He had already fought at Gallipoli with the 17th Battalion before being wounded in action. He was subsequently transferred to the 55th, which fought at Fromelles. In early 1917, he was hospitalised and on his return on 3 April 1917 was transferred to the 33rd Battalion. Corsie was wounded in action (gunshot wound to finger) on 8 June 1917 at the Battle of Messines in Belgium, was later wounded (gassed) on 17 April 1918 in the Villers-Bretonneux sector of France and sent to hospital in England. He again rejoined his battalion on 18 July 1918 and was wounded in action for the third time (severe gunshot wound to left arm and back) on 10 August 1918 during the final Allied push on the Hindenburg Line. Fortunately, he survived all that and returned to Australia on 19 April 1919.[171]

24 April 1916, Monday

Still in Cairo [in detention]
and I wished that
I had stayed
there [Cairo] for good
as I am sick and tired of
the desert

Yo Ho
& Bottle
Of Rum [CBH II 24/4/16]

26 April 1916, Wednesday

Returned to camp [at Ferry Post]
and was tried by
Lt Col McConaghy
of 55 [Battalion] and fined

1 days pay and
Two days 2 field
Punishment amount
ing to 15/- [CBH II 26/4/16]

Col McConaghy
Cut my gear off me
& took all the mom[en]tos he could
where I was (skittled) [CBH II 26/4/16]

Some time after the original entry, Charlie had added next to McConaghy's name, "HE DIED Somme".

From Charlie's Statement of Service, it notes that he committed the crime of:

> breaking camp and remaining absent without leave from 0600 till tattoo [and was awarded] 2 days field punishment and forfeited one days pay.

Over the next few days Charlie made some random notes:

29 April 1916, Saturday

Building of a man

8 heads Equal height

Head equals breadth
of two feet.

10 Hands equal height

Better late than ever

Every dog has his day

Still waters run deep [CBH II 29/4/16]

30 April 1916, Sunday

No pastry can beat rice
pudding – Beatrice

She had nice berth and
Voyage Bertha

The bird lined her nest
with moss – Ernest

On the step – hers were
selling Stephen

Her Bertha was made
of fine lace – Herbert [CBH II 30/4/16]

1 May 1916, Monday

A king who was long
Besieged MafeKing

A King who torments
others ProvoKing

A merry uproarious
King RollicKing [CBH II 1/5/16]

Meanwhile, preparations were underway for transferring to the Western Front in France.

6 May 1916, Saturday

What with inspections
and looking
through kits bags
is just about
made me sick

Every man lost
his sheep skin
The Heads said
that we could not
carry too much
they don't carry
theirs so there you are [CBH II 6/5/16]

7 May 1916, Sunday

Told by the Colonel's
Chaplin that we are
leaving for
Moaski Tuesday
and embarking
for France on
Thursday but
I think that the
Colonel tells lies [CBH II 7/5/16]

8 May 1916, Monday

Had good swim to-day
in Canal I was
chasing boats and
diving for Hours
It was about 1.30°
in sun. To-night
there's concert on
in mess shed
all the West Indian
Troops are invited
They're fine lot of
Fellows Speak good English
[CBH II 8/5/16 and also CBH I 60]

Back on duty there was nonetheless also some relief from the searing heat via swimming in the Suez Canal. The reference to "West Indian Troops" probably refers to Indian troops who were from the western part of the sub-continent.

11 May 1916, Thursday

Who wants
To be

Ned Kelly [CBH II 11/5/16]

This is an unusual entry, Ned Kelly being a famous bushranger in the late 19th century in the New South Wales and Victorian colonies.

14 May 1916, Sunday

> If you join the
> Army, Don't Join
> the Infantry
> Its for the Goats [CBH II 14/5/16]

Another member of B Company to reflect at this time on joining the infantry was Lieutenant Percy Chapman, a former student from Glen Innes, NSW. He had originally been a trooper in the 1st Light Horse Regiment but had impressed his superiors at Gallipoli and was promoted to second lieutenant in the infantry. He wrote to his family:

> News came through today about the third Batt., which is now in the trenches in France. I have told you that when I came to the third Batt., another Light Horse fellow came with me, and when the Batt. Was split up he remained with the third and I came to the 55th. Well, he is dead. Killed in action. Fortune, they say, is a blind Goddess. The funny part is that it seems so hard to realise that death may come at any time. I don't for a minute believe that I will get killed. Soldiers all seem to become fatalists and the majority optimistic ones at that. It's a way they have in the Army.[172]

Charlie's diary continues:

15 May 1916, Monday

> Out of Blankets 3am
> bacon & biscuits
> drink tea and
> off we popped to the trenches
> only 12 miles

arrived there at 9.30.
Just about done
No water
Sinai Penninsula
is no Bunch of
roses for Charles [CBH II 15/5/16 and also CBH I 60]

16 May 1916, Tuesday

Landed at the trenches
and just about dead
with thirst & hunger
My God will I ever
forget the flies & Land
had about 2 hours sleep
through the night.
The flies work overtime
they are worse than
Shrapnel. [CBH I 62 and also CBH II 16/5/16]

17 May 1916, Wednesday

Not so bad now
I am cooking for N° 8
Platoon also acting
Quartermaster The
heat at present is
140° in shade
My God the Sinai
Penninsular is no
Good to me
Landed back at
Spinx Camp 9.20
after days [CBH II 17/5/16 and also CBH I 64]

On the ground the troops had to suck it up and bear with the treatment that was being meted out to them. Over the next few days Charlie reported on conditions in the trenches:

18 May 1916, Thursday

Camped at Spinx
behind the trenches
Terrible dry. Helped
to erect a marquis
& had a sleep
Dreamt I was playing
football but was woken
by somebody calling
mess orderlys.
Marched out to the
trenches on fatigue. [CBH I 64 and also CBH II 18/5/16]

19 May 1916, Friday

Back in trenches not
so bad as last ones more
water and tucker message
came round that party
of arabs where 1500
yds off
Dreamt that Roy & Harry were dead
had about two drops of rain
if we wash or shave
we get crimed
don't I wish it would rain [CBH II 19/5/16 and also CBH I 64-65]

Roy will be his brother Leslie Roy Hardy. Harry may be his other brother John Henry Hardy.

20 May 1916, Saturday

Back in Spinx Camp
from trenches. Warned to
go back to Hogs Head
Rest Camp 4 miles across
the desert to relieve 3
men on Guard. Very
hot to-day about 120°
in shade last two
days it was cool about
100 in shade I hope
we are not long on
this front [CBH II 20/5/16]

21 May 1916, Sunday

Got orders to move back
to Hogs Back camp
3 miles from first line
of trenches put on
a Water Guard with
Jim Egan and others
not bad show either
Rumoured that
that the 55 [Battalion] is moving
back to Ferrys
Post on Wednesday [CBH II 21/5/16]

After the name "Egan" Charlie wrote, apparently after the event, "(KILLED)".

22 May 1916, Monday

Warm again and
not much tucker
to spare to any

Bagman that should
pass Never mind
I will soon be
out of Gypos
Land amongst
the Iron Foundry
and Shrapnel [the Western Front in France] [CBH II 22/5/16]

23 May 1916, Tuesday

How stiff got warned
that we were
to be Relieved
by the 53rd Battn
another march
back to the trenches
to-night.
I wish I could
get some letters
from Australia [CBH II 23/5/16]

24 May 1916, Wednesday

Back at Spinx
Camp Behind trenches
Rumoured that we
are leaving here on
the 8 June for France [CBH II 24/5/16]

25 May 1916, Thursday

Had touch of dysentery
and got Medicine
& Duty by doctor
I was pretty crook

Picture postcard sent to Charlie's brother Roy stating on the reverse: "To Dear Roy, From three of the wounded at Gallipoli. Charlie Egypt 1915-16". Charlie is seated on right. (From Hardy family collection)

but Glad to say
That I am at present
much better [CBH II 25/5/16]

28 May 1916, Sunday

[We] are leaving
tomorrow
[Give] way to
the Tommies
[to take] our places
[We were handed] out 100 rounds [CBH II /5/16]

29 May 1916, Monday

[Good bye] Egyptian [desert]
Good bye Sinai Peninsula
[Good bye] Spinx Camp
[Good] bye Lemnos
[Good bye] Meddelsen
I am not [the last] for once [CBH II /5/16]

The reference to "Meddelsen" may refer to Lieutenant Berrol Mendelsohn, who was an officer in the 55th. He may have been Charlie's platoon leader and with the move to France maybe there were changes which Charlie was happy with. Mendelsohn was to be killed on the night of 19/20 July 1916 at the Battle of Fromelles in the rearguard action, aged 25. It was later reported by Private F. Johnston of A Company, 55th Battalion, that "I was with him on the night of 19.7.16 at Fleurbaix in the charge, when he was hit by a shell, and only lived a few minutes, and I saw him just before he died and again after he was dead. He did not seem to suffer. He was a game man all right. This happened in the 3rd line of German trenches, and as we had to retire, his body would have been left in the German trench."[173]

Charlie's diary continues:

30 May 1916, Tuesday

I am not
[the last] for once
left since Penninsula
this morning [left] around
5.30 am and
arrived at Ferry Post
at 10.30 distance
about 14 miles
how glad I am to
be here now we
can have good wash
in the Suez Canal [CBH II /5/16 and CBH II 30/5/16]

31 May 1916, Wednesday

Camped on the old
Brigades ground [CBH II 31/5/16]

1 June 1916, Thursday

Got issued with
all new clothes
for France but
its nothing compared
with the old
material we were
issued with
12 months ago [CBH II /6/16]

2 June 1916, Friday

Div[isional] Inspection by
Brigadier Pope and
we was the Best
battn on the Ground

Swimming Parade
at 4 o'clock
but I went
down to the canal
before hand
with the lads [CBH II /6/16]

3 June 1916, Saturday

Sent our uniforms
away on the
transport so it
will be clean
when we get to
France
Minus Chats [CBH II /6/16]

"Chats" was a slang word used for vermin that infested clothing.[174]

5 June 1916, Monday

Haven't had
any letters since
April I think
that the Postal
Staff must be
short of tucker
and devour
them it seems
funny [CBH II /6/16]

6 June 1916, Tuesday

Supposed to go away
to-day but it don't seem so

had bonser swim to-day at
present I am waiting
for pass

Yo Ho
&
Bottle
of
Beer [CBH II /6/16]

7 June 1916, Wednesday

Russians had
another good win
as paper goes
only 51,000
prisioners if they
keep taking any
more there'll be
no Germans left
for us to kill [CBH II 7/6/16]

The Russian "win" that Charlie refers to will be the successful offensive mounted by Russian General Aleksei Brusilov against the Austro-Hungarians in the area of western Ukraine. The attack began on 4 June 1916 (only a few days before Charlie's note) and involved the wholesale surrendering of thousands of Czech troops, not Germans as Charlie mentions. Charlie also says the newspaper reported 51,000 prisoners. The final tally was over 70,000. It has been described as "the greatest Russian victory of the war".[175] Amusingly, at the end of the page, Charlie seems to have written some time after the original entry of "if they keep taking any more [prisoners] there'll be no Germans left for us to kill" – "What Rot".

8 June 1916, Thursday

Lord Kitchener Death
reported to-day
Was on his way to
Russia on board
the HMS Hampshire
and was either
torpedoed or hit
by mine all
hands lost
General Roberts
takes command [CBH II 8/6/16]

The great wartime leader, Field Marshall Lord Herbert Kitchener, was killed on 5 June 1916 when the cruiser H.M.S *Hampshire* was sunk. In all, 737 died. His death was a huge shock. He had been travelling to Russia to discuss the war effort with the Russian Czar. Kitchener was not replaced by "General Roberts" as Charlie has been told. He had been Secretary of State for War and not a general in the High Command. He was in fact replaced by David Lloyd George, who was to later become Prime Minister (replacing Herbert Asquith on 6 December 1916). "General Roberts" will probably be a reference to Lieutenant General Sir William Robertson who had previously been appointed the Chief of the Imperial General Staff in December 1915 and was already the senior general in the Army. Having said that, this is a remarkably accurate report by Charlie. Along with the previous extract and a lot of other entries in Charlie's diary it shows how the world of communications had rapidly changed in the previous half century, with major world events being reported across the globe in a matter of days.

To the more mundane, Charlie's next entry was another attempt at poetry:

9 June 1916, Friday

My Little red Rose
Yesterday I went into the flower [shop]
and I ask the man:-
"How much -a you want
for-a one red-a rose in da window
The flower [man] he look, and say: 2/-
each
Then I say ; I canna pay-a so
much mak a little cheap
The flower man he say
"oh no, no cheaper theyre 2/- each
I go outside and look-a in da window
at the nisa reda roses and pretty [CBH II 13/6/16]

soon a young lady come a
Beautiful young a lady and
she see da pretty flowers
and she-a say a
"oh the pretty reda-roses
How much.
The flower man he see the
nice young a lady and he
say 6^d each
The lady buy one Reda
Rosa and she go away [CBH II 14/6/16]

I still look in da window
The flower man say "I tella
you before there 2/-
Then I say mak "a little
cheaper of me signor
The flower man he say no no
no cheaper. 2/- each

what for you want-a red-a rose
I say I tell you what for
I want-a the red rose
I had leetle girl-a once [CBH II 15/6/16]

and-a she was Just like dis
so high and because she
look-a so much lika dis
flower we call-a her Rosa
we were so happy to gether
me – da mamma and-a
da leetle Rosa – but one a
day da mamma she die
signor I bury her quick
away away in da country
and a leetle Rosa and me [CBH II 9-16/6/16]

were left alone
How much I loved that a child
and every night when I
comma a home from
da work-a I go da hill a top
and I saya Hello Rosa
and she say a froma a
winda up a high Hello papa
and-a every night signor I
go thata way from da work
and I say just a like [CBH II 9/6/16]

I always Hello Rosa but
there was no hello papa
she was no-a there signor
she was dead
I bury a my leetle Rosa
by the mamma and I

have been alone Signor
I just a wanta a one a
red a rose to put on da
grave of my leetle Rosa
that is all signor [CBH II 10/6/16]

that is all signor
Scuse me to taka a too
mucha of youre time
Signor scuse me
What you say Signor
whole bunch-a nothing
the whole bunch for me
for nothing thank you
Signor thank a you
Thank-a you [CBH II 11/6/16]

12 June 1916, Monday

Jim Egan is up
before the Colonel
for dealing out
stoush to the
Police Sgt Yours
Truly and few
others are the
main witnesses
28 days 2nd F.P. [ie field punishment]

I deliveres
A bomb
to the
Policeman [CBH II 12/6/16]

Again, after the name "Egan" Charlie has written after the event "(Killed)".

17 June 1916, Saturday

Same
As [before]
A.W.L. [ie absent without leave] [CBH II 17/6/16]

18 June 1916, Sunday

A.W. L. [CBH II /6/16]

Lost my Disc and
chain also the medal
Alma Latham gave me. Was swimming
In canal and
Egan & mob were
ducking me and
the chain broke [CBH II 21/6/16]

19 June 1916, Monday

Left Ferry Post to-day
and landed at
Moaski where we
expect to be for about
24 Hours I hope so [CBH II /6/16]

Leaving Moaskir
to-night for Alexandria
then for France
Good bye to Egypt
For Good I hope [CBH II /6/16]

After months on the frontline on the Sinai Peninsula, Charlie and the 55th Battalion were finally heading off to the festival of death in France or, as Charlie called it in an earlier extract: "the Iron Foundry and Shrapnel"

8

France 1916

"Back again at Front Line"

The 55th Battalion was eventually given its marching orders and headed off to France on 19 June 1916. It was an anxious time for Charlie and his mates. He and many of the others were now veterans so they actually had a sense of what they were heading into. They had seen the carnage at Gallipoli and the reports of casualties on the Western Front were not hidden from them. If they read the newspapers they knew that by mid-1916 many hundreds of thousands of British Empire troops had already died or been wounded in the mud of France and Belgium. Still, things were only to get worse, as one of the most deadly battles in world history – the Battle of the Somme – was just about to be launched by the British on 1 July 1916. That was only 12 days away and Charlie and his mates would be some amongst many who paid the consequences for the failure of this offensive.

Charlie's diary continues:

20 June 1916, Tuesday

> Arrived at Alexandria
> and embarked on to the
> the S.S. Caledonia
> its scotch ship and
> you can guess that
> it's a starvation ship [CBH II 20/6/16]

S.S. *Caledonia* (reproduced from Royal Dublin Fusiliers extracted at www.dublin-fusiliers.com on 13 August 20200

Some time after the War, Charlie annotated this page writing "plenty of porridge & shortbread" [CBH II 20/6/16]. Charlie's comrade in B Company, Private Robert Harpley, also wrote:

> We were pleased to leave the cussed boat. I never had such starving in my life – the last three days we had only hardship biscuits and tea and very small portion of "burgoo" [a porridge].[176]

It should be noted again that these maritime crossings were not holidays. There was a constant U-Boat threat and men had to wear life jackets at all times. These also substituted as pillows for sleeping.[177] In fact this very ship, the SS *Caledonia*, was sunk by a German submarine on just such a trip to Marseille six months later, on 4 December 1916.[178]

Charlie's diary continues:

24 June 1916,

> Don't
> Ask ? [CBH II 24/6/16]

25 June 1916, Sunday

Twelve months to-day
since I left Australia
and at present I am
at Malta awaiting
to move off to France
Had good swim at Malta Beautiful
Blue water

Only land Sharks [CBH II 25/6/16]

26 June 1916, Monday

Left Malta about
5.30 and was
met by 3 Destroyers
convoyed us about
as far as the Italian coast
then was picked up by French
Cruiser [CBH II 26/6/16]

27 June 1916, Tuesday

Weather still
Warm but
expect to find
it cooler in
day or so
as we expect to arrive in
France on the 28th if all's
well [CBH II 27/6/16]

28 June 1916, Wednesday

Arrived at France
to-day but can't

do anything
but Growl no
tucker and very
little water to drink [CBH II 28/6/16]

After the War, in his laconic way, Charlie annotated this passage with the question: "What about beer?" [CBH II 28/6/16]

Private Herbert Allen of the 55th records:

> Amid much playing of the Marseillaise and the cheers and emotions of the French crowd we entrained. The Battalion was one big smile.[179]

Charlie recorded:

30 June 1916, Friday

Entrained to-day
for the Australian
over seas base
expect 3 days
journey before
we get out of the
rattler Thiennes
17 miles back of
Firing line [CBH II 30/6/16]

After the War, Charlie annotated this passage with the words: "Turned out later to be the firing line". [CBH II 30/6/16] The newly formed Australian 5th Division was being sent to a relatively quiet stretch of the Western Front, dubbed the "nursery", because it supposedly allowed new troops to familiarise themselves with trench warfare without being under constant attack. In fact, as we will see in the next chapter, it had been the site of furious bloody battles in 1915 and was soon to be again. Thiennes was a small French village.

Charlie's narrative continued:

1 July 1916

On board the
Rattler and I don't
mind 3 days of it
as the country
is the prettiest
I have ever seen
talk about farms
they are Beautiful
the Paris Express
Just passed as
Speeding about
70 miles an Hour [CBH II 1/7/16]

Private Allen remarked:

> The Battalion … wondered if this was the Garden of Europe. Not an inch of ground was wasted. Tilled land, rich crops, lush grass, tall trees, broad streams, prosperous villages and towns everywhere.[180]

Another from the 55th, Private Frank Brown, wrote:

> Never did anyone enjoy 63 hours travelling more than I. The glorious green country, rich with orchards of cherry, pear and other fruits seemed like home. Everyone became enraptured with the miles of vegetation … and a more happy crowd of troops would be hard to find.[181]

Charlie humorously talked about going AWOL to Paris:

2 July 1916

Round
About
Paris
Waiting to

Jump off
but the
train is too
fast [CBH II 2/7/16]

The 55th battalion arrived at Thiennes on 3 July at 2.30am.

As Private Harpley from B Company also recorded:

> As soon as we got out of the train we could hear guns roaring – they seem to be firing almost incessantly.[182]

The next day they immediately began training in bayonet fighting, musketry, and response to gas attacks.[183]

Charlie was obviously also meeting the locals:

7 July 1916

Jacques Leclercq
25 rue des Vasions
Montalaine Oises
France
Georges Danrut
A
Chiennes Nord

Gave my tucker
to those named
They looked starved [CBH II 7/7/16]

Louis Laurans French
Remarques Victoricux

Borg-Saint- Audiol
Ardeche
France

Could write book on this
last few days but it's
too much trouble

Just ask me to explain
about the above address [CBH I 100]

And troops from around the Empire:
J Coleman
Dublin

J Thompson
London East

T. Cunningham
John St
Dundalk
Co. Louth
Ireland [CBH I 100]

At this stage Charlie and the Battalion must have been briefed on what their forward movements would be. After only a few days, the Battalion was moved to the front line near Fleurbaix:

8 July 1916

Billeted at
Thiennes, Estaires,
Sailly, Back St Muir
Under Fire [CBH II 8/7/16]

As the 55th Battalion diary says:

> 9th [July 1916] 8 a.m. The Battalion with the rest of the 14th Brigade A.I.F., left its billets in THIENNES and route marched to ESTAIRES about 22 kilometres distant … and Estaires reached at 5.00 p.m.[184]

As Private George Gill of the 55th noted:

> It is all narrow streets, few nice shops … We are now very near the firing line but outside the town everything looks peaceful enough … Have had a look around this place but are not impressed at all. … Estaires is not altogether free of gas

> attacks … most of the inhabitants appear to be possessed of gas helmets but do not appear to have much fear of gas.[185]

From Estaires the 55th marched with the 54th Battalion 11 kilometres to another village – Sailly sur la Lys – under the cover of darkness, on 10 July, starting at 8.30pm and arriving at 11.30pm. As the Battalion diary noted:

> Progress was slow and cautious owing to enemy aeroplane activity and the proximity to the firing line. Men remained in billets during the day and in view of the activity of enemy aircraft were not permitted to wander or loiter in the streets.

As Charlie recorded it:

10 July 1916

> Don't ask [CBH II 10/7/16]

Then, at 8.30pm on 11 July, the Battalion moved forward once again, settling into the trenches around 1.00am the following morning. As the Battalion diary records it:

> The Battalion commenced its march of the final stage to the trenches, going vice BAC ST MAUR, and took over the position of the front line, sections 37 to 41 at the time held by the 45th Battalion of the 12th Australian Infantry Brigade. The position which the Battalion now held lay, roughly, 4 miles to the south of Armentieres, and formed the outside of a horseshoe salient, the distance between our trenches and the enemy's at this point being about 300 yards.
>
> During the day there was little activity beyond artillery exchanges.
>
> Casualties. One man wounded by rifle grenade explosion.

The length of 300 yards is equivalent to three football (soccer) fields. That is not far at all when someone is shooting at you.

Charlie's diary continues:

11 July 1916

Arrived at another
billet early this morning
not as good as the last one
Plenty of bombs
and Fritz is beginning to think
that Australians
like plenty of fight [CBH II 11/7/16]

12 July 1916

Back in firing line
I don't know
the name of it
all I know [is] that
at the rear of us
there once stood the
longest convent
in world but now
there's only the
wall around it
standing [CBH II 12/7/16]

It is not entirely clear as to what convent Charlie is referring. It is most likely the Abbey of Saint Vaast that had been badly damaged in fighting during 1914. Private Herbert Harris also wrote:

> Tonight into the firing line. God this is a rotten game … so if this is my last entry good bye.[186]

For the next day Charlie simply wrote:

13 July 1916

Don't ask [CBH II 13/7/16]

This was an important day for the new 55th Battalion. The Battalion diary says:

> Intelligence reports that the trenches opposite us are occupied by the 21st Bavarian Regiment. Enemy bombarded CONVENT AVENUE and BOUTILLERIE AVENUE at intervals between 2 p.m. and 7 p.m. Gas Alert at 11.30p.m.
>
> Casualties 1 man Killed: 1 wounded – through bursting shell.[187]

This was the first man killed in the Battalion. It was a Private Edward McKenna. Particularly for those who had not been in combat before this was sobering news.

Charlie's diary continues:

> 14 July 1916
>
> Back again at front Line carrying Bombs [CBH II 14/7/16]

These "bombs" will be the Mills hand grenade. They were introduced in May 1915 and were the standard issue 4-second fuse, metal fragmentation bomb. In addition, according to the family recollections of Charlie's postwar stories, by the time he was on the Western Front he was a Lewis gunner. The normal weapon for Australian troops was the short magazine, Lee Enfield 0.303 inch calibre rifle which was considered a superior weapon to the German Mauser. The Lewis gun was a 0.303 inch calibre light machine gun that could be carried by one man, and was introduced into the British Army in 1915.[188]

Charlie's diary entries for the period 15 July to 18 July (the day before the Battle of Fromelles) are very succinct.

> 15 July 1916
>
> Don't ask [CBH II 15/7/16]
>
> 16 July 1916
>
> Don't Ask [CBH II 16/7/16]
>
> 17 July 1916
>
> Same as [CBH II 17/7/16]

18 July 1916

? [CBH II 18/7/16]

What was happening on those four days? They were learning that the Western Front against the Germans was another level higher in the horror of War. As Charlie's comrades in the 55th Battalion recorded it, the bombardments were constant. Private Harris said:

> Just finished dinner when Germans began sending sausages over. Got so hot were ordered to dugouts. The shells bursting not 20 yards away and covering us with mud – a lot of men hit. [189]

And later:

> Have been working all night on fatigues … since coming into the trenches have had six hours off in 34 and haven't fired a shot yet, nothing to fire at. Where I am sitting one fellow had his hand smashed. … Have got a little dugout of my own. At any rate it is drier than the last one where the walls were dripping wet and slugs climbed all over face.[190]

While Private Gill noted:

> Early in the evening we were entertained by a big German gun or guns which I think was trying to fix up our battery. It fired about sixty shells which must have been 9 [inches] at least. We could trace the course of the shells which went over our place and landed some distance away and would burst with an awful explosion. Although it was some distance away, we could feel the rush after each explosion.[191]

The 55th Battalion diary says:

> 14 July: Our Artillery caused much damage to enemy parapets & they are busy repairing same. Enemy artillery very active during afternoon and evening. CONVENT AVENUE again shelled. We sent out patrol from 10.30p.m. to 2.30 a.m. 14/15th

Casualties. 1 man wounded during artillery bombardment.

Enemy snipers very active during evening & used many flares.

15 July 9 p.m.: Troops holding line to our right made Gas attack on enemy. Some of the gas drifted across 55th Battalion lines, and Gas Helmets had to be called into use. No casualties.

Relieved by 6th Bn Shropshires Light Infantry between 11 p.m. and 2 a.m. Battalion moved into billets in BAC ST MAUR. A very heavy bombardment took place after the gas attack but no losses were incurred by the Battalion in withdrawing.

16 July: Battalion now in billets and being utilised for fatigues, carrying ammunition, stores etc. up to the front line preparatory to an attack on the enemy's trenches.

17th & 18th July: These two days were occupied in the same way.[192]

The next two days were to be a horrible bloodbath for the 55th.

9

Fromelles/Fleurbaix 1916

"Most expensive & terrible battle"

The Battle of Fromelles, from 19 to 20 July 1916, has lived in infamy in Australia for over a hundred years. It is famous for being a military disaster that resulted in the heaviest casualty list for the Australian army in a single day. Although other battles in the War were to have accumulated higher totals over a number of days, Fromelles has a particular place in Australian history.

It is worth recounting the overall state of affairs on the European theatre of war at this stage. The open warfare on the Western Front of 1914, with large movement of troops in the Battles of Mons and the Marne, and the "Race to the Sea", was by now far in the past. The battles of 1915, such as the Battles of Neuve Chapelle, Second Ypres, Aubers Ridge, Loos, Champagne, and Vimy Ridge, showed that little headway had been made by either side due to the dominating power of artillery and machine guns. There was also a stalemate on the southern front, between Austro-Hungary and Italy. Far away on the German Eastern Front against the Russians, the Central Powers were not making progress. The Brusilov Campaign, which has been previously referred to, had made some headway against the Austro-Hungarians, although Russia struggled to match the Germans themselves after their significant losses to them starting in 1914 with the Battle of Tannenberg. Despite all this, at the beginning of 1916, the German High Command believed that they now had a chance of ending the War by 1917.

The German plan of attack developed by General Erich von Falkenhayn was to bleed the French Army dry by attacking what they perceived to be a weak point around the town of Verdun. Von Falkenhayn, as the Chief of the German General Staff, was the overall commander in chief, albeit under Kaiser Wilhelm II. He was an experienced professional Prussian General, who had been too young to participate in the Franco-Prussian War of 1870 (as had his predecessor in the position, Helmuth von Moltke), but had fought in the 1901 Boxer Rebellion in China. At the beginning of the Great War he actually held a political position as the Prussian Minister for War. Although comparatively junior in Army rank, he had succeeded von Moltke in September 1914, when the former had had a nervous breakdown after the enormous military clashes of that year and the failure of the Germans to deliver their anticipated knockout blow with the Schlieffen Plan to encircle the Allies in Belgium and Northern France.

In February 1916, Germany began attacking the Verdun sector in what was to prove to be an utter charnel house of death and destruction. The French put up a heroic resistance and both countries suffered appalling losses. In light of this, the Allies decided that the British would assist their French comrades by making a separate thrust into the German lines in the Somme River sector to take advantage of the weakened German army. It was more than just a diversion, but a plan to break through the German lines, move back to mobile warfare, and end the War. The Battle of Fromelles was to be a subsidiary battle to this larger Battle of the Somme.

Just to clear up the dual name, "Fromelles/Fleurbaix", straightaway: throughout history battles often have had two names depending on which side of a conflict is writing about it. The British initially called this battle Fleurbaix because they were attacking from the direction of that French village which was on their side of the trench line. Equally, the Germans referred to it as the Battle of Fromelles because that village was directly behind the area of attack on their side and was one of the targets of the offensive. During the 1920s British and

Australian historians began to adopt the German name for the battle. Why is not completely clear. But, by the time the *Official History of the AIF in 1916* by Charles Bean was published in 1929, he was using this name.

Charlie Hardy entered the Battle of Fromelles as a Lewis gunner but was badly wounded on 20 July 1916. It was to end his active participation in the War, and it is apparent from his diary entries that he retained bitter resentment about what occurred and the poor way such a tremendous action was essentially covered up.

The following passage appears in Charlie's War Diary, which would seem to have been written sometime after the War had concluded, most likely in 1919.

> The Battle of Fleurbaix
> July 19th 1916
> France
> Very little is Known of the battle of
> Fleurbaix it was never fully
> reported for sufficient reasons it
> was perhaps deemed inadvisable
> to disclose the details of our
> newly arrived AIF unit or the
> extent of our loss to the Enemy
> It was described in most English
> newspapers in light lines and was
> variously called a lively Skirmish
> a stirring attack or a big raid
> For dogged self Sacrificing courage
> and extent of casualties it ranks
> with other record trench battles
> Pozieres & Bullecourt. On strict
> examination will probably be the
> most expensive & terrible

Australian troops, Fleurbaix, France, 1916
(reproduced from Australian War Memorial, extracted at www.awm.gov.au on 13 August 2020)

battle ever fought by the AIF.
& the most desperate. One thing is
absolutely certain it tops the lists
for casualties for the time engaged
Many AIF officers of experience
declare that they never Knew
Australians to fight better Certainly
they were never confronted with a more
difficult problem not over
at Lone Pine, Gallipoli. As the
casualty list of Pozieres came to
Australia at the same time there was
certain vagueness about the geographic
-cal details of Fleurbaix There are
still many people who think that
their sons or Brothers fell at pozieres
whereas they fell at Fleurbaix Our
heroic dead who fell in this first
trench battle are entitled to their
little bit of history their place
on our hall of Fame
it is fitting therefore that
amid our rejoicing for peace

The veil of mystery should be lifted
From this glorious action, and
that Fleurbaix should take its
place in the lists of outstanding
Australian battle. The 5th Div
has nothing but glory from such
a revelation. it has made History
Bapaume, Lagnicourt Polygon Wood
Menin Road & many another place

list should have Fleurbaix inscribed
on its banners
On arrival in France
the 5th Div [was moved] up to front line in Flandres
via Estaires, Saille-sur Lys & went into the
trenches On a very exciting night of
July 11th '16
it occupied a sector
South of Armatrees to Bois Grenier
Commonly called the nursery
because newly arrived AIF
units were sent there for training
in trench warfare while holding
the line

it was a bit quiet
because both sides seemed to
Recognise that advance either way
was impossible at this point
British & Germans held strong ground
With marshy ground between &
We laboured under the disability
Of being unable to fire into [the town of] Lille
Because of the presence of French
Women & children whilst the big [German]
Guns of Lille could fire on us
All along the sector we daily watched
The gradual demolition of fine big
Churches by the systematic
Bombardment of the Bosche

The advice given by the British officers
when we took over was if you
leave the bosche alone he will leave

you alone Keep watch, strengthened your
positions but don't get too lively.
This advice given was treated
With mild contempt by most
of the AIF units as they arrived
for they all wakened up Fritz

For their turn its was the optimism of the
Command that an advance was possible
& then there was the glory of being the
the first Australians to go into pitched
battle in France.

We were to attack
from [the town of] Bois Grenier on two mile
front. Our objective being the village
of Fromelles held by the Germans
British Divisions were brought up
From the terrible fighting at Ypres
To hold the front line while we
Went over the top We were out
For two days. Organising before the
battle Zero hour being 6pm on
July 19th 1916 for three days our
Guns had been wire cutting
All along the sector & there was three
hours bombardment to which the Germans
replied by counter battery fire
which was very successful

in some cases our gun crews
Had to be removed & one gun was
struck & the whole pit wrecked
We had an initial piece of bad
luck for a German H. P. [ie shell] found

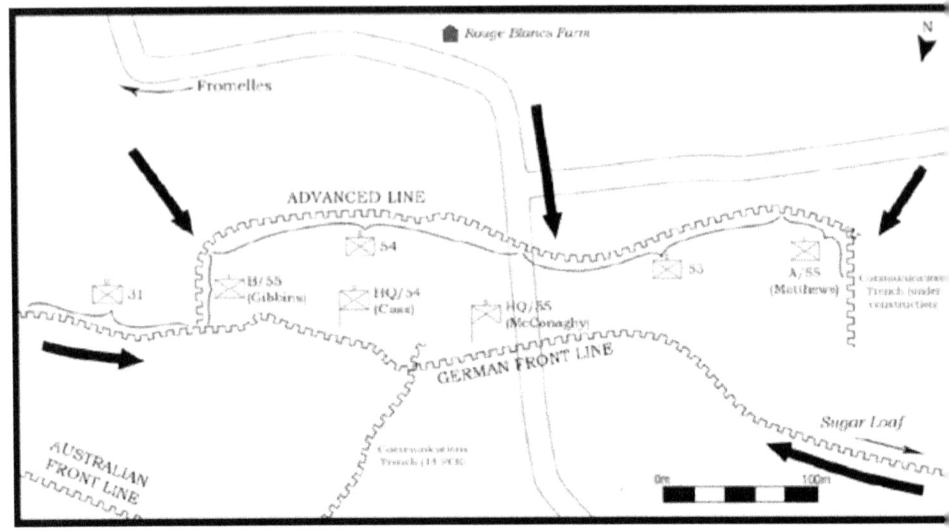

Battle of Fromelles (Fleurbaix), France, 19-20 July 1916
(reproduced from Cook 2014, 37)

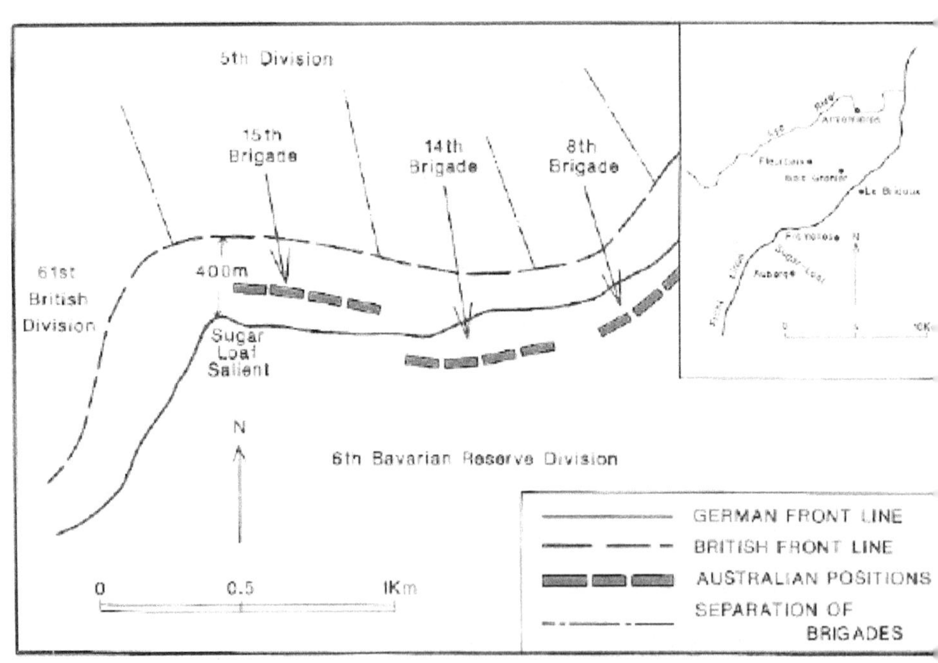

Battle of Fromelles (Fleurbaix), France, 19-20 July 1916
(reproduced from Virtual War Memorial Australia extracted from www.vwma.org.au on 13 August 2020)

one of our bomb reserves which
went up in yellow smoke
Punctually at 6pm the first wave
went over the parapet with
bayonets fixed being at once
subjected to tremendous cannon
fire from the German line high
explosives shattering our works
& doing much damage in
fact I think Fritz fired all
the Ironmongery he could
find in Germany. It was
much worse ordeal than the
landing at Gallipoli

Although we appeared to have
Artillery superiority for some
time when the attack was made
we discovered such enemy
Artillery concentration which proved
As German prisoners afterwards
told us that they expected
the attack at this
place & time Having advanced
through the German fire our
infantry were now confronted
with swampy ground & the
German second line trenches indicated
on our maps could not properly
be identified They had in some
cases been flooded In spite of the
loss by the bombing of the German
Exports our troops were not to be

Denied and by 7pm all
The German trenches were captured
& Colonel Cass [C.O. 54th Battalion] was installed
in the headquarters of a German
Battalion many of our men
Got right through to Fromelles

from the first we were in
difficulty in regard to transport
Two parallel roads lead to the front
They were visible & were swept
by gun fire There were advance
dressing stations on each of the
roads in the ruined farm houses
which we called Rifle Villa &
Beacon House Saps emerged near
Both & soon a ceaseless stream
Of wounded began to pour into
these dressing stations me
being one. All around the
dressing stations they were lying
in the open where I see many
of my pals whom I had served
months in the line with go west
with terrible wounds which I
think they would not have
lived long if [not treated]
then, There was many individual
deeds of heroism Captain
Gibbons led his bombers
whom I belonged
forth again & again until
he fell Lieut Mendalshon fought on

though he was wounded fight on
to his death Lieuts Cummins.
Folkard & Matthews carried right
through into enemy lines
near were wounded they
were done & were captured by
Fritz Two commanders fell and Capt [chaplain]
Maxted M.A. was killed by a piece
of shell. Our Battn [the 55th] which had gone
out to consolidate had to undertake the
duty holding back the Boche when
at last our Brigadier Colonel
Pope gave the order to retire
it was with difficulty that our own
could be induced to retire from
some places as they did not
understand the General position
it was orderly. Much booty machine
guns, maps, official orders with
over 100 prisioners.

Then our maxims
were pushed to the rear but our
lewis gunners stayed to the last
to cover the retirement
one of our most pathetic
difficulties was retrieving
many wounded men who lay in swampy
gullies The stretcher bearers
recovered a number & as the
battle died away a small
party went out under a red
cross flag to ask for leave

to bury the dead
they were met by a German officer who
conducted them to Headquarters
where Fritz officer at once
photographed them whilst they
waited for a message from the
German O.C. They were told
that we could get our wounded
if we showed the white flag
which we of course refused to do

In spite of rifle fire However
all through the 20th our
bearers at the risk of lives
were bringing in our own wounded
They were sent up in trollies
or carried on stretchers & we
had a sad day of helping
the wounded & burying the dead
when the fight was
over men lay about in
battle stupor cause by the weariness
they were quite
oblivious of the danger of passing
gun teams or mobile ambulances
& one could roll or move them
to places of safety without
awakening them
So passed our first Battle in France
it proved the strength of the
German position which was
Never again attacked at This point
possibly it prevented the Germans

from sending men and guns to
the Somme. Most of all it proved
that the 5th Div had the same
high courage as the 1st
This has since been confirmed
in many a battle
after Fleurbaix we settled down in that
sector to raids confined to
groups of not more than
60 specially trained men
in this way we caused much
loss to the enemy & kept
them guessing
it was a terrible & expensive battle but it has
its share in the heroic events
Which finally broke the
German spirit & led to
Victory

The Casualties numbered
9,400 (killed) out of
12,00
IN LESS THAN
8 HOURS [CBH I 122-133]

Initially, it would seem that the above was a completely original piece that Charlie penned himself. Indeed, parts of this passage have been quoted in Cook's book on the 55th Battalion and attributed to Charlie.[193] However, research revealed that it was in fact largely transcribed in hand by Charlie from an article published in the *Sydney Morning Herald* on Saturday, 19 July 1919. It was written by Senior-Chaplain James Green CMG. I have included it because Charlie actually made quite a large number of edits to the original article, most notably inserting personal references to his own story and involvement in B Company's rearguard action and the heroics of their commanding officer, Captain Norman Gibbins. Just as an example, I note that he inserts:

in fact I think Fritz fired all
the Ironmongery he could
find in Germany.

And:

Captain Gibbons
led his bombers
whom I belonged
forth again & again until
he fell

And:

soon a ceaseless stream
Of wounded began to pour into
these dressing stations me
being one. All around the
dressing stations they were lying
in the open where I see many
of my pals whom I had served
months in the line with go west
with terrible wounds which I
think they would not have
lived long if [not treated]
then,

The references to the number of casualties at the end of the passage have also been added by Charlie and, of course, adds a strong final note of poignancy to the passage. Charlie would probably have known Reverend Green. It is not beyond the realms of possibility that as a veteran of the battle he was a key witness who talked to Green to help him compile the article.

So what actually happened during the battle? While the sense of the Battle is well described in the above passage, there is a lot of important detail missing.

The passage accurately refers to the arrival of the Australian 5th Division, including Charlie's 55th Battalion, in the Sailly-Sur-la-Lys sector and its move into the trenches on 11 July 1916.

The passage alleges that:

> The advice given by the British officers
> when we took over was if you
> leave the bosche alone he will leave
> you alone. Keep watch, strengthened your
> positions but don't get too lively.
> This advice given was treated
> With mild contempt by most
> of the AIF units as they arrived
> for they all wakened up Fritz
>
> For their turn its was the optimism of the
> Command that an advance was possible
> & then there was the glory of being the
> the first Australians to go into pitched
> battle in France.

This would principally lay the blame for what was to turn out to be a very badly planned attack principally on the shoulders of the Australian commanders. The history of the assault is somewhat more complicated and originated at much higher levels in the British hierarchy.

The Battle of the Somme began 18 days earlier on 1 July 1916. The first day of casualties alone was horrendous, with the British losing 57,470 of which 19,240 died. And the carnage continued as the days proceeded. The commander of the British Forces, General Douglas Haig, asked Lieutenant General Henry Rawlinson, commander of the British 4th Army Group, the principal leader on the Somme front, to devise attacks that would ease German resistance to the major thrust by diverting their attention and resources away from the Somme. Rawlinson in turn asked his colleagues for options. Some 80 kilometers north of the principal attack on the Somme, Lieutenant General Sir Charles Monro, the new commander of the 1st Army (whom we previously saw in thc Gallipoli Campaign), on 8 July detailed Major General Richard Haking, the commander of the XI Corps, to meet Rawlinson's request. Haking dusted off a plan that he had previously proposed to attack the strategically important heights of Aubers Ridge not far from the German-held French town of Lille and also Fromelles. It was a ridge of high ground that commanded the region and was a distinct advantage to the occupying German army. A principal subsidiary target was to first capture the Sugar Loaf heights that were in front of the British lines and to the north west of the Aubers Ridge. As this part of the British sector straddled the dividing line between the 1st and 2nd Armies, agreement was also sought from General Herbert Plumer, commander of the British 2nd Army, which the Australian 5th Division had recently joined.

Of the above men, the only one we have mentioned in any depth before is Monro. Douglas Haig was the commander of the British Expeditionary Force on the Western Front. Prior to this promotion, on 10 December 1915, after the sacking of General Sir John French, he had been commanding general I Corps in 1914 and later that year promoted to command the British 1st Army. He had had a distinguished career serving in India; with Kitchener in the Sudan, including the 1898 Battle of Omdurman; and the Second Boer War.[194]

Henry Rawlinson was also a career soldier. He had served in India and was also at the Battle of Omdurman and in the Second Boer War. At the beginning of the Great War, he was made commanding officer of the British 4th Division, then of the IV Corps in 1915, and of the 4th Army in January 1916.[195] Similarly, Richard Haking was a career soldier who had seen active service in Burma and the Second Boer War. At the start of the Great War he was given command of the British 5th Brigade on the Western Front and had received a head wound at the Battle of the Aisne in September 1914. After recuperating, he was promoted, given command of the 1st Division in December 1914, and led it in the Battle of Aubers Ridge in May 1915. In September that year he was promoted to command XI Corps of the 1st Army.[196] We will have more to say about Haking.

Herbert Plumer also served in India and the Nile expedition in the Sudan in 1884, where he was in the battles of El Teb and Tamai. He fought in the Second Matabele War and led the relief column at the Siege of Mafeking in the Second Boer War. In the Great War he had taken command of V Corps and took part in the Second Battle of Ypres in 1915. He was put in command of the 2nd Army in May 1915.[197]

Haking proposed to mount a limited attack with three divisions. It was to start with a significant bombardment that would then be followed by a substantial infantry attack on the German trenches. It was not very different from the plan of attack for the Battle of Aubers Ridge on 9 May-16 June 1915 that had ended in failure and resulted in some 11,000 British casualties. Other attacks in the Aubers Ridge sector, namely the Battle of Neuve Chappelle on 10-12 March 1915 and Battle of Festubert on 15 May 1915, had also been unsuccessful. Having noted this, it is worth mentioning that there is a genuine debate amongst military scholars about the plan. Lee for one believes that while the end plan was badly executed the attack itself was a rational strategic proposal based on tactical doctrine at the time, including the limited objectives and the knowledge that there would be sizeable casualties.[198]

Monro rejected the plan on 12 July as he was hoping for alternatives closer to the Somme. Haig's headquarters, however, remained insistent on some sort of action as soon as possible, in light of the ongoing Somme battle and proposed an "artillery demonstration". Haking was then asked to prepare a plan that simply involved a sustained artillery bombardment, although there was some doubt that enough artillery could be spared for this operation. While work on this was proceeding, Major General R.H.K. Butler, Haig's Deputy Chief of Staff and Chief of Operations, conferred with Monro at his headquarters on 13 July and it was agreed to go back to a combined infantry and artillery attack. It was initially proposed to start the bombardment on 14 July and make the infantry attack on 17 July. But more prevarication surfaced and on 16 July Haig informed Monro and Plumer via Butler that he wanted them to proceed only if they believed that they had adequate resources, particularly artillery. It was up to them whether to proceed or not. Monro and Plumer agreed to proceed and Butler promised as much artillery ammunition as possible.

The plans were somewhat thrown into further disarray because Haking did not actually receive the artillery support he was promised. To top it off, a large proportion of it was to be supplied by largely inexperienced artillery from the Australian 4th and 5th Divisions. This is not unimportant given the critical role that artillery played on the Western Front. Because of this, Hacking reduced the attacking force from three to two divisions, across a smaller front. This resulted in substantial rewriting of orders just days out from the assault and ultimately a degree of confusion for divisional and brigade commanders. The final plan of attack was for the British 61st Division from 1st Army accompanied by the Australian 5th Division from the 2nd Army to attack the German trenches. While Lieutenant General Sir William Birdwood, the commander of I Anzac Corps, had reservations, he was not directly involved in the planning and was himself in the Somme sector many miles to the south. The same is true of his chief of staff, Brigadier General Cyril Brudenell White. The commander on the spot in charge of the Australian 5th Division (which was temporarily transferred from 2nd Army to be part of the British XI Corps), General McCay, agreed to the plans. An example of the confusion was that the British Division was fully aware that this was an operation "to prevent the enemy from moving troops southward to take part in the defence of the Somme" and that both the artillery and infantry preparation were not to be done in secrecy so that the Germans were aware of what was going on. However,

McCay was not made fully aware of this and so he emphasised to his brigade commanders the need for secrecy and the importance of the advance. Having said that, the fact that the Germans occupied the Aubers Ridge and the high ground meant that it was hard to maintain a secret buildup from them.

The Germans facing the British were from the 6th Bavarian Reserve Division which was part of the German 6th Army commanded by Field Marshall Crown Prince Rupprecht of Bavaria. The Division was led by Lieutenant General Gustav Scanzoni von Lichtenfels, who was a career Bavarian artillery officer appointed commander in December 1914.[199]

The detailed British plan of attack can be simply described. Across a front of some 4½ kilometers the British 61st Division of the 1st Army (182nd, 183rd, and 184th Brigades) and the Australian 5th Division of the 2nd Army (8th, 14th, and 15th Brigades) would advance in a south easterly direction to capture the German lines with the Sugar Loaf heights, in the centre of this front, as a principal objective. The British occupied the western half of the front (with men from Warwickshire, Gloucestershire, Worcestershire, Oxfordshire, Buckinghamshire and Berkshire) and the Australians the eastern (with the New South Welshmen of the 14th Brigade, Victorians of the 15th Brigade and mixture from the 8th Brigade). In the Australian sector the initial advance would see the 59th and 60th Battalions of the 15th Brigade at their furthest west, the 53rd and 54th Battalions of the 14th Brigade in the middle, and the 31st and 32nd Battalions of the 8th Brigade on the far east of the line of attack. In the middle, the 55th Battalion was kept in reserve, as were other battalions across the Australian sector. In all some 15,000 men were committed to the attack. It is believed the Bavarians had as many as 30,000 facing them from their fortified positions. The area was saturated with water with the groundwater level being basically at the surface. Both sides therefore had to rely principally on "trenches" that were actually above ground fortifications or breastworks that were protected by sandbags and other piled up dirt.

The attack started off with an intensive artillery bombardment of some six hours. As referred to in Charlie's diary entry, this prompted a retaliatory bombardment from the Germans which caused varying damage to the British lines. In the Australian sector, the 15th Brigade was relatively unscathed, but the 14th and 8th Brigades received a pummeling with the 53rd and 54th Battalions losing over 60 men during this period. Likewise, the 31st and 32nd Battalions lost many men and the 31st Battalion's ammunition dump was destroyed with a direct hit. This may account for the reference in Charlie's diary: "We had an initial piece of bad luck for a German H. P. [ie shell] found one of our bomb reserves which went up in yellow smoke". Further, it was to become immediately apparent that the British bombardment had failed to silence the Bavarian artillery and mortars or to sufficiently cut their barbed wire defences.

The British attack began between 5.45pm and 6.00pm. It was staggered to take account of the varying length of no-man's-land between their trenches and that of the enemy. In some parts of the line, the Bavarians abandoned their first line of trenches and when the Australians reached the second line they found that they were flooded. Only the Australian 14th Brigade, made up of the 54th Battalion led by Lieutenant Colonel Walter Cass, and 53rd Battalion, initially led by Lieutenant Colonel Bert Norris, were able to get this far. Indeed, the hail of Bavarian bullets and bombs had stopped the Australian 15th Brigade, led by Brigadier Harold Elliot (nicknamed by his men "Pompey" after the illustrious Roman general), and a large proportion of the 8th Brigade, led by Brigadier Edwin Tivey, in their tracks before they could get to the Bavarian trenches. The British 61st Division had for the same reason made virtually no ground at all. In the case of both Brigades, this was in retrospect totally forseeable. They had been assigned the task of directly taking the heavily fortified Sugar Loaf. Almost all the officers and NCOs of both the 59th and 60th Battalions of the 15th Brigade were casualties. For example, 35 of 39 officers of the 59th Battalion either died or were wounded. [200]

The result was that the 14th Brigade's western and eastern flanks were both exposed to the full force of the Bavarians. As the only senior officer in the front line (Norris had died from machine gun fire in the first 20 minutes of the battle[201]), Cass called for support. Colonel Pope, commanding the 14th Brigade, sent in the available reserves, which were the men of the 55th Battalion. The mission at this stage was to boost the exhausted men of the 54th and 53rd with fresh troops and if possible consolidate the position.

Charlie, as a member of B Company, 55th Battalion, was part of the reserve. B Company, which, as we have previously noted, was led by Captain Norman Gibbins, was dispatched around 7.30pm to the second line of the Australian trenches at the 300 yard mark as a reserve to follow-up on the advance of the 53rd and 54th battalions.

As Lieutenant Chapman of B Company recorded it:

> Our special job was practically that of pioneers of our Brigade. Two [other Battalions] were to make the charge while we were to follow and dig the communication trench between the captured German trench and our own.
>
> For about six hours our Artillery stormed the enemy trenches – Boom – Boom – Boom it thundered, all the afternoon – the windows of the houses where we were situated rattled in their frames – while great clouds of smoke rose from the bursting shells – A and B [companies] were to dig the communication trenches while C and D [companies] were split up into fatigue parties to carry supplies etc across. Captain Gibbins led us – and we could not have had a better leader.
>
> We marched along the road in single file – keeping to the right under cover of the hedge as much as possible – and about five minutes interval between platoons, till we got to the communication saps leading to the main trench: in these we were slightly congested owing to supplies going forward – and wounded coming back.[202]

"Saps" were the trenches dug by the troops to connect other trenches.

As the 55th Battalion historian Matthews has noted, casualties quickly mounted up:

> During the move to the front Private Sydney Bell was killed by a shell burst, the shrapnel from the same explosion ripping Sergeant Jack Doyle's right foot so badly he never again walked properly. Sergeant George Blunt had his legs shattered by a shell; he was carried back to an aid station where his lower limbs were amputated but the wounds proved fatal. Lieutenant Roy Goldrick had his face and neck lacerated by shell splinters. For most of the battalion this was a true baptism of fire.[203]

Chapman continued his narrative:

> The first wounded man I saw was one lying on the road with a bullet wound through the stomach. The sight seemed to bring me the first indication that there we were actually going into battle – a slight feeling of sickness crept over me – and I felt annoyed with myself, but it soon passed. In the sap a shell landed among our front party – but we could not stop, one poor chap was blown to pulp, bits of legs and arms were scattered about. I trod on his head by mistake as I hurried by – and it gave under my foot like a sponge – others were lying about moaning and groaning – but all feeling had left me now – I passed dead men without feeling pity or remorse. We lined up in our support-trench, and here bombs were handed out to each man – after which Capt. Gibbins gave the order to scale the parapet – and away we went.[204]

As one of Charlie's other comrades in B Company, Private Harpley, recorded the events:

> We were each issued with hand grenades … then came the supreme moment. The order was then given 'leap the parapet and charge'. My God, it required all the nerve available. I set my teeth and over we went, we had only gone about 20 yards when we encountered our barbed wire having to delay here

> in getting through we lost a few for the shrapnel and machine gun and rifle fire was terrific. However, on we went, there were dead and wounded everywhere. About 300 yards and we were into the German front-line, some were left to clear this up and on we went through more barbed wire to the [advanced] trench. It was in this last stretch … that a lot were lost. Poor Penfold was shot there through the head.[205]

Private John Bain of B Company later recorded that he spoke to Gibbins just before they set off:

> His last words he said to me before going into action were "Well! Bain, you are going into action that will be pretty hot. But if you get out of it alright you will have something to talk about all your life".[206]

Gibbins led from the front and courageously risked all. According to the *Official History*, at this stage of the battle:

> Even in the Australian line Captain Gibbins of the 55th, coming forward with his company to garrison the front trenches in place of the attacking waves, found troops retiring. "No good – you can't get up there", said their leader [an officer of the 53rd]. "The 55th can!" was Gibbin's reply as he led his men on.[207]

As Gibbins was described in the *Official History*:

> Six foot four inches in his boots, a gaunt, brave, humorous, cool-headed Australian, bank manager in civil life, older than most company officers, but an athlete, promoted from the ranks at Anzac.[208]

After this initial rush through no-man's-land, the men of the 55th, including B Company, were directed to build a communications trench from the front line of the Australian advance back to their own lines. Again, because it was often above ground, this was particularly hazardous and had to be done under constant enemy fire.

As Chapman described the actions of B Company:

> Each man carried fifteen sand-bags – and most had a pick or

> shovel, so on arriving at "No Mans Land" it did not take us long to settle down to work.[209]

However, at around 9.30pm, pressure from the Bavarian counter attack was so great on the Australian advance that 5th Division commander, General McCay, agreed to commit the 55th Battalion A and B companies further forward and hand over the entrenching to 14 Field Engineers. The 56th Battalion was employed in running supplies and shepherding wounded back to the Australian lines. Charlie's B Company was sent to cover the eastern/left flank of what remained of the Battalion and A Company under Lieutenant John Matthews to the western/right flank of the 53rd. With this, the various gaps in the line in this immediate part of the battlefront were filled and there was now a continuous line between A Company in the west, across the remained of the 53rd and 54th Battalions to B Company on the eastern flank.[210] In fact, this was in fact a desperate position. While there was a sustained rifle and bomb throwing assault on the Bavarians, the reply was even more ferocious. Men were to die left, right and centre, while to the men on the ground there was great confusion.

As Chapman described B Company's actions:

> But an order came through from the front that they wanted reinforcements so off we went again. Our road was strewn with dead men lying as they had fallen – mostly face downwards, and heads towards the enemy – their yellow-white complexions – blue finger nails and clear staring eyes gazing into vacancy telling that Death had for some time taken his toll. We reached the German trench about the point B. and found that the 54th were occupying a small trench in front, B.C.D. This was dug out of sand-bags – Fatigue parties were told off to carry sand-bags – ammunition and bombs from our own trench, others were sent to the machine gunners to dig emplacements for their guns, and by morning we felt a little safer than when first we got into that muddy little trench.[211]

When B Company arrived at the 54th's eastern flank they discovered that there was a large gap of some 250 metres between them and the 32nd Battalion of the 8th Brigade. In fact, the 31st Battalion, which was between these two units, had retired and created a break in the Australian line that risked being filled by Bavarian troops. A Company found the situation no better. They were on the extreme western flank of the advance. As stated above, the Australian 15th Brigade and the British 61st Division had made no progress and A Company were now partly surrounded by German bombers. Although, in the fog of war, the frontline commanders of the 14th Brigade were not aware of the true picture and hoped that there was simply a gap between them and a possible 15th Brigade advance.

As Gibbins reported to Lieutenant Colonel McConaghy in command of the 55th after arriving in the front line:

> We hold front line with 54th. C.O. 54th (Cass) in next trench in rear. 53rd on our right. 31st and 32nd on our left. Consolidating positions as fast as possible. Sending back to rear trench by parties of ten under N.C.O.'s for ammunition and sandbags. We want Very pistols, flares, and sandbags (plenty). Have 54th Lewis guns and five of our own under Sergeant Colless for counter-attack. Each of my men have three bombs, but require more. Expect a counter-attack shortly. Anyway, we can hold them easily.
>
> N. Gibbins, Capt., O.C. "B" Company
>
> Sergeant Colless doing good work – my officers also of course. Would like you to say something to this man (ie the bearer of the message). He is doing splendid work.[212]

At this stage of the battle, Charlie would be one of the five Lewis gunners under Sergeant Colless that Gibbins referred to in the above message.

Another member of B Company to record the events was Private Archie Winter. He stated:

> My mates were scattered in all directions … Vin Baker, Fred

> Carpenter and self managed to keep together. … We were not there long before we volunteered to go back for sandbags. Being between the German lines we had to move when getting across the parapets. There were dead men everywhere. It being our first actual fight and seeing some ghastly sights, made us feel peculiar for a while but soon wore off. … Fritzy was making it interesting with his artillery. We made several trips back for sand.[213]

McConaghy had himself joined the front line at 10.10pm. He assessed that the situation was far from well. He met with Lieutenant Colonel Cass of the 54th, the senior officer, in a nearby dugout. In the confusion of battle, they were both unclear of the exact circumstances and so McConaghy sent a number of officers across the battlefront to gather information. Based on these reports he was able to establish that only the initial charge of the 14th Brigade had succeeded. The 8th Brigade had only had partial success and there was basically no contact with the 15th Brigade. Without being entirely sure – in fact the two colonels bickered about the true state of affairs – it also now appeared to them that the 53rd, 54th and 55th battalions might be in a bulge in the line that would be hard to defend as well as being heavily exposed to a German counterattack to their rear from both the left and the right.

Fighting continued, with Lieutenant Chapman describing a gruesome event that involved himself and Gibbins:

> Gib and I were sitting on the parapet of the front trench we had captured while men were busy filling sandbags with earth and mud building the parapet, when in our rear staggering through the gloom we saw a man – he came about 10 yards towards us, and then staggered & started to crawl. I thought it was one of our men so went out to him. Poor beggar I have seen worse looking mess ups but he was bad enough – his left eye was gone – as for the rest of him I could not tell what else was wrong except that he was a mass of blood and looked

> as if he had been through a sausage machine. He pleaded something in German – I don't know what, it was hardly a plead – it was a moan, or a prayer – so I gave him my hand to hold and said nicely as I could "All right old chap". He kept pushing towards the trench all the time and as it was rather awkward getting along on one hand and two knees while I held the other hand, I let go. Whereupon the poor mangled brute got up on his knee – put his hands together & started to pray! "Oh cruel – cruel" Gib said when he saw the poor beggar – Gib was with him all the time also. But as I looked at him the thought struck me: "How can men be so cruel?" I got on one side of him and Gib the other and we helped him along. He was determined to get into our trench as a black scarab beetle is to get out of your fingers when you catch him round the lamp at night – only he felt a bit worse – he was covered all over with wet cold blood.

By 11.00pm the senior officers of the 55th met with McConaghy and Cass in the latter's trench. Gibbins was reasonably upbeat and maintained that on the east/left flank B Company had established contact with the 8th Brigade and was consolidating the position. Major Robert Cowey (McConaghy's deputy), who had scouted across the line, was less sanguine about the west/right flank. A particular problem was the flooding of trenches, waist deep in some cases, and the increasingly muddy bog that they had to defend. At this stage, the decision was taken to simply consolidate the 14th Brigade's position. Meanwhile, the Bavarians had started easing their attack so they themselves could prepare for another attack in the early hours of 20 July.

Private Harpley noted:

> We worked all night on this and were well dug-in by 1 a.m. on the morning of the 20th.[214]

During the very early morning, Cass was able to briefly raise contact via field telephone with 14th Brigade HQ. It was now much clearer that the 15th Brigade had largely failed in its advance and that the 14th Brigade was entirely exposed on its east/right flank.

The Bavarians renewed their counterattack in earnest in the early hours. They approached from the ruined farm at Rouge Blancs and concentrated on the left/east flank and the line held by the remnants of the 54th Battalion. Major Cowey, who again had the task of reconnoitering the line, reported back to McConaghy that the Australian line was crumbling and that he should withdraw his forward command post further. McConaghy initially rejected the accuracy of the information and refused this advice. Cowey then reported to Cass, who accepted the report but ordered Cowey to collect reserves and return to the front line. The problem was that there were no reserves to hand.

Shortly afterwards, McConaghy reversed his decision and also thought of collecting more men to fill the gaps emerging. He summoned Gibbins, and half of B Company under Lieutenant Ken Wyllie was ordered to help shore up the right flank. But, as Chapman later observed:

> As he [Wyllie] got up to go thud came something against his side and he rolled over grasping his side. 'They've got me Chappy, they've got me' he said as I held up his head. They carried him to the main German trench and from there to our own trench.[215]

All through the darkness of the early morning desperate fighting between the Bavarians and the Australians continued in the area of the bulge in the line. Trenches were won and lost in succession.

Soon after, on the east/right flank, the men of A Company and of the 53rd Battalion were sighting Bavarians flanking them and approaching their rear. Lieutenant Farmer of A Company and men of the 53rd launched a bomb throwing counterattack and slowed their progress. Nevertheless, the Bavarians gained the upper hand and the Australians were pushed back. Their flank had been turned.

It was in this particular fight that Lieutenant Berrol Mendelsohn of B Company was killed.

Soon after, Lieutenant Cecil Agassiz of the 55th Battalion, together with one of the Lewis gunners in his platoon:

> Turned his gun to the rear, and, resting it high above the trench on the shoulder of Corporal Stringfellow, opened upon these Germans. The gunner was presently shot through the head, but Agassiz continued to fire over the corporal's shoulder, with the result that the Bavarians were forced under cover, and remained suppressed for the next hour or more.

Meanwhile, the Bavarians kept on attacking, trying to encircle the exposed position. By around 3.45am, the battle was continuing in earnest. Captain Arblaster, now commanding officer of the 53rd after Norris had been killed, tried to rally the situation by leading a charge. This failed and he was mortally wounded.

At around 4.00am on 20 July, Cass and McConaghy conferred again in the midst of this desperate situation. Cass ordered a bayonet charge accompanied by rifle fire. McConaghy protested and argued that bombs were the only real solution. During this dispute Cass ordered another subordinate to proceed and, with men of both the 54th and 55th Battalions, a charge occurred driving back the Bavarians some 20 metres. But this was a very limited success and could not be sustained. At the same time, following orders, McConaghy also organised a charge and Gibbins ordered Lieutenant William Denoon of B Company to take 51 men, although McConaghy ensured that they were each supplied with three additional bombs. The charge occurred at 4.30am after Denoon had the men throw bombs at the Bavarian lines. Most likely, because of this concerted bombardment, the enemy reeled back from the Australian attack and some 80 metres were secured. This relieved the immediate pressure that the Bavarians had been putting on the vital Australian communications trench back to their own lines.

Over on the east flank, with the remainder of B Company, Lieutenant Percy "Bob" Chapman recorded the fighting at dawn:

> Coming through the dusk [ie dawn] on our left [ie the east] we saw Germans. Our machine guns opened fire. But word came from the right that they were our men. During the night some of our men had been found stripped of their clothing and apparently spies were sending false messages. However, although we accounted for a good many, the enemy got in our left. Then came the sound of bombing. We were being driven in on either flank. … As they came our artillery was shelling them, in a body left the trench and retired to our lines. I got to the tail end just in time to get them back again but the majority left.
>
> Capt Gibbins came along then and we both went round the trench and found it all clear. The men were then extended on the left again – but still the bombers came.
>
> "Get as many bombs as you can – and come with me" said Gib. So I got all the bombs I could – called to some men to follow. Gib led the way on the outside of the parapet. We shifted those bombers – but poor old Gib got a wound in the head and had to retire. [Lieutenant] Robinson turned back to our own trench to get reinforcements – but they would not come. I took charge of the bombing party and as the Bosches had dropped bombs for the present and taken to rifle fire we had to take shelter in the trench. We waited there for perhaps a quarter of an hour ready to bomb Fritz should he come again.

While it is not clear, some reports are that Gibbins had been hit in the forehead with a German hand grenade that had not exploded or at least he had not suffered from the blast. Still, he needed to go to get bandaged.

Dawn was around 5.00am. McConaghy had much earlier requested more support and men from the 56th Battalion, which had taken over the duties of maintaining the communication trench, supplied much needed men, despite the orders from General McCay that these men should not be "thrown into the fight". As the *Official History* recorded it:

> With Lieutenant S.A. Pinkstone of the 55th they took position in the recaptured trench, and they beat down the Bavarian attack and for the time being thoroughly subdued the enemy in his old front line.[216]

While this was occurring, at 5.00am the commander of the Australian 5th Division, Major General McCay, was meeting with his superiors, General Monro and Lieutenant General Haking, at the latter's headquarters. It was well known by now about the failure of the 15th Brigade and 61st Division the previous day. McCay had also just received an update from the front of how bad the situation was for the 14th Brigade and that the 8th Brigade had withdrawn to the Australian lines. Monro ordered that the attack be abandoned and that Colonel Pope direct the 14th to withdraw immediately. Pope didn't receive this message until 6.30am.

Meanwhile, Cass, via runner, was able to inform Pope at 6.15am that first light had allowed his men to temporarily stabilise their position; With Cass being fully aware that a retreat would need to occur, he started sending back the valuable machine guns and ordered McConaghy to make ready a rearguard for when the order was given. This task was assigned to Gibbins and B Company.

As a result, McConaghy sent Gibbins a written message that stated:

> Capt Gibbins and 55th officers. You must prepare for an orderly retirement. We are unprotected on our flanks. Hold first Hun line [ie the old German front line] until further orders.[217]

While Cass had not actually given the order to retreat, the *Official History* concludes that:

> Cass did not intend that the rear-guard should immediately take position in the old German front line, but he was by this time utterly worn out by strain and fatigue, and it is possible that he did not make the point clear to McConaghy.[218]

Gibbins, quite reasonably, interpreted McConaghy's order to have immediate effect. He grabbed his men and remaining Lewis gunners from the advanced front trenches and moved them back to the top of the vital communications trench that met the old German front line trenches. The communications trench (that B Company had started at the beginning of the battle) was the only relatively safe route that the men of the 14th Brigade could use to get back to their own lines. With the dawn, anybody risking travel above ground outside this protective trench would be a sitting duck for enemy fire. The unfortunate consequence of this move back to the communication trench was a substantial weakening of the front line (before the retreat order came) that allowed the Bavarians to advance quickly into the gaps.

All across the line the Australian position began crumbling. Private George Gribbon of A Company, 55th Battalion, noted that at this time:

> Somebody hoisted a white flag in the trench on our left rear. Lieutenant Agassiz promptly fired on the flag with the machine gun and ordered the men to open fire on it with their rifles.[219]

Cass ordered the final retreat at around 7.50am on the morning of 20 July. It was only at this time that he received the message from Colonel Pope to retire. This was almost three hours after Monro had issued the command. The delay was an indication of how much the situation had deteriorated. Pope had to send seven runners in succession to get the message through.

These last moments were a frantic dash by men, many attempting to bypass the overcrowded communications trench and risking death in no man's land. Many died as a result.

Privately Harpley describes the consequences of bypassing the trench:

> The order came for us to retreat to our line, this we had to do across about 200 yards of open country under heavy machine gun and rifle fire and shrapnel. Oh! The whole turnout was absolute hell. The bullets were cracking all around us yet most

> of us got over. ... There I got into a bay with some of the 56th Batt. There were eight of us, four were on the fire step and the remainder were sitting down when a shell burst right on the parapet and killed [two] and wounded all the rest except myself. I was knocked silly for a time but managed to crawl out.[220]

As noted, Gibbins and 55 men of B Company were to cover the withdrawal. Lieutenant Chapman recorded what happened next:

> But the order came to retire – so I went back to the point B and sat on the parapet. I borrowed a rifle from one of the troops passing and sniped at Fritz till he got up to me with his bombs. It was then time to go so I had to. My return is a bit blurred. I remember picking my way through barbed wire with rifles cracking around me. At one place the grass in front of me was shaking and quivering. I looked at it for a second and realised that a machine gun was playing through there – so I jumped and hurried on. I got in all right and as the trench was becoming too crowded I sent what 55th men I could back into the support. As soon as the enemy saw our men making use of the sap they opened fire with high explosives. "Crack – Crack" came whistling over our heads – but we leaned against the parapet and were comparatively safe.[221]

Sergeant Bert White, leading a Lewis gun party, noted:

> [Gibbins] was quite cheery and moving freely amongst his men, although he was wearing a bandage around his head. At the time Capt Gibbins was but a few yards from me and most of the infantrymen had retired. I was suddenly brought back to my senses by hearing Captain Gibbins call, "Come on all you gunners". I immediately picked up my spare parts and followed him.[222]

Unfortunately, Gibbins was not to survive. Like others, he decided to bypass the congested trench and leapt up over the parapet. He was immediately shot in the head and died instantly. Chapman paid his respects to Gibbins:

> Capt. Gibbins was shot through the head while coming in. I have never known a braver man than he. If ever a man died bravely – doing his duty – old Gib did.[223]

Gibbins was aged 38 but was not awarded any medals for his gallant actions. At least one historian has conjectured that Cass blamed Gibbins for initiating the wholesale retreat by moving to the head of the communications trench too early.[224]

That was not the view of McConaghy, who stated in his official report on the battle:

> Col. Cass detailed me to organise a rearguard action. I kept Capt. Gibbins and 4 other officers, and about 50 men to do this, and it was due to the very fine action of these men that the remainder of the garrison were able to get across no man's land with comparatively few casualties. They fought very valiantly, and their leader, Capt. Gibbins, was killed, and 2 officers and 25 men of the party are missing.[225]

The verdict in the *Official History* was clear:

> The responsible task of rear-guard commander could not have fallen to a more suitable man. Combining the gentlest of natures with a stern sense of discipline and duty, Gibbins possessed the firmest possible hold upon his men, who almost worshipped him.[226]

The withdrawal was to continue. Private Winter recorded:

> Got the signal to retire. This must have been about 8 a.m. That's where a good many men were killed. In the retirement I found myself with Colonel [McConaghy] and RSM [Regimental Sergeant Major]. They went along a sap and we who were there followed. The sap was half full of mud and nothing but dead men. The boys suffered even when they attempted to cross the parapet.[227]

Sapper Smith of the 14th Field Engineering Company recorded

in an article after the War that he had witnessed the following confrontation:

> Colonel Pope (14th Brigade) and Lieutenant Colonel Cass (54th Battalion) came along the new [communications] trench and through our cutting in the breastwork. Both of these officers had been across to the enemy lines. Col. Cass was obviously over-wrought and distressed. He and Pope were having a heated argument about the attack and Col. Cass unburdened his mind. "I tell you that it was wholesale murder, they have murdered my boys". "Oh pull yourself together man, this is war!" "This is not war they have murdered my boys."[228]

Historian of the 55th Battalion, Matthews, notes that this report is probably inaccurate in that Pope was never in the front lines during the battle. But he does believe that Smith confused McConaghy with Pope and notes that, in his account of the battle, Cass mentioneded that he met McConaghy at around this time and "when I reached our own front-line I found McConaghy going for my men for leaving me behind".[229]

Although there were some stragglers, the Australians were back in their lines by 10.30am, minus the dead and some 400 captured by the Bavarians. Chapman concluded:

> Well so ends the first fight. I am the only officer left in B Company. About 25% of the Battalion are either killed or wounded – but our losses were light in comparison to some, the 60th Battalion have only 61 men and 1 officer left.[230]

The 55th Battalion War Diary recorded in its typically succinct style:

> 19th 4.30 p.m.: Received final orders for the attack on German lines this afternoon.
>
> Marched out of billets to join in attack which was launched about 6 p.m.
>
> The attack was successful and the German trenches were car-

ried. The trenches were held during the night and communication established with our lines. Owing to strong counter attack by the enemy, and to being exposed on both flanks a retirement was necessary and this was effected.

20th 7 a.m.: The losses were heavy, but the battalion, four fifths or more of whom were strangers to battle, acquitted itself honorably in its first engagement, and returned with 40 German prisoners.

Casualties:	Killed	2 officers	35 other ranks
	Died of wounds		5 ditto ditto
	Wounded	5 ditto	149 ditto ditto
	Missing	4 ditto	139 ditto ditto

This is a statement of casualties as known on 31st July 1916. Many of the missing will undoubtedly be proved to have been killed – and others wounded in their trenches are doubtless prisoners of war.

Chapman took command of B Company after the battle. He was awarded the Military Cross for the Battle of Fromelles due to "conspicuous gallantry during an action. He repeatedly led bombing attacks along the enemy's trenches and fought them back long enough to enable many of our wounded to reach safety". He was wounded in action later in 1916 and subsequently promoted to Captain on his return to the front. Unfortunately, he went missing, presumed killed, in the fighting around Bapaume, France on 12 March 1917.[231] When his body was eventually found in a German trench he had his gun in his hand surrounded by three dead German soldiers.[232]

In fact there was immediate recognition of the heroics of the men at Fromelles:

> More than 200 men won medals. The Australian 5th Division won 11 Distinguished Service Orders, 46 Military Crosses, 35 Distinguished Conduct Medals, 50 Military Medals, 36 Mentions-in-Dispatches and 15 foreign awards.[233]

Meanwhile, recriminations flowed. McCay sacked 14th Brigade commander Pope the next day. It is understood that when Pope was summoned to meet McCay he could not be woken and McCay, very possibly unfairly, said he was drunk and dismissed him. It was known that there had been acrimony between the two so it is not inconceivable that McCay had other reasons. But it is worth noting that Pope was later recalled to command the 52nd Battalion in the Battle of Messines in 1917.[234]

Colonel Walter Cass, the commanding officer of the 54th Battalion, also suffered from the battle. According to his biographer, "after Fromelles he broke down in health and was evacuated to England where he later held an A.I.F. administrative command. … Cass was mentioned in dispatches twice during the war and appointed C.M.G. in 1916. He was demobilised in April 1917".[235] Major Robert Cowey received no awards for his leadership in the crisis, but was put in temporary command of the 55th Battalion in early 1917. Unfortunately, he received a severe gunshot wound to his left foot which had him out of the front line for the second half of 1917. After returning to the Front, he served out the War and was mentioned in dispatches for gallantry.

In his report on the battle, Haking considered that the rawness of the Australian troops, inexperienced in Western Front trench warfare, and the lack of spirit of the British troops, accounted for the high level of casualties. He wrote:

> The artillery preparation was adequate. There were sufficient guns and sufficient ammunition. The wire was properly cut, and the assaulting battalions had a clear run into the enemy's trenches.[236]

None of this is borne out by the analysis of military historians.[237]

Haking continued:

> The Australian infantry attacked in the most gallant manner and gained the enemy's position, but they were not sufficiently trained to consolidate the ground gained. They were eventually

> compelled to withdraw and lost heavily in doing so. ... The 61st Division were not sufficiently imbued with the offensive spirit to go in like one man at the appointed time. Some parts of the attack were late in deploying. ... With two trained divisions the position would have been a gift after the artillery bombardment.[238]

Lastly, he wrote:

> I think the attack, although it failed, has done both divisions a great deal of good, and I am quite sure as a result of the attack that the Germans are not likely to move troops away from the front for some time.[239]

Again, historians have questioned his claim about deterring the Germans in moving troops. There is good evidence that the Germans knew exactly that it was a feint and were not tricked. In fact, written orders noting that it was a feint were found by the Bavarians on a dead British officer. Nevertheless, the assessment that the troops were under-prepared may be correct. After all, the Australians had been in the front line for only a matter of days before being committed. The generals knew this before the attack. Still, whether "two trained divisions" would have made all the difference is highly questionable.

15th Brigade commanding officer Brigadier Elliot later wrote:

> One of the best of my commanding officers was killed and practically all my best officers, the Anzac men who helped to build up my Brigade, are dead. I presume there was a plan at the back of the attack but it is difficult to know what it was. I can only say – it was an Order. I trust those who gave the order may be made to realise their responsibility.[240]

The verdict of history therefore falls heavily against Haking (and his superiors for placing confidence enough in his plan for it to proceed). While Haking never received a further promotion from Corps commander to Army commander, he continued to command the XI Corps for the remainder of the War, on both the Western Front and in Italy, when it was re-deployed there.

In Australia, the finger was also pointed at McCay as a culprit in the debacle. However, as Bean concluded in the *Official History*:

> Moreover, since the Australian nation does not differ from other democracies in its tendency to search for scapegoats, and a small section of the press saw no unfairness in publishing, then or since, without verification, damning statements or implications mainly contained in soldier's letters – the blame for the enterprise was thrown upon an unpopular but entirely innocent leader, General M'Cay. It is probably true that in the case of the Fromelles offensive M'Cay welcomed the early chance of commanding his division in action; but, even had he been as thoroughly opposed to it as were White and Birdwood, the general appeal made by his [British] superiors for assistance to the force struggling on the Somme might well have prevented any opposition on his part to the plans of his superiors.

To Australia this was an important battle. To the British it had lesser importance. It is worth putting in context the size of the operation. Compared to the two divisions committed by the British Army at Fromelles, the Allies committed 19 in the Battle of the Somme. Over five months, the latter battle saw some 400,000 British casualties, 200,000 French and 600,000 German.

Not generally known is that, on the other side of this deadly battle, was one of the most infamous figures in the history of the 20th Century – Adolf Hitler.

When Charlie's B Company of the 55th Battalion joined the fray and fought its way to the front of the attack to help members of the 54th Battalion make a tactical retreat back to British lines, as has been previously mentioned, they were facing troops of the 6th Bavarian Reserve Division. Part of the 6th was Gefreiter (Corporal) Hitler's own regiment – the 16th Bavarian Reserve Infantry Regiment (16th BRIR

– also known as the List Regiment, named after their first Colonel). Hitler was a "meldegänger" – an army messenger or dispatch runner.

In the action described above, it will be recalled that when the Australian troops of the 53rd and 54th Battalions moved forward into the second line of German trenches they had moved too far, beyond all the other Australian troops. They were now susceptible to a German flanking attack that would attempt to completely surround them. That, in fact, was undertaken by the 16th BRIR, although it is not because of this that Hitler was in the lines in front of the Australian forces. Instead, as a messenger, his job was to run between bodies of troops to convey the written messages of commanding officers. It was a highly dangerous occupation and during the war Hitler was to win both the coveted German Army medal, the Iron Cross, Second Class, and also First Class, in recognition of this.

During the Battle of Fromelles, he was directed to, first, travel between his regiment and the 17th Regiment to the West of them, and then later to the 21st Regiment to the East. In doing so, he crossed in front of the German trenches that the Australian troops had temporarily captured. It does not bear to think of one of the greatest "What Ifs?" of world history: if a bomb or bullet from B Company had hit Hitler it might have changed the course of further human tragedy in World War II.

As Private Balthasar Brandmayer of the 16th BRIR, a colleague of Hitler who ran messages with him during the battle, recorded in his memoirs:

> We carried message after message from and to the trenches. Glaring flares lit our way. The Australians stormed for the fifth time vainly across the battlefield. Those who escaped the rain of bullets from our machine-guns, found certain death in the hurricane of the German artillery fire.

He went on:

> I dashed with Hitler to the battle HQ of the 17th Regiment. He

> scarcely gave me time to get my breath back [before] we ran on to the 21st Regiment. … Grenades chased us through the darkness of the night; we rolled in time with them into a water-filled mine-crater. The light of a high-flying flare first gave us an instant of orientation again. "Now push on!" said Hitler and we scrambled up the crater wall. Wet through to above the chest our trousers and shirts stuck to our bodies. And how we froze! The envelope and paper we handed the regimental commander were soggy. He was scarcely able to decipher the report.[241]

The German troops were both appreciative and damning of the Australian troops. A correspondent for the Berlin newspaper, the *Norddeutsche Zeitung* wrote shortly after the battle:

> The English troops who took part in the action were Australians. For the most part they are war-volunteers and amongst them were many well-to-do farmers, strong youthful men, who undoubtedly attacked with great bravery and proved themselves clever and tenacious in close fighting.[242]

On the other hand, both Germans and Australians shared accusations of the ill treatment of each other's combatants. In the official 16th BRIR report of the battle it states:

> Under these conditions the recovery of the large number of prisoners has become extremely dangerous for us. The number of our losses incurred while undertaking this task is a result of the perfidiousness of the enemy, as they first feigned surrender and then resume combat when we come close to them.[243]

Before leaving the account of the Battle of Fromelles, there is another extract from Charlie's diary. He notes it is "clipped from Sydney paper 1919". It is a striking passage and conveys the deep feelings that he had for the conduct of the battle and the poor leadership displayed.

Fleurbaix
Clipped from
Sydney paper
1919
Regarding the Fleurbaix Fromelles battle
let me voice a heartburn felt
by many. The Fifth Division
were the first Australian troops
over the top in France. This was
on the terrible night of 19 July
1916. Fifth Division Veterans
who have seen most of the fighting
in France acclaim it the Hell
of their experiences. They say,
God knows how we came
through and they say it
reverently. Those who
find pride in the Glory of
Pozieres should remember how
much is due to Fleurbaix.
The attack was made to draw
the Germans off Pozieres

But of what cost to the fifth Div
and yet in our lists eloquently
citing no Australians great
battles Fleurbaix. Instead of
having first place is passed over
why why should that immortal
sacrifice be as silent as many
who went forth unflinching to
certain death that night
why should these martyrs weeping

by their empty tomb know yet
another heart thrust that their
sons deeds are forgotten why
should the men who came
through not have this recognition
To where more
Australian blood was spilled
than any other of our battle
grounds where more homes
were rendered desolate
and more hearts knew the
crucifixion of war than ever
before or since what homage on
Honour can be too time. [CBH I 105-106]

10

France & England 1916

"Not arf painful"

Within a matter of hours, Charlie's active service in the war was over, although he would not know that for a few more months. He would have to endure agonies as his shattered arm would undergo many operations as the months went on.

As Charlie wrote:

> Wounded at Armitrees, Western Front by German Bullet
> On July 19th 1916 [CBH I 63]

And further:

> Wounded in
> left arm
> at Flanders
> Both Bones
> Broken and wound
> Clean through
> As big as Half crown
> not arf Painful [CBH II 19/7/16]

According to his service file, though, he was actually wounded some time during the action on the morning of 20 July 1916.

20 July 1916, Thursday

> Operated on in
> France by Lt Col

Out of 12,000 men
there was only
3,000 got back
Without injury
Not bad for
Start in France

Operated on
by Lt Col McLauren [CBH II 20/7/16]

The doctor who operated on him would be a Canadian medico named Lieutenant Colonel Murray McLaren, who was in charge of the No 1 Canadian General Hospital that was based in Étaples in France at the time[244]

Charlie sounds as though he received the very best of attention and so did not lose his arm. As one Australian nurse, Elsie Tranter, who worked in the Étaples area, was to write:

> At present our work in the theatre is hard and we have very long hours. Today I had to assist in ten amputations, one after another and I seem to hear that wretched saw at work whenever I try to sleep. We see mostly ghastly wounds and all day long we are inhaling the odour of gas gangrene. How these boys suffer. This war is absolute hell. We can hear the guns quite plainly from here.[245]

Charlie's Diary entries for 21 to 23 July simply have a written "s", which is interpreted as "sick". On 24, 26 and 27 July, he has one word "dopey". It's "s" again from 29 July until 2 August, when it changes to "blotto" between 3 and 7 August.

According to Charlie's service record, the original operation he received occurred at the 2nd Canadian Stationary Hospital in Outreau, France, on 22 July. He was then moved to the port at Boulogne on 24 July and is embarked on the Hospital Ship H.S *St David* to arrive in England the next day. The *St David* was another hired ship converted into a hospital. It was originally built by the Great Western Railway to transport passengers between Fishguard in Wales to Rosslare in Ireland.[246]

25 July 1916, Tuesday

Arrived at Duston
War Hospital
England [CBH II 25/7/16]

Duston War Hospital was a converted mental asylum in Northamptonshire.

28 July 1916, Friday

Operated on to-day
at Duston [and placed in] infirmary
Dr Boon Civil Doctor
Doing well

[Dr Boon is a] Yank & a Man [CBH II 28/7/16]

As can be appreciated, there are no diary entries for a number of days until he finally notes:

9 August 1916, Wednesday

Still under
the Dope [CBH II 9/8/16]

Then it is simply back to a simple "s" for "sick" between 10 and 20 August.

21 August 1916, Monday

At last I awoke [CBH II 21/8/16]

He records the names of others in the hospital with him. One appears to be from Leeds and another from County Meath in Ireland.

22 August 1916, Tuesday

Pte M. Scholey

28 Mosely Place
Woodhouse Leeds

Sgt W Evans
44 Mansel Trce
Old Road
Meath S.W. [CBH II 22/8/16]

He also records the death of one of his close friends:

Bill McFarlane
Got killed at Pozaries
July 24th 16 [CBH I 66]

23 August 1916, Wednesday

Still under Dope [CBH II 23/8/16]

24 August 1916, Thursday

Nurse F Edmonds
Ward I
Like Myself Dopey [CBH II 24/8/16]

25 August 1916, Friday

To-day six years
ago my dear
Mother left us [CBH II 25/8/16]

On 29 August, he wrote a letter to Moa Llwellyn that still survives. He said:

29 August 1916, Tuesday

Northamptonshire War Hospital
Duston
Northampton England
Aug 29th 1916

My Dear Moa

I received some
more of your letters and was
very pleased indeed to
hear from you. I am still
at the above hospital
awaiting to be transferred
to Harefield Park Hospital
My arm is going on grand
and by the time you receive
this I most likely I will be
better I am getting my photo
taken when I go on leave
so I won't forget you
I was playing Football
Yesterday and got my arm
Hurt and its [just] shocking
painful this morning So
I hope you can understand
this scribble If you see
any of my sisters tell them
I am going on well

It seems to be a character trait of Charlie's to be a bit reckless. This extract is yet another example of that. He has been shot in the arm and is apparently suffering agonies, yet decides to play football and exacerbate the pain. Shortly after, he is transferred to a new hospital, the Australian Auxiliary Hospital at Harefield Park, Middlesex:

5 September 1916, Tuesday

Left Northampton
and arrived at
Harefield Park

same day arm
very bad [CBH II 5/9/16]

6 September 1916, Wednesday

Operated on my
arm again very
sick and painful [CBH II 6/9/16]

He soon wrote another letter to Moa Llwellyn that still survives. He said:

10 September 1916, Sunday

Aus[tralian] Auxiliary Hospital
Harefield Park
Middlesex England
September 10.

My Dear Moa

Five more welcome
letters arrived today just as
I was about to go through some
agony with my dressing
I have taken bad turn again
and they operated on my
arm for the third time
Think I have had my go
at operations Today I feel
much better Sister of our
Ward told me that I was
going home I hope that's
true It's much better going
home with wound than
those who went home from
Egypt with nothing wrong

Photo of walking wounded 1916. Charlie is seated on left with face partially obscured (reproduced from Hardy family collection)

with them, I think that if
they send one home I've
done my bit don't you?
I'll shake [all] those
Cold Footers up
I didn't mention about your
Photos Well Moa. They are
Bonnie. Please excuse this
Scribble and mistakes as I
Writing on my back and
its pretty hard Well I'll
Draw to close and will write longer one next time.
I remain
Yours sincerely
Charlie

It is worth noting, where he says above:

> It's much better going
> home with wound than
> those who went home from
> Egypt with nothing wrong
> with them, I think that if
> they send one home I've
> done my bit don't you?

It indicates some anxiety that he is feeling as to whether he deserves, or is worthy, to be coming home. He answers his own question by noting that the wound does indicate that "I've done my bit".

This conclusion is heightened by the context of the next sentence where he says:

> I'll shake [all] those
> Cold Footers up

This would appear to refer to those "shirkers" back in Sydney who had not volunteered to join the army. It will be recalled that in the bitter poem he wrote in Egypt, titled "My Brother that Stayed at 'ome", he talked of:

> My oath [h]e'll make yer sick
> But [h]e wont risk is blooming [h]ide
> Why [h]is [h]earts a frigid zone
> And his feet are blooming Icebergs
> me brother who stayed at home [CBH II 14-22/2/16]

The diary then includes an unusual entry. For the first time, he mentions his future wife Indiana (Indie) Llewelyn. Indie is Moa's older sister. Based on the recollections of the family, this could possibly have been written at a later date than indicated. This is a conclusion that you might come to when you consider that, according to Charlie's detailed cataloguing of letters sent and received for over two years, none have been to or from Indie.

5 October 1916, Thursday

> Theres only
> One women in
> World that I
> love dearly &
> that is going
> to be my wife
> & that is
> Indie Llewelyn
> One of the best
> Charles Hardy [CBH II 5/10/16]

He wrote another letter to Moa. It said:

6 October 1916, Friday

> Australian Auxiliary Hospital No. 1
> Harefield Park

Harefield
Middlesex
Oct 6. 16

My Dear Moa
Just few lines to
let you Know that I may
be home some time in
November or December for
Six months furlough
My arm is still bad but
that won't stop me from
having good time.
I have made friends with
several English Girls here
but Moa they are too slow
& got no Go in them.
Why the Australian Girls
Run rings round them.
I hope you can understand
this as I am racing
to catch the Mail.
Best Luck & Wishes to Your
Mother & Sister Not forgetting yourself
Very sincerely Charlie XXX

Interestingly, Charlie believes at this stage that, while he is being shipped home, it is only for "six months furlough".

10 October 1916, Tuesday

Major Sampson
Got killed in
Raid at Fleurbaix
Also our O.C. [ie officer commanding]
Captain Gibbons [CBH II 10/10/16]

We have previously referred to Major Sampson at the beginning of our story. Sampson served at Gallipoli where he was wounded in September 1915 and shipped to England. On his return to active service on 27 May 1916, he was transferred to the 53rd Battalion. It was while serving with them that he was killed in action at the Battle of Fleurbaix on 19 July 1916, aged 28.[247] Reference was also previously made to Captain Norman Gibbins in the last chapter.

It is worth here noting the fate of Charlie's battalion.

After the Battle of Fromelles, the 55th Battalion, along with the rest of the 5th Division, stayed at the front in this sector for another two months, taking casualties but not committed to any major actions. However, the future battle honours of the Battalion are a reflection of how the War proceeded for the AIF on the Western Front.

Early in 1917, the 55th were assigned to the Somme Valley and advanced when the Germans strategically retreated to the Hindenburg line in 1917 and it took part in the Second Battle of Bullecourt. Later in 1917, it moved with other Australian forces to the Ypres sector of Belgium and took part in the battle at Polygon Wood on 26 September 1917. Later still, the Battalion moved to the Corbie sector of France and, with the rest of the 14th Brigade, took part of the defence north of Villers-Bretonneux, courageously holding their ground during the German Spring Offensive of 1918. This offensive was the last throw of the dice of the Germans after their Western Front was reinforced with some 55 divisions, due to the Russian Bolshevik Government leaving the War.

This was a critical turning point in the war. When the German offensive ran out of steam, the Allies moved to the attack in the late summer of 1918. This was the Hundred Days Offensive. After years of stalemate, the Allies had finally developed a strategy for combined artillery bombardment and the use of the newly invented tanks and overwhelming aircraft superiority to overwhelm the Germans and return to mobile warfare. Also critically important was the arrival of the Americans. By October 1918, 10,000 US troops were arriving a day, some 300,000 a month.[248] The collapse of German morale, with brewing civil war on the home front and widespread exhaustion and hunger, was also decisive.

As historian Martin Gilbert summarised it:

> The fighting therefore went on, but Germany could no longer influence the outcome of the negotiations by its actions on the battlefield. In the 100 days since the Allied offensive had opened at the beginning of August, Germany's power had been broken not by dissent or revolution behind the lines, or by political intrigue, as later nationalist and Nazi politicians were to claim, but by the military superiority of the Allied armies. In those hundred days the British army, and its Dominion forces, had captured 186,000 German prisoners and 2,800 guns. The French had captured 120,000 prisoners and 1,700 guns, the Americans 43,000 prisoners and 1,400 guns, and the Belgians 14,000 prisoners and 500 guns. The combined total of 363,000 prisoners and 6,400 guns constituted a quarter of the German army in the field, and one half of all of its guns. The war making power of Germany, even to defend its borders, was within a few days of collapse.[249]

As part of the 14th Brigade, the 55th Battalion played its role in capture of Peronne during the Battle of Mont Saint-Quentin on 2 September, finally taking part in the Battle for the St Quentin Canal, between 29 September and 2 October 1918, which saw the Australian Corps with US and British troops, led by Lieutenant General Monash, break through the Hindenburg Line. This was its last major battle and during it Private John Ryan was awarded the Victoria Cross.

The Battalion was resting out of the line when the Armistice was declared on 11 November. It was merged with the 53rd Battalion on 10 March 1919 and then disbanded on 11 April. Over the course of the War, the Battalion suffered 1,835 casualties of whom 507 were killed. When you consider that, as a starting point, an Australian infantry battalion began the War with a strength of just over 1,000 men, you can see the awful casualty rate.

Meanwhile, for Charlie, his story moved in a different direction to that of his Battalion. According to his service records, he was discharged from the 1st Auxiliary Hospital on 16 October 1916 and embarked the same day on the hospital ship, H.S. *Karoola*, at Southampton bound for Sydney. The ship was originally enlisted as a troop carrier from the Melbourne firm McIlwraith McEachern, but was quickly converted to a hospital ship.

During the long voyage Charlie made notes of places he had visited:

Aden	Zeitown
Port Suez	Abbasich
Port Said	Cairo
Alexandrie	Luna Park
Cairo	Sudan Desser
Heliopolis	Portiarno
Lemns island	Rest Gully
Mudros	Shrapnel Gully
Embros	Lone Pine
Gallipoli	Walkens Ridge
Anzac	Quinns Post
Cape Helles	Steels Post
Suvla Bay	Gully Ravine
Gaba Tepe	Kondi
Sedd-El Bahr	Sarpey
Achi Baba	Olive Green
Turks Head	Malta
Salonicka	Marseilles
Mastaffa	Lyons
Gazieh	Thinnes
Terrys post	Back St Much[?]

Hogs Back	Sailly
Rail Head	Estares [CBH I 150]

Places of Interest
To Me

1914-15-16-17

Liverpool Camp

Aden	Paris
Port Suez	Glenbrook
Port Saad	Thiennes
Cairo	Estaires
Alexandria	Sailly
Heliopolis	Bact. St Muir
[?]eitoum	FleurBaix
Semmes LSD[?]	Armentrires
Anzac	Bailleue
Mudros E&F	Outreau
Imbros	(Sneece) Boulonge
Turks Head	Calais
Ghezirch	Dover
Ishmalia	Diiston
Sinai Desert	North Hampton
Ferry Post	London
Malta	Southhampton
Marseille	Durban

[CBH I 90]

<u>France</u>

Fleurbaix

Armitrees

Boulonge

Outreaux

Doner

Northampton
London
Middlesex
Southampton
St Vincent
Durban
Cape Town
Freemantle
Sydney
Melbourne

[CBH I 157]

And the number of boat journeys across various oceans and seas:

Pacific Ocean	2
Indian	2
Red Sea	1
Mediterranean Sea	4
Aegean Sea	2
Atlantic Ocean	1
English Channel	1 [CBH I 151]

Next, various ships he had been on:

H.M.S.	*Ceramic*	left	Sydney
" "	*Sutarnia*	"	Alexandria
" "	*Osmanian*	"	Lemnos
" "	*Eramine*	"	Gallipolil [CBH I 152]

And the badges he had collected:

Badges collected on
Battlefield

Royal Field Artillery	Badge
Kings own Scottish Borders	"
German Infantry	"

East Yorks Pioneers "

Numerals

N.Z.M.R. New Zealand Mounted Rifles

R.M.L.I. Royal Marine Light Infantry

5th Bedford Terri Regiment

7 German Badge

26th Mountain Battery (Indian)

7th Essex

Royal Munster Fusiliers

Leinster Royal Canadian

R.A.M.I.

Connaught Rangers

Royal North Lancashire

Bedford

Army Ordinance

Manchester

[CBH I 155]

Next, a sad record of mates who had died or been wounded at Gallipoli:

Killed at Popes Post

Gallipoli

B Coy 19th Batt 5th Brigade

Killed	Wounded
Reub Whiteman	myself
Dick Feeney	Les Hastwell
Corp Wilson	Bill Dwyer
Andy Berry	Steve Lincoln
Major McNamanery	Lieut Anderson
Sgt Taylor	Harry Hind
A[rthur]-Mason	Sgt Francis
Clyde Compton	Major Sampson

Major Sherbon
Lieut Cohen

C Burns
Carl
Bob Brown
C.L. Davis [CBH I 30]

And:

> Clyde Compton got killed
> in early part of
> Gallipoli Campaign. [CBH I 69]

Of these men, Corporal Wilson, Sergeant Taylor, Private Mick Arthur-Mason, Major Sherbon, Major Sampson, Lance Corporal Les Hastwell, Corporal Bill Dwyer and Corporal Bob Brown have already been mentioned. Although it is worth noting in passing that Major Sherbon's name must have been mistakenly added after the rest as he didn't die at Gallipoli but in France. Sherbon was killed in action at the Battle of Flers in the Somme sector on 14 November 1916, aged 23. He was posthumously awarded the Military Cross.[250] Regarding Sherbon's death, it was later recorded by Private Albert Woodford of the 19th Battalion:

> The left flank, B Compnay, under command of that most gallant of soldiers Major Ivan Sherbon MC, in years but a boy but worshipped by his men, had to form up on a tape outside the trench to conform with the remainder of the battalion. The strain of the last hour's marching was intense. We arrived just in time. Poor Sherbon was killed, shot through the body while supervising the forming up of his company.[251]

Of the other men listed, Major "McNamanery" was actually Major James Whiteside Fraser McManamey who had been the commanding officer of B Company. He was from Wilsons Point, NSW, and had been a barrister before the War. Unlike most men recorded here, he was married. He had been a commissioned part-time officer for 20 years in the Citizens Militia and prior to enlisting had been the commanding officer of the 38th Infantry Regiment. He was killed in action in the trenches below Hill 60 on 5 September 1915, aged 53.[252] His death was considered a "cruel loss". As the 19th Battalion historians have noted:

> The second in command [of the Battalion], Major James Whiteside Fraser McManamey was killed by shrapnel near the front line. At age 53 he was older than the average officer in the unit but he had considerable previous militia service when he enlisted. He was known as "father" and his genial disposition and care for the needs of the men was sorely missed. McManamey had practised as a barrister in civilian life and had been the President of the NSW Rugby Union. He was as active rugby referee and had played in the first NSW versus Queensland interstate game. His presence along with quite a number of other rugby players led to the unit being known in its early days as "the rugby battalion". James McManamey provided a good counterpoint in style and character to the CO, Mackenzie, who was considered somewhat rigid and eccentric.[253]

"Lieut Cohen" was in fact Captain Francis Coen. Like Major McManamey, he was also a barrister, in this case from Yass, NSW. After Gallipoli, he was transferred to the 18th Battalion and was killed in action at the Battle of Pozières on 28 July 1916, aged 32.[254]

Private Reuben George Whiteman, like all below, was from B Company, 19th Battalion. Unusually, he was born in Wellington, New Zealand, and was a sailor before the War. He died of wounds on 10 October 1915, aged 20.[255] Dick Feeney was Private Richard Feeney, from Parramatta, Sydney, and was a farm hand on enlistment. He was killed in action on 22 September 1915, aged 30.[256] Andy Berry was Corporal Andrew John Berry, originally from Young, NSW, where he had been a labourer. He died of wounds on 11 September 1915 at Hill 60, aged 25.[257] And Clyde Compton was Private Reginald Clyde Compton, who was from Goulburn, NSW, and had been an engine driver. He was killed in action on 19 September 1915, aged 26.[258]

Of the wounded, who included Charlie himself, was Steve Lincoln and Private Francis Cameron Lincoln. He was also from Balmain, Sydney, and was a railwayman before the War. He later fought in France where he was wounded. Finally, he was gassed in May 1918 and returned to Australia on 6 December 1918.[259]

"Lieut Anderson" was Robert Cairns Amos Anderson from Lindfield, Sydney. He was a university student on enlistment and was later promoted to Captain and mentioned in dispatches, winning the Order of the British Empire. He returned to Australia on 24 December 1918.[260]

Corporal Harry Stanley Hind was from Manly and had been a carpenter just before the War. He was hit by a bullet in the foot at Gallipoli on 31 August 1915 and repatriated to Australia soon after. Back on home soil, he remained in the 19th Battalion until October 1916 when he was discharged. However, in April 1918 he reenlisted and joined the Sea Transport Staff of the AIF as a corporal and was shipped to England, serving there until the War ended. He returned to Australia on 5 April 1919.[261] The Sea Transport Staff, as the name suggests, were responsible for coordinating the shipping to transport troops to the Front and back when wounded or otherwise.

"Sgt Francis" was Sergeant Leonard Arthur Francis, originally from Kentish Town, England. He had been a steward in Wagga Wagga, NSW, and was married. Francis had previously spent three and a half years in the 8th City of London Territorials. He received both a gunshot wound to the abdomen and the right thigh at Gallipoli on 26 August 1915 which were serious enough to see him return to Australia on 20 October 1915.[262]

Private Charles Henry Burns was a carpenter, born in Christchurch, New Zealand, and was one of the few married individuals on the list. In September 1915, he was transferred to the 4th Field Company Engineers as a sapper and promoted to lance corporal; but this was reversed "at own request". After Gallipoli, he subsequently suffered a serious gunshot wound to the head near

Pozières on 1 September 1916 and these wounds resulted in his returning to Australia on 12 November 1916.[263]

"Carl" will most likely be Private Karl Matson of B company who was from Kiama, NSW, and a pattern maker. He received a gunshot wound to his hand at Gallipoli, but later rejoined the Battalion and served in France and Belgium. While in action in France he suffered a gunshot wound to the buttock on 14 November 1916 but again returned to the Front. He spent much of 1917 being repeatedly absent without leave and then being subsequently punished. Interestingly, he was discharged from the Army in January 1918 for being "not a British subject". His file says that he returned to Australia on 5 April 1918. Of note is that his service record also shows that his wife (who lived in England) wrote to the Army on 27 August 1918 asking where her husband was, as she had lost contact with him.[264]

Lastly, C. L. Davis was Private Charles Lindsay Davis, who was not just wounded in action at Gallipoli, but actually died of his wounds. He had been a carpenter and was from Adamstown, NSW. He received a gunshot wound to the abdomen on 9 September 1915 and died at Mudros later that day, aged 19.[265]

In contrast, the journey home was a blessed relief for Charlie, every day of steaming taking him further away from the horrors of the Western Front.

The diaries pick-up again after the departure via ship for Australia, with nothing recorded between 11 and 22 October 1916. During the voyage he notes:

> Southampton to
> Cape Verde 7 days
> Cape Verde to
> Durban 14 days
> Durban to Freemantle
> 14 days
> Freemantle to Melbourne
> 7 days

Melbourne to
Sydney 2 days [CBH II 3/5/16 and also CBH I 63]

Then he writes:

23 October 1916, Monday

Arrived at St Vincent Island belonging to Portugal. no
sooner our anchor
was down [natives]
came around us
in thousands selling
all sorts of curios
Arm in very
good condition [CBH II, 23/10/16]

There are then no entries between 24 and 27 October until he notes:

28 October 1916, Sunday

We are to cross
the Line at 7.30
to night sea
fairly calm
Arm in good
condition [CBH II, 28/10/16]

There is further silence until:

3 November 1916, Friday

Was impressed
to have risked
interview as
soon as possible
having made
at entes[?]

endure[?]
instrument
has said
eh[?] would
has[?][CBH II, 3/11/16]

On:

6 November 1916, Monday

Passed Cape Good Hope
to-day not very
rough passed Cape
at night [CBH II, 6/11/16]

Eventually they arrived in Durban:

9 November 1916, Thursday

Went ashore to-day
had fine time we
went round Durban
by tram cars
the nicest place
I've seen since
I left home. [CBH II, 9/11/16]

Always family oriented, he notes:

10 November 1916, Friday

Roy's Birthday
Had another good time
The Mayor of Durban
Invited us to spree
at Mitchell Park
Durbans Zoo
Plenty to eat & drink

& young ladies to
chat to went to
the Beach later
on Day [CBH II, 10/11/16]

More time in Durban:

11 November 1916, Saturday

Left Durban to-day
for Freemantle
we had plenty of
young ladies to
see us off
fairly rough
saw six whales [CBH II, 11/11/16]

Travel across the Indian Ocean:

12 November 1916, Sunday

Terrible sea running
The Sister is sick
and most of the
patients I am OK [CBH II, 12/11/16]

As Charlie's service record notes:

3/12/16 returned to Sydney

According to newspaper reports, the return of a hospital ship was a major event back in Australia. For example, when the same ship, the H.S. *Karoola*, returned on 3 December 1915, it was reported:

> Wounded soldiers from the hospital ship Karoola, which arrived in the bay on Friday afternoon, disembarked early on Saturday morning, and were conveyed through the streets in motor-cars before being taken to the Base Hospital. The enthusiasm shown by citizens on the arrival of every steamer with men from the front shows no signs of slackening, and

> despite the early hour of the procession – the men were landed at half past 8 o'clock – the streets were thronged. … Fifty-six motor cars, provided by the Automobile Club, were waiting on the pier and the [170] returned heroes were speedily accommodated with comfortable seats and driven through the city.[266]

In Charlie's case, he was home just in time for Christmas celebrations.

War medals: 1914-15 Star, British War Medal 1914-1920, Victory Medal 1914-1919
(reproduced from Matthews and Wilson 2010, Research Disk)

11

Sydney 1917, the Depression and World War II

Sydney was heaven on earth compared to what Charlie had recently been going through. He was initially assigned to "Training and Combined Base Depots, 3rd Auxiliary Hospital". This hospital, in the Sydney suburb of Randwick, was probably the Prince of Wales Hospital, which was used as a military hospital during the Great War.

The diagnosis was good and bad.

> X Ray Report of
> Wounds
> Skigram shows –
>
> Old Fracture of middle
> of both bones of forearm
> that of radius oblique
> with good boney unions
> Fragments in good position
> but for some overlapping
> and consequent of
> shortening lower end of
> upper fragment slightly
> projecting in Palmar
> direction fracture of
> ulna transverse
> Fragment united on
> Palmar aspect by

dense bony callus
in good position on
doosal aspect
Hightly between [CBH I 119]

Fragments with small
exostosis projecting
doosal from lower &
upper Fragment
Several small metallic
particles of relation of
of ulna at seat of
injury

W.B. Dight Capt
Rado
Randwick Hospital
1917 [CBH I 120]

It was a good diagnosis in that his wounds were healing, although bad in the sense that it was the end of the adventure, as he was no longer able to hold a rifle properly. It is understood that he was not suited to a desk job and was officially discharged from the Army on 22 March 1917. His service records note that, as to conduct and character, he was "Good", and was being medically discharged for "Bullet wound in left arm".

So what of Miss Hinemoa Llwellyn of Balmain, his correspondent during the War? During the War young women were asked to write to troops serving overseas. Whether there had been any prior contact is not known, but Moa Llwellyn wrote to Charlie. She would have been 15 when she started corresponding in 1915. There are references to her letters throughout the diary. According to the oral history in the family, it is understood that he had come back to Australia with the hopes of marrying Moa. However, she did not reciprocate his affections, as she was more interested in women than in men, and he ended up marrying her sister Indiana. Nonetheless, for some unknown reason, he gave Moa his precious War Diary. She held onto it for the rest of her life, living until age 101. Just before she died, she sold it to the State Library of NSW for $5,000. Maybe there is nothing more to this than that he felt grateful to her, all those years later, as one of the few people who actually wrote to him while he was in the trenches. Perhaps he gave the diary to Moa in hope that she could use her connections to get it published. For, under the stage name Louise Homfrey, she was a famous actress appearing in many films and episodes of Australian television series in the 1960s and 1970s like *Homicide*, *Division 4* and *Matlock Police*, as well as being a radio presenter on stations 2KY, 2GB and 3KY. She received a Medal of the British Empire (MBE) for her work in music, film and television. According to her niece, Amanda, she "started and recorded for all the Australian libraries, 'voice books' for all vision impaired Australians and eventually became blind herself".

So it wasn't Moa that Charlie married, but her older sister Indie. At the time of their marriage, Indie Llewelyn lived with her mother and sister in Balmain, a working class suburb of Sydney. Their son Douglas was born on 23 February 1918 in time to be there for the end of the war. As Charlie recorded it in his diary:

> Armistice Signed
> ~~Peace Declared~~ on
> Monday 11 Nov 1918
>
> Indie & Douglas have gone
> into Manly to celebrate
> I have just come
> home from work CBH [CBH I 62]

Even the last day of the conflict saw mass casualties and ruthlessness from the Allied generals. While the Armistice was signed around 5.45am, early morning French time, the Allied Supreme Commander, French Marshal Ferdinand Foch, would not allow the cessation of hostilities until the exact time of 11.00am. In the delay there were some 10,940 casualties with 2,738 deaths on all sides, mainly due to artillery fire. However, Foch was to be prescient about the state of affairs, when he later declared: "This is not a peace treaty it is an armistice for twenty years".[267] Likewise, British Prime Minister, David Lloyd George, questioned his military advisors on 13 October 1918 on "whether the actual military defeat of Germany and the giving to the German people of a real taste of war was not more important, from the point of view of the peace of the world, than a surrender at the present time when the German armies were still on foreign territory".[268]

After the War, Charlie made more lists of his fallen comrades:

> Killed in Action
> France
>
> Capt Gibbons
> Lieut Col McConachy
> Jim Egan
> Ned Edgely
> Ted Murphy
> Bill McFarlane
> George Stewart
> Arch McPherson
> Major Sampson
>
> Many Others
> Too Numerous
> to mention [CBH I 71]

Gibbins, Egan, Murphy, McFarlane and Sampson have already been mentioned. Of the others, "Lieut Col McConachy" was actually Lieutenant Colonel David McConaghy of the 55th Battalion to whom we referred before. He was transferred to the 54th Battalion as commanding officer on 18 December 1917, was wounded in action, and died on 9 April 1918 in the Battle of Villers-Bretonneux during the last great German offensive (the Spring Offensive or

Kaiserschlacht) of the War, aged 31. As Charles Bean described it in the *Official History*:

> Early on April 9, in a heavy bombardment (possibly associated with "diversions" for the Lys offensive or the attack on Hangard), the headquarters of the 54th on Hill 104 were hit. Lieut.-Colonel D.McF. McConaghy – young veteran of Anzac – and his intelligence officer, Lieutenant H.E.G. Staples, being mortally wounded, and the adjutant, Captain N.B. Lovett, killed. McConaghy's second-in-command, Major R.D. Jack who was away as liaison officer with the 9th Brigade, was killed in the same bombardment.[269]

Ned Edgley was Private Norman Edgley of the 53rd Battalion. He was a shoemaker from Melbourne, and died of wounds on 7 July 1918 at Morlancourt, in the Somme sector during the final stages of the German Spring Offensive of that year, aged 25.[270] George Stewart was Private Joseph George Stewart of D Company, 18th Battalion. Also from Manly, he had been a carter before the war and died of wounds on 17 April 1916, not long after his battalion arrived at the Western Front in France, aged 22.[271]

Arch McPherson was Private Archibald Colin McPherson of the 56th Battalion, yet another Manly boy and a baker before the War. He fought in France and suffered a gunshot wound to the arm on 1 November 1916 during fighting in the Armentières sector. He was again wounded on 23 April 1918 with severe "gas burns" during the Second Battle of Villers-Bretonneux and died of those wounds on 9 May 1918 whilst in England, aged 26.[272] It is worth reflecting on a rare note in his service file describing in detail his funeral at a cemetery in Birmingham:

> The coffin was conveyed to the cemetery on a Gun Carriage drawn by 12 men of the R.A.M.C. The coffin was draped with the Australian Flag, and was followed by twelve of his comrades from the Hospital who placed flowers on the grave. The "Last Post" was sounded at the graveside by a Bugler of the

> R.A.M.C. Administrative Headquarters, A.I.F. London, were represented at the funeral.[273]

McPherson's file also notes that his personal luggage never reached his family in Australia as it:

> Was included in a consignment shipped from England per S.S. "Barunga", which vessel was lost at sea, with all cargo, as a result of enemy action.[274]

Charlie also made an additional list:

Mates Killed in action
France & Gallipoli

Jim Egan
Spud Murphy
George Stewart
Arch McPherson
Bob Furness (Prisoner)
Clyde Compton
Dick Devlin
Reub Whiteman
Andy Berry
Billy Burridge
Harry Badmington
Dick Badmington
Roy Quick [CBH I 74]

Of these names, most have been mentioned earlier. Spud Murphy is Private Edward Murphy of the 55th Battalion, who has already been noted. Of the rest, Billy Burridge was Private William Thomas Burridge of the 25th Battalion who was a stockman from Gin Gin, Queensland. He received a gunshot wound to the back on 27 October 1917 in the Ypres sector of Belgium and died on 1 November 1917, aged 28.[275] Private Harry Duff Badmington was from the 20th Battalion. Before the War he was a labourer from Manly and was killed in action in the area of the Ypres Salient on 9 October 1917, aged 23.[276] His older brother

Dick was Private Richard Charles Badmington of the 53rd Battalion. Before the War he was a carpenter from Manly. He died of disease on 14 October 1918 in Cologne while a Prisoner of War, aged 29.[277] Roy Quick is most likely Private Francis Henry Quick of the 56th Battalion-who was from Petersham, Sydney, and was a clerk before signing up. He was killed in action at the Battle of Fleurbaix on 20 July 1916, aged 30.[278] It is not clear who Bob Furness was.

Of interest, we still have a letter that Charlie received on 17 February 1920 from his Irish pal, Thomas Cunningham, who lived in Dundalk, County Louth. Cunningham served in a number of famous regiments during the war including the 6th Battalion, Royal Irish Rifles, the Royal Irish Regiment, and the King's Own Scottish Borderers. He enlisted on 11 November 1914, served in action with the Mediterranean Expeditionary Forces and the BEF in France and saw out the War, being discharged in 1919. Charlie met him on the Western Front.

Cunningham wrote:

> Dear Charley
>
> I am more nor sorry for not writing
> [missing part]
> and then a long march into Germany
> so I may tell you that only we played
> ourselves. There we be got dead [?]
> So I don't think I have a lot to say
> This time only I was going to send you
> A little shamrock but it is on the
> Late side just now. But if God spares
> all of us doing well you shall have it
> next time Don't forget old sport, but let
> Please let me know if there is much work out there as I have
> Not done a bit once I came home
> For if things are good out there
> I will take it on

> The public houses are open just now
> And I have just the price of 2 pints and I
> must go and get them.
> Well Charley all for the
> present. Hoping this will find
> you in the best of health
> [?] ever me at present
>
> I remain your old chum

There are a few anecdotes concerning Charlie's life after the Great War. His daughter Diane remembers:

> Indie played piano for silent movies. They went for a dance every Saturday night at the Masonic Hall.
>
> Further, there would be concerts at home. Indie played the piano, Dad would juggle phonograph records, breaking them, Diane on violin, Yvette on banjo, Yvonne also on violin and Doug would tap dance.
>
> The Depression was tough on Dad, but we always had food, always had shoes. During the Depression he worked for "relief" on the roads. I recall that one day he got hit with a pick in the buttock. It was a clean wound. He just poured some iodine on it and that was it.
>
> I recall that during the Depression we had the gas cut off because we couldn't meet the payments. The gas man cut the pipe. Then Dad would use bicycle tubing to close the gap while mum cooked dinner and I would wait outside watching for the gas inspector.

By 1938, Charlie worked as a station or shearer's cook near Wilcannia in outback New South Wales, which he followed up as a station cook on a property in South Australia between February and May 1939, and between 1 May and 15 September as a polisher at the Forestry Commission of NSW in Sydney. That last date is relevant.

Australia entered World War II on 3 September 1939. Charlie

signed up within days on 13 November at the age of 44. He was made a private in the 2nd Garrison Battalion. How he managed to do this given his arm injury from the Great War is not explained, although it may explain the reason for his early discharge for being "medically unfit" on 12 April 1940.

Later records show that Charlie worked as a seaman "on his majesty's service" (O.H.M.S.) on the R.M.S. *Queen Mary* between 13 June 1941 and 16 August 1941, out of the Port of Sydney. Later to be dubbed the "Grey Ghost", the *Queen Mary* was one of the largest passenger ships in the world and was requisitioned by the British government to be converted into a troop ship. This is the same ship that now sits permanently docked at Long Beach in California.

This turn of events may account for the story that Diane recounts when Charlie headed off on the R.M.S. *Queen Mary* for the Middle East. His son Douglas, who had signed up as an official army correspondent and photographer, was at the same time on the troopship R.M.S. *Queen Elizabeth* that was also departing Sydney. Diane recalls that, as they were leaving, the band on the dock played "We're off to see the wizard". She was later told that, when the commanding officers realised that they had a father and son on separate ships departing from Sydney Harbour, a flying fox was rigged up to send Douglas over for a visit to his father and say his farewells. This occurred on 27 June 1941. They headed for the Port of Aden and disembarked in the Middle East on 31 July.

Charlie had signed up as a cook. But as Diane said, "He wasn't really a cook. He could burn water". According to how Charlie related the story to his daughter, the authorities could also figure this out and he was sacked when they reached port and put on the next ship home. Back in Australia, according to Diane, he joined the Volunteer Defence Corps (the Australian equivalent of the British Home Guard) and was part of the "Old and bold" during the rest of World War II.

By August 1942, he was working again as a French polisher under contract for the Department of Information in Pitt Street.

On 18 September 1943, he noted in a letter to his son Douglas, who was then serving in New Guinea, to "Look out for Sergeant Alwyn Hardy, he's in the Censors Office in your town also his brother. Most likely you have met them by this. He wrote to me some time ago and I answered same".

Charlie's son is worthy of a biography in his own right. He had been a child protégé and when young had acted in a number of successful Australian-made films, notably the *Dad and Dave* features, based on the books by Steele Rudd. He became a cinematographer and joined the army in that capacity. As he was only five feet tall, this specialist skill allowed him an exemption to join. He was assigned to a photography unit and was on the front line in the Middle East with the 9th Division 2nd AIF during 1941 and 1942, including the siege at Tobruk. He was later shipped to Papua New Guinea and was at Morotai in Indonesia and later Borneo and served until 1945. He was responsible for much of the film footage subsequently seen by civilian audiences from those combat zones and was promoted to the rank of sergeant. After World War II, he ran his own production company – Southern Cross Films – making a number of feature films, and also worked for the BBC and the Australian Broadcasting Commission (ABC) on a number of projects. He died in 1993.[279]

Diane left home in 1943 to join the Air Force at the age of 17. She later married and had two children. Charlie's other daughters, Yvonne and Yvette, also married and had children and grandchildren.

As the years passed, the Great War faded into the background. At the time of their telling it was never known for sure whether some of Charlie's stories were true or not whenever he reminisced about fighting in the trenches. Later, when his granddaughter was small, he would also tell a story about being bayonetted by the Japanese. This was obviously not true as he did not serve in the Pacific Theatre in World War II. Overall, the family recollection is that there were many stories, of which some were gruesome, but mostly funny. Unfortunately, all these stories are now lost to time.

Epilogue

For his service in the War, Charlie was awarded the 1914-15 Star, the British War Medal and the Victory Medal. World War I was to have been the defining event of Charlie's life. As with so many veterans, he went straight back to civilian life. We can only imagine the torments he may have suffered in his dreams over the years. He had spent two years and 243 days in the AIF, of which two years and 162 days were abroad. Now he returned to his profession as a French polisher. His granddaughter Amanda recalls as a child often going to the back shed in the garden and noting the strong smell of shellac. He also undertook some sign writing.

An amazing fact is that he named his marital home at 3 Peacock Street, Seaforth, a war service home, after the battle where he received the awful wound that ended his wartime service. His granddaughter, unaware of the link with the battle, had always thought the name Fleurbaix was simply meant to reflect the beautiful garden – a basket of flowers – they had surrounding the house.

Did he name the house after the battle for any particular reason? His family did not know. Was it some dark joke or something more straightforward, because, in the end, being wounded at Fleurbaix (or Fromelles) was his ticket to life. Chances are that had he stayed in the trenches he may never have made it back to Australia. Many of his close mates died in the subsequent Battle of Pozières. Therefore, to have the name "Fleurbaix" on a brass plate next to his front door – something he might see more than once a day – was possibly a reminder of serendipity in life.

He was a keen fisherman, owned a boat and would sail out "fishing for salmon and sharks" off Manly. His daughter Diane recalls that he remained "a bit of a larrikin" and that, when she was a child, heading off with him one day for fishing. They didn't catch any fish, so on the way home they ducked into a fish and chip shop to buy some freshly caught fish so he could say to Indie, "this is what we caught today".

Diane recalls that, for years after the War, he would pick little bits of bone out of his forearm. This was a lasting legacy of the shattered radius from 1916. Unfortunately, according to Diane, "he would often drink to excess and could be a bad tempered drunk". In fact, "He brewed with pears and the tops would sometimes blow off the bottles. He would often buy a big quart bottle of beer from the hotel on Manly wharf", plus "he always had a cigarette hanging out of his mouth". Nonetheless, on the up side, "he didn't ever swear". She noted that he was quite philosophical about life and, "If you used to hurt yourself he would repeat the old saying 'crack hardy', that is to say 'get on with it'".

Charlie's last years were to present him with another trial. Whether it was in any way directly related to his war service is not known. He developed diabetes and gradually lost both legs as surgeons removed, first his feet, and then more and more of both his left and right limbs. As his daughter Diane noted, "bit by bit they chopped his legs off". In the end, he actually died on the operating table in the last in a series of these operations, on 30 March 1973, aged 79.

Charlie was not a big fan of Remembrance Days, not marching with the other diggers on ANZAC Day. Although he must have had some pride in what he did, as he allowed his granddaughter Amanda to march while wearing his medals. As she says: "I [would] take Pa for a walk". Although when these commemoration days came around he would reflect to his family on "the futility of war" and the fact that "no one wins".

Australia's broader contribution to the First World War is breathtaking. From a population of less than five million, some

417,000 Australians volunteered and enlisted. By the war's end, in November 1918, over 61,000 had been killed in action, with a further 155,000-plus wounded, making the nation's casualty rate the highest in the British Empire. It is worth noting again: every one of these Australians was a volunteer. It is easy to get lost in the enormity of these figures; to lose sight of the very personal and tremendous sacrifice of each and every one of these individuals, their families, and their communities.

Rural and regional Australia was particularly hard hit by the sacrifices. It is easy to form the view that the men and women who served at Gallipoli and throughout the First World War were superhuman – that they possessed qualities that made them 'natural' warriors, or better placed to deal with the horrors of war. The truth is that these young men and women were ordinary people placed in extraordinary circumstances. This is the true tragedy, and, indeed, the true glory, of their sacrifice. They were young people from our cities, towns, villages and regions. They were confronted with the full horror of war and conducted themselves with honour. I like to think of them as extraordinary, ordinary Australians.

One of these extraordinary, ordinary Australians was Charlie Hardy.

Another extraordinary, ordinary Australian was one of my great-uncles, Bill Browne, who served on the Western Front, endured the horrors of the Battle of the Somme, and won a Military Medal in 1918. I was very privileged to have known him when I was a little boy.

The 55th Battalion, in which Charlie spent the second half of his war, was principally raised in southern New South Wales, mainly on the Monaro Plains region and the Snowy Mountains. A hundred years later, I represented that area in the Australian Parliament and was very proud to have taken part in Centenary commemorations of the Anzac Landings in 2015.

It included events by the Bega Historical Society and the Cooma-

Monaro Centenary of Anzac dinner was held at the Cooma Ex-Services Club. This historic dinner was a fine and memorable salute to the men and women of the Cooma region. While only a small town of less than 2,200 people in 1915, several hundred enlisted from the Cooma district, with 53 of them making the ultimate sacrifice. There was a memorial at the Bombala Cenotaph with a striking sculpted rock centrepiece surrounded by boulders symbolising the 34 World War I deaths. On Anzac Day I attended a moving dawn service in Bega where the Bemboka light horse troop emerged from the predawn mist creating a poignant and stunning opening for the 600 locals in attendance. I joined locals in Narooma, Bergalia, and Moruya. In Moruya, I attended the launch of six documentary films detailing the lives of five servicemen and one nursing sister from the local region, who served during the Great War. I then attended the morning service in Batemans Bay, where approximately 2,000 people gathered to commemorate the Centenary. A particularly moving part of the ceremony was when special scrolls were given to families and descendants of a group of 26 fallen diggers who enlisted in Batemans Bay and are buried overseas. My final engagement for the day was in Braidwood. Some 465 men and women from the Braidwood district volunteered and went to the Great War, but 88 did not return.

Over the years, I have visited the cemeteries at Villers-Bretonneux in France and Gallipoli, and these experiences have left an indelible imprint on my mind. But so too does standing amongst your community, with young and old, on Anzac Day, and reflecting on those extraordinary, ordinary Australians to whom we owe so much.

The reminders of the Great War are ever present. Just in the surrounding suburbs, where I live nowadays in Sydney, the road names are a daily reminder of the battles and military commanders. A quick survey found the following in the area of Ryde: ANZAC Avenue; Mons Avenue; Arras Parade; Amiens Street; Gaza Road; Maxim Street; Haig Avenue; Monash Road; Beattie Avenue; Birdwood Street; Hamilton Crescent; Chauvel Street; Lavarack

Street; Morshead Street; Ryrie Street; Sturdee Street; Rowell Street; Blamey Street; Northcott Street; and Berryman Street.

In writing this book, I pay tribute, not just to the veterans of the Gallipoli campaign, or Fromelles, nor, indeed, just the Great War. It is a tribute to all the men and women who have served our nation in all wars, conflicts and on peacekeeping operations – the extraordinary, ordinary Australians to whom we owe so much.

Lest we forget.

Bibliography

The bibliography is divided into two parts. The first consists of the primary documents, including Charlie Hardy's war diaries, Army service documents and his letters. The secondary sources are some of the principal works on Australia's involvement in the War, although many more texts were consulted regarding the great conflict.

Main Primary Sources

Hardy, Charles B., *War Diary I*, unpublished notebook, State Library of NSW (designated CBH I in the text)

Hardy, Charles B., *War Diary II*, unpublished notebook, (in author's possession) (designated CBH II in the text).

Hardy, Charles B., *Soldiers Pay Book for use on Active Service*, State Library of NSW

Hardy, Charles B., Army Service File 1915-1917, National Archives of Australia

Hardy, Charles B., Army Service File 1940-1941, (in author's possession)

Hardy, Charles B., Various letters to friends, (in author's possession)

5th Brigade, Australian Imperial Force unit war diaries, Australian War Memorial, Item numbers 23/5/9, March 1916

19th Battalion, Australian Imperial Force unit war diaries, Australian War Memorial, Item numbers 23/36/1, March 1915 to 23/36/6, February 1916

55th Battalion, Australian Imperial Force unit war diaries, Australian War Memorial, Item numbers 23/72/1, February 1916 to 23/72/6, July 1916

Main Secondary Sources

Armstrong, Natalie (2014), *The Men from Snowy River*, Delegate Progress Association, Delegate

Atabaki, Touraj (2016), "Persia/Iran", *International Encyclopedia of the First World War*, 2 May 2016, extracted from online at www.encyclopedia.1914-1918-online.net on 3 September 2020

Bean, Charles E. W. (1941a), *The Story of ANZAC from the outbreak of the war to the end of the first phase of the Gallipoli Campaign, May 4, 1915,* The Official History of Australia in the War of 1914-1918, Volume I, 11th edition, Australian War Memorial, Canberra

Bean, Charles E. W. (1941b), *The Story of ANZAC from 4 May 1915 to the evacuation of the Gallipoli Peninsula,* The Official History of Australia in the War of 1914-1918, Volume II, 11th edition, Australian War Memorial, Canberra

Bean, Charles E. W., (1941c), *The Australian Imperial Force in France 1916*, The Official History of Australia in the War of 1914-1918, Volume III, 12th edition, Australian War Memorial, Canberra

Bean, Charles E. W., (1941d), *The Australian Imperial Force in France, 1917*, The Official History of Australia in the War of 1914-1918, Volume IV, 11th edition, Australian War Memorial, Canberra

Bean, Charles E. W., (1941e), *The Australian Imperial Force in France during the Main German Offensive 1918*, The Official History of Australia in the War of 1914-1918, Volume V, 8th edition, Australian War Memorial, Canberra

Beaumont, Joan (ed) (1995), *Australia's War 1914-18*, Allen & Unwin, St Leonards

Beaumont, Joan (2001), *Australian Defence: Sources and Statistics*, The Australian Centenary History of Defence, Volume VI, Oxford University Press, South Melbourne

Blair, Dale (2005), *No Quarter: Unlawful Killing and Surrender in the Australian War Experience 1915-18*, Ginninderra Press, Port Adelaide

Brandmayer, Balthasar (1933), *Meldegänger Hitler*, Franz Walter, Überlingen a. Bodensee

Cameron, David W. (2011), *Gallipoli: The Final Battles and the Evacuation of Anzac*, Blue Sky Publishing, Newport

Carlyon, Les (2006), *The Great War*, Macmillan, Sydney

Clark, Chris (2010), *The Encyclopaedia of Australia's Battles*, Allen & Unwin, Crows Nest

Coates, John (2001), *An Atlas of Australia's Wars*, The Australian Centenary History of Defence, Volume VII, Oxford University Press, South Melbourne

Cook, Tim (2006), "The Politics of Surrender: Canadian Soldiers and the Killing of Prisoners in the Great War", *The Journal of Military History*, Vol. 70, No. 3, July 2006, pp. 637-665

Cook, Timothy J. (2014), *Snowy to the Somme: A Muddy and Bloody Campaign, 1916-1918*, Big Sky Publishing, Newport

Dwyer, Philip (2015), "Anzacs behaving badly: Scott McIntyre and contested history", *The Conservation*, Australian Broadcasting Corporation, 28 April 2015, extracted from online www.theconversation.com on 14 August 2020

Falconer, John Harold (1916), *On Active Service*, extracted online at www.users.tpg.com.au on 13 August 2020

Feltman, Brian K. (2010), "Tolerance as a Crime? The British Treatment of German Prisoners of War on the Western Front, 1914-1918", *War in History*, Vol. 17, No. 4, November 2010, pp 435-458

Ferguson, Nial (1998), *The Pity of War*, Penguin Books, London

Ferguson, Nial (2004), "Prisoner taking and Prisoner Killing in the Age of Total War", *War in History*, Vol. 11, No. 2, April 2004, pp 148-192

Fitzsimons, Peter (2017), *Fromelles & Pozières: In the Trenches of Hell*, Penguin Random House, North Sydney, 2017

Gatfield, John, and Landels, Richard (2015), *The RSL Book of World War I*, Harper Collins Publishers, Sydney, 2015

Gilbert, Martin (1994), *The First World War: a complete history*, Henry Holt and Company, New York

Hardy, Mabel (1959), *History of the Hardy Family in South Australia*, typescript booklet, State Library of South Australia, Adelaide

Helgason, Gudmundur (2020), *Ceramic*, extracted online at www.uboat.net on 16 August 2020

Hodges, Paul D. (2006), "The British Infantry and Atrocities on the Western Front, 1914-1918", Birkbeck College, University of London, PhD Thesis, London, 2006

Holmes, Richard (1985), *Firing Line*, Jonathan Cape, London

Hopper, Tristin (2018), "The forgotten ruthlessness of Canada's Great War soldiers", National Post, 12 November 2018, extracted online at www.nationalpost.com on 14 August 2020.

Jones, Edgar (2006), "The Psychology of Killing: The Combat Experience of British Soldiers during the First World War", *Journal of Contemporary History*, Vol 41, No. 2, 2006, pp 229-246

Keegan, John (1976), *The Face of Battle*, Jonathan Cape, London

Kelly, Fran (2014), "Claims Australians executed prisoners in WWI engagement", *Radio National Breakfast* broadcast transcript, Australian Broadcasting Corporation, 11 September 2014, extracted from online at www.abc.net.au on 14 August 2020

King, Ernest (1916), Diary, at www.users.bigpond.net.au/rhearne

King, Johnathan (2010), *The Western Front Diaries: The ANZACs' Own Story, Battle by Battle*, Simon & Schuster Australia, Sydney 2010

King, Johnathan (2014), *Gallipoli Diaries: The ANZACs' Own Story, Day by Day*, Scribe Publications, Brunswick, 2014

Kramer, Alan (2017), "Atrocities", *International Encyclopedia of the First World War*, 24 January 2017, extracted from online at www.encyclopedia.1914-1918-online.net on 14 August 2020

Lee, Roger (2010), *The Battle of Fromelles 1916*, Australian Army Campaigns Series 8, Army History Unit, Canberra, 2010

Library and Archives Canada (2012), "Canadian Army Medical Corps", Guide to Sources Relating to Units of the Canadian Expeditionary Force 1914-1919, Toronto

Lindsay, Patrick (2008), *Fromelles; Australia's Darkest Day and the Dramatic Discovery of our Fallen World War One Diggers*, Hardie Grant Books, Prahran, 2008

Lynch, E.P.F., (edited by Will Davies) (2006), *Somme Mud: The War experiences of an Australian infantryman in France 1916-1919*, Random House Australia, North Sydney, 2006

Matthews, L.D. (1979), "Cass, Walter Edmund Hutchinson (1876–1931)", *Australian Dictionary of Biography*, Volume 7, (MUP), 1979

Matthews, Wayne and Wilson, David (2011), *Fighting Nineteenth: History of the 19th Battalion, AIF, 1915-1918*, Australian Military History Publications, Canberra, 2011

Monash, John (1923), *The Australian Victories in France in 1918*, Lothian Book Publishing, Melbourne

Moorehead, Alan (1989), *Gallipoli*, Macmillan Australia, Crows Nest, 1989

Grant, R.G. (2018), *World War I, The Definitive Visual Guide*, Dorling Kindersley, London

Scott, Ernest (1936), *Australia During the War*, The Official History of Australia in the War of 1914-1918, Volume XI, Australian War Memorial, Canberra, 1936

Shermer, David (1973), *World War I*, Octopus Books, London

Stevenson, Robert (2015), *The War with Germany*, The Centenary History of Australia and the Great War, Oxford University Press, South Melbourne, 2015

Sumner, Ian (2011), *Anzac Infantryman 1914-15: From New Guinea to Gallipoli*, Osprey Publishing, Oxford

The Gazette (Montreal) (2006), "Canadian soldiers frequently executed German fighters trying to surrender during WW1", *History News Network*, 22 October 2006, extracted from online at www.viu.ca on 14 August 2020.

Unkles, James (2018), *Ready, Aim Fire: Major Francis Thomas, the Fourth Victim in the execution of Lieutenant Harry "Breaker" Morant*, Sid Harta Publishers, Glen Waverley, 2018

Wilcox, Craig (2010), "Breaker Morant: The murderer as martyr", in Stockings, Craig (ed)(2010), *Zombie Myths of Australian Military History, University of New South Wales*, Sydney, 2010

Williams, John F. (2005), *Corporal Hitler and the Great War 1914-1918: The List Regiment*, Frank Cass, Oxford, 2005

Weber, Thomas (2010), *Hitler's First War: Adolf Hitler, the Men of the List Regiment, and the First World War*, Oxford University Press, Oxford, 2010

Endnotes

1 The "First" Australian Imperial Force (AIF) served in World War I, the "Second" AIF served in World War II.

2 State Archives & Records, NSW ANZAC Centenary, NSW Government, www.nswanzaccentenary.records.nsw.gov.au extracted on 12 August 2020.

3 Ibid.

4 Ibid.

5 Quoted on *The Great War*, The Great War Channel, atwww.youtube.com, extracted 11 September 2020.

6 Stevenson 2015, 98.

7 Beaumont 2001, 274.

8 Scott 1936, 874.

9 Hardy 1959, 6.

10 Matthews & Wilson 2011, 21.

11 See "Victor Horatio Buller Sampson", *The AIF Project*, UNSW Canberra, at www.aif.adfa.edu.au, extracted on 8 September 2020.

12 See "Francis Coen", *The AIF Project*, UNSW Canberra, at www.aif.adfa.edu.au, extracted on 16 September 2020.

13 See "Ivan Brunker Sherbon", *The AIF Project*, UNSW Canberra, at www.aif.adfa.edu.au, extracted on 8 September 2020.

14 See "William Kenneth Seaforth Mackenzie", *The AIF Project*, UNSW Canberra, at www.aif.adfa.edu.au, extracted on 8 September 2020 and "Lieutenant Colonel WKS Mackenzie, 19 [B]attalion, AIF", Australian War Memorial, at www.awm.gov.au, extracted on 12 November 2020.

15 Scott 1936, 870.

16 Ibid., 874.

17 Matthews & Wilson 2011, xii.

18 Ibid., 9.

19 Ibid., 15.

20 Falconer 1916.

21 Lynch 2006, 1.

22 Falconer 1916.

23 Helgason 2020.

24 Matthews & Wilson 2011, 22.

25 See William Thomas Dwyer, Army Service File 1915-1917, National Archives of Australia.

26 Falconer 1916.

27 Hodges 2006, 192.

28 Quoted in "The Gallipoli Campaign 1915", The History Room, www.youtube.com extracted 27 August 2020.

29 Quoted in Strachan, Hew (2004) The First World War, television series, Wark Clements, Hamilton Films and Channel 4, London.

30 Coates 2001, 42.

31 See "General Sir John Monash", *The AIF Project*, UNSW Canberra, at www.aif.adfa.edu.au, extracted on 17 November 2020.

32 Cecil Aspinall-Oglander, 1992, Military Operations Gallipoli: May 1915 to the Evacuation, Imperial War Museum and battery Press, London, 46, 53 quoted in Wikipedia article on Gallipoli Campaign at www.wikipedia.org on 28 August 2020.

33 Falconer 1916.

34 Quoted in Matthews & Wilson 2011, 25.

35 King 1916.

36 James Dunley, Army Service File 1915-1916, National Archives of Australia.

37 "H.M.T. Osmanieh", Troop Ships, *Follow the Twenty-Second*, at www.anzac-22nd-battalion.com, extracted 10 September 2020.

38 Falconer 1916.

39 See "Sir Herbert Vaughan Cox", Australian War Memorial, at www.awm.gov.au, extracted on 17 November 2020.

40 Falconer 1916.

41 Lieutenant Colonel Alfred Ernest Chapman, ANZAC Biographies, at www.anzac-biographies.com extracted on 25 September 2020.

42 Private Ernest King, AIF diary, Australian War Memorial 315 419/008/027.

43 See "Frederick Jerry Wilson", *The AIF Project*, UNSW Canberra, at www.aif.adfa.edu.au, extracted on 8 September 2020.

44 See Amanda Laugesen (editor), Glossary of Slang and Peculiar Terms in Use in the A.I.F., Australian National University, School of Literature, Languages and Linguistics, www.slll.anu.edu.au extracted 20 July 2020.

45 Lieutenant Frank Boyden, quoted in Matthews and Wilson 2011, 32-34.

46 Moorehead 1989, 247-248.

47 Sumner 2011, 52.

48 See "Sir Henry de Beauvoir de Lisle", First World War.com, at www.firstworldwar.com, extracted on 17 November 2020.

49 See "Hampton Prout Woolcott", *The AIF Project*, UNSW Canberra, at www.aif.adfa.edu.au, extracted on 8 September 2020.

50 See "Colonel Harold Pope", *The AIF Project*, UNSW Canberra, at www.aif.adfa.edu.au, extracted on 20 September 2020.

51 Private Ernest King, AIF diary, Australian War Memorial 315 419/008/027.

52 See "Brigadier General William Grant", *General Officers of the First AIF*, at www.aif.adfa.edu.au, extracted on 16 September 2020 and 9th Light Horse, *First World War, 1914–1918 units*. Australian War Memorial. Retrieved 15 September 2010.

53 Leslie Raymond Pountney, Army Service File 1914-1915, National Archives of Australia.

54 *Macquarie Port News*, July 15, 1915.

55 Quoted in Ferguson 2004, 154.

56 Beaumont 1995, 157.

57 Hodges 2006, 6-7.

58 Feltman 2010, 441.

59 Cook 2006.

60 See Hopper 2018.

61 Cook 2006, 661.

62 Ibid., 659.

63 Ibid., 663.

64 Ibid., 656.

65 Monash 1923, 229.

66 Hodges 2006, 7.

67 Quoted in Hew Strachan, (2004) *The First World War*, television series, Wark Clements, Hamilton Films and Channel 4, London.

68 Bean 1941c, 262-263.

69 Ibid.

70 Ibid., 268-269.

71 Quoted in Hodges 2006, 99-100.

72 Ibid., 74-75.

73 Ibid., 74.

74 Ibid., 75.

75 Bean 1941a, 267.

76 Quoted in Kevin Fewster (1983), *Gallipoli Correspondent: the frontline diary of C.E.W. Bean*, Allen & Unwin, Sydney, 83.

77 Quoted in King 2010, 165.

78 Quoted in Blair 2005, chapter 4.

79 Quoted in Ferguson 1998, 383.

80 Quoted in Carlyon 2006, 450.

81 Carlyon 2006, 451.

82 Ibid.

83 Ibid.

84 Bean 1941d, 772.

85 Ibid.

86 Ibid.

87 Keegan 1976, 51.

88 Quoted in Carlyon 2006, 483-484.

89 Feltman 2010, 447.

90 Holmes 1985, 382.

91 Blair 2005, introduction.

92 Feltman 2010, 448-449.

93 Ferguson 1998, 374-376.

94 Frank Maxwell (1921) *A Memoir and Some Letters*, edited by Charlotte Maxwell, John Murray, London, quoted in Feltman 2010, 450.

95 "Historical Note on Killing of Prisoners in World War I (1916)", LHCMA, Liddell: 11/1948/24, quoted in Feltman 2010, 455.

96 Quoted in Feltman 2010, 454.

97 Quoted in Ferguson 2004, 157.

98 Ferguson 2004, 158.

99 Ibid.

100 Ibid.

101 Ibid., 159.

102 Ibid.

103 Ibid., 148.

104 Ibid., 149-151.

105 Quoted in King 2010, 174.

106 Ibid., 246.

107 Wilcox 2010, 29-49.

108 Unkles 2018.

109 See "William Norman Arthur-Mason", *The AIF Project*, UNSW Canberra, at www.aif.adfa.edu.au, extracted on 8 September 2020.

110 See "Thomas Hope Sanders", *The AIF Project*, UNSW Canberra, at www.aif.adfa.edu.au, extracted on 8 September 2020.

111 19th Battalion Australian Imperial Force unit war diaries, Australian War Memorial 23/36/2, October 1915.

112 Matthews & Wilson 2011, 44.

113 See State Library of Victoria, "The rush to enlist", *Australia & WW1*, at www.ergo.slv.vic.gov.au, extracted on 12 November 2020.

114 19th Battalion Australian Imperial Force unit war diaries, Australian War Memorial 23/36/3, November 1915.

115 Hampton Prout Woolcott, Army Service File 1915-1919, National Archives of Australia.

116 Quoted in Cameron 2011, 204.

117 See "Richard Linton", Virtual War Memorial Australia, at www.vwma.org.au, extracted on 2 September 2020.

118 He is the author's now long-departed Grandfather.

119 Feltman 2010, 439.

120 Ibid., 438.

121 Bean 1941b, 843.

122 See Amanda Laugesen (editor), Glossary of Slang and Peculiar Terms in Use in the A.I.F., Australian National University, School of Literature, Languages and Linguistics, www.slll.anu.edu.au extracted 18 September 2020.

123 Bean 1941b, 846.

124 Ibid.

125 Quoted in Cameron 2011, 247.

126 Lee 2010, 150.

127 Feltman 2010, 439.

128 Beaumont 2001, 269.

129 Quoted in Cameron 2011, 285-286.

130 19th Battalion Australian Imperial Force unit war diaries, Australian War Memorial 23/36/4, December 1915.

131 See "Jesse Herbert Taylor", *The AIF Project*, UNSW Canberra, at www.aif.adfa.edu.au, extracted on 13 September 2020.

132 Matthews & Wilson 2011, 432.

133 Ferguson 1998, 198.

134 Ibid., 201-202.

135 See "1913 The Battle of Lemnos", *Age of Steel and Coal*, at www.sites.google.com/site/ageofsteeland coal, extracted on 17 November 2020.

136 Reginald Rupert Hoare, Army Service File 1915-1917, National Archives of Australia.

137 19th Battalion Australian Imperial Force unit war diaries, Australian War Memorial 23/36/5, January 1916 and 23/36/6, February 1916.

138 Thomas Hansen Shurey, Army Service File 1915-1916, National Archives of Australia.

139 5th Infantry Brigade Australian Imperial Force unit war diaries, Item numbers 23/5/9, March 1916.

140 See "19th Battalion". *First World War, 1914–1918 units*. Australian War Memorial. Archived from the original on 13 March 2011. Retrieved 19 March 2009.

141 See Matthews & Wilson 2011.

142 William John MacFarlane, Army Service File 1915-1917, National Archives of Australia.

143 7th Brigade, Australian Imperial Force unit war diaries, Item numbers 23/7/7, March 1916.

144 Daniel Joseph Ryan, Army Service File 1915-1916, National Archives of Australia.

145 See www.mariecorelli.org.uk

146 Atabaki 2016.

147 Robert Brown, Army Service File 1915-1919, National Archives of Australia.

148 Matthews & Wilson 2011, 423.

149 William Tom Bastin, Army Service File 1915-1919, National Archives of Australia.

150 John Shepherd Ryan, Army Service File 1914-1919, National Archives of Australia.

151 Hartley Elmer, Army Service File 1915-1920, National Archives of Australia.

152 Leopold Joseph Geddes, Army Service File 1915-1919, National Archives of Australia.

153 Arthur Henry Darley, Army Service File 1914-1919, National Archives of Australia.

154 See "Royal Navy Officers" extracted at www.naval-history.net on 19 September 2020.

155 See Errol Cappie Nepean Devlin, *The AIF Project*, UNSW Canberra, at www.aif.adfa.edu.au, extracted on 14 September 2020.

156 55th Battalion Australian Imperial Force unit war diaries, Item numbers 23/72/1, February 1916 and 23/72/2, March 1916.

157 See "David McConaghy", *The AIF Project*, UNSW Canberra, at www.aif.adfa.edu.au, extracted on 16 September 2020.

158 C.D. Coulthard-Clark (1983), "Irving, Godfrey George Howy (1867-1937)", *Australian Dictionary of Biography*, Vol 9, Melbourne University Press, 441-442.

159 Christopher Wray (2002), *Sir James Whiteside McCay: A Turbulent Life*, Oxford University Press, South Melbourne.

160 See "Norman Gibbins", *The AIF Project*, UNSW Canberra, at www.aif.adfa.edu.au, extracted on 8 September 2020 and Norman Gibbins, Roll of Honour, Australian War memorial, at www.awm.gov.au extracted on 20 September 2020.

161 See "Major General Godfrey Irving", *The AIF Project*, UNSW Canberra, at www.aif.adfa.edu.au, extracted on 20 September 2020.

162 55th Battalion, Australian Imperial Force unit war diaries, Australian War Memorial, Item numbers 23/72/2, March 1916.

163 See "Robert William Harpley", War Diary 1915-1916, Australian War Memorial 315 419/044/018.

164 Ibid.

165 Cook 2014, 27.

166 See "Colonel Harold Pope", *The AIF Project*, UNSW Canberra, at www.aif.adfa.edu.au, extracted on 20 September 2020.

167 Cook 2015, 362.

168 55th Battalion Australian Imperial Force unit war diaries, Item numbers 23/72/3, April 1916.

169 James Michael Egan, Army Service File 1915-1918, National Archives of Australia.

170 "Edward Peter Murphy", *The AIF Project*, UNSW Canberra, at www.aif.adfa.edu.au, extracted on 8 September 2020.

171 Phillip Clarence Corsie, Army Service File 1914-1919, National Archives of Australia.

172 See "Percy Wellesley Chapman", typescript copy of diary entries, March 1915 to June 1916, Australian War Memorial, 2016.30.61.

173 See "Berrol Mendelsohn", *The AIF Project*, UNSW Canberra, at www.aif.adfa.edu.au, extracted on 8 September 2020.

174 See Amanda Laugesen (editor), Glossary of Slang and Peculiar Terms in

Use in the A.I.F., Australian National University, School of Literature, Languages and Linguistics, www.slll.anu.edu.au extracted 20 July 2020.

175 Shermer 1973, 142.

176 See "Robert William Harpley", War Diary 1915-1916, Australian War Memorial 315 419/044/018.

177 Matthews & Wilson 2011, 75.

178 See "RMS Caledonia", *Wrecksite*, at www.wrecksite.edu, extracted on 17 November 2020.

179 See "Herbert D. Allen", diaries 12 February-30 September 1916, Australian War Memorial, 224 MSS183.

180 Ibid.

181 See "Frank Cecil Brown", diaries, Australian War Memorial, 1DRL/0160.

182 See "Robert William Harpley", War Diary 1915-1916, Australian War Memorial 315 419/044/018

183 55th Battalion Australian Imperial Force unit war diaries, Item numbers 23/72/5, July 1916.

184 Ibid.

185 See "George Thomasson Gill", diaries, State Library of NSW, ML MSS2765.

186 See "Herbert Henry Harris", diaries, State Library of NSW, ML MSS 2772.

187 55th Battalion Australian Imperial Force unit war diaries, Item numbers 23/72/5, July 1916.

188 Lee 2010, 64-66.

189 See "Herbert Henry Harris", diaries, State Library of NSW, ML MSS 2772.

190 Ibid.

191 See "George Thomasson Gill", diaries, State Library of NSW, ML MSS2765.

192 55th Battalion Australian Imperial Force unit war diaries, Item numbers 23/72/5, July 1916.

193 Cook 2014.

194 See Gary Sheffield (2015), "Haig, Douglas", International Encyclopedia of the First World War, at www.encyclopedia.1914-1918-on-line.net, extracted 15 October 2020.

195 See "Sir Henry Rawlinson", extracted at Firstworldwar.com, on 15 October 2020

196 Lee 2010, 194-195

197 See "Herbert Plumer", extracted at Firstworldwar.com, on 15 October 2020.

198 Lee 2010, 88-98.

199 "Gustav Scanzoni von Lichtenfels", The Prussian Machine at www.prussianmachine.com, extracted 9 October 2020.

200 Lee 2010, 142.

201 See "Lieutenant Colonel Ignatius Bertram Norris", Anzac Biographies, at www.anzac-biographies.com, extracted on 10 October 2020.

202 See "Percy Wellesley Chapman", typescript copy of diary entries, 26 July 1916 to 9 March 1917, Australian War Memorial, 2016.30.612.

203 Matthews 2014, 37.

204 See "Percy Wellesley Chapman", typescript copy of diary entries, 26 July 1916 to 9 March 1917, Australian War Memorial, 2016.30.612.

205 See "Robert William Harpley", War Diary 1915-1916, Australian War Memorial 315 419/044/018.

206 Quoted in Matthews 2014, 36.

207 Bean 1941c, 389.

208 Ibid., 408.

209 See "Percy Wellesley Chapman", typescript copy of diary entries, 26 July 1916 to 9 March 1917, Australian War Memorial, 2016.30.612.

210 See Bean 1941c, 403.

211 See "Percy Wellesley Chapman", typescript copy of diary entries, 26 July 1916 to 9 March 1917, Australian War Memorial, 2016.30.612.

212 See Bean 1941c, 408.

213 Matthews 2014, 44.

214 See "Robert William Harpley", War Diary 1915-1916, Australian War Memorial 315 419/044/018.

215 See "Percy Wellesley Chapman", typescript copy of diary entries, 26 July 1916 to 9 March 1917, Australian War Memorial, 2016.30.612.

216 See Bean 1941c, 420.

217 Bean 1941c, 431.

218 Ibid.

219 Matthews 2014, 53.

220 See "Robert William Harpley", War Diary 1915-1916, Australian War Memorial 315 419/044/018.

221 See "Percy Wellesley Chapman", typescript copy of diary entries, 26 July 1916 to 9 March 1917, Australian War Memorial, 2016.30.612.

222 See "Archibald Thomas Winter", Diary 1916, Australian war Memorial PR89/163.

223 See "Percy Wellesley Chapman", typescript copy of diary entries, 26 July 1916 to 9 March 1917, Australian War Memorial, 2016.30.612.

224 Matthews 2014, 57.

225 55th Battalion Australian Imperial Force unit war diaries, Item numbers 23/72/5, July 1916.

226 Bean 1941c, 431-432.

227 See "Archibald Thomas Winter", Diary 1916, Australian war Memorial PR89/163.

228 William Smith (1936), "Sapper's Diary: The Battle of Fromelles", *Reveille*, 1 July 1936, Vol 9, No 11.

229 Matthews 2014, 57

230 See "Percy Wellesley Chapman", typescript copy of diary entries, 26 July 1916 to 9 March 1917, Australian War Memorial, 2016.30.612.

231 See "Percy Wellesley Chapman", *The AIF Project*, UNSW Canberra, at www.aif.adfa.edu.au, extracted on 15 October 2020.

232 Matthews 2014, 90.

233 Lindsay 2008, 147.

234 Bean 1941c, 447.

235 Matthews 1979.

236 Carlyon 2006, 96.

237 See for example Carlyon 2006, Lee 2010, Lindsay 2008, and Fitzsimons 2015.

238 Carlyon 2006, 96.

239 Ibid.

240 Quoted in Lindsay 2008, 158.

241 Brandmayer 1933, 48-58 quoted in Williams 2005, 142.

242 W. Scheurmann, "The Battle of Fromelles – From our War Correspondent – W. Scheurmann", *Norddeutsche Zeitung*, 1 August 1916, quoted in Williams 2005, 145.

243 Quoted in Weber 2010, 147.

244 Library and Archives Canada 2012, 73.

245 Nurse Elsie Tranter quoted in Armstrong 2014, 79.

246 "S.S. St. David 1st W.W. Hospital Ship", Images of Industry, *National Museum of Wales*, at www.museum.wales, extracted 12 September 2020.

247 See "Victor Horatio Buller Sampson", *The AIF Project*, UNSW Canberra, at www.aif.adfa.edu.au, extracted on 8 September 2020.

248 Gilbert 1994, 481.

249 Ibid., 499.

250 See "Ivan Brunker Sherbon", *The AIF Project*, UNSW Canberra, at www.aif.adfa.edu.au, extracted on 8 September 2020.

251 Quoted in Matthews & Wilson 2011, 154.

252 See "James Whiteside Fraser McManamey", *The AIF Project*, UNSW Canberra, at www.aif.adfa.edu.au, extracted on 16 September 2020.

253 Matthews & Wilson 2011, 36.

254 See "Francis Coen", *The AIF Project*, UNSW Canberra, at www.aif.adfa.edu.au, extracted on 16 September 2020.

255 See "Reuben George Whiteman", *The AIF Project*, UNSW Canberra, at www.aif.adfa.edu.au, extracted on 16 September 2020.

256 See "Richard Feeney", *The AIF Project*, UNSW Canberra, at www.aif.adfa.edu.au, extracted on 16 September 2020.

257 See "Andrew John Berry", *The AIF Project*, UNSW Canberra, at www.aif.adfa.edu.au, extracted on 16 September 2020.

258 See "Reginald Clyde Compton", *The AIF Project*, UNSW Canberra, at www.aif.adfa.edu.au, extracted on 16 September 2020.

259 Francis Cameron Lincoln, Army Service File 1915-1919, National Archives of Australia.

260 See "Robert Cairns Amos Anderson", *The AIF Project*, UNSW Canberra, at www.aif.adfa.edu.au, extracted on 16 September 2020.

261 Harry Stanley Hind, Army Service File 1915-1919, National Archives of Australia.

262 Leonard Arthur Francis, Army Service File 1915-1916, National Archives of Australia.

263 Charles Henry Burns, Army Service File 1915-1916, National Archives of Australia.

264 Karl Matson, Army Service File 1915-1918, National Archives of Australia.

265 Charles Lindsay Davis, Army Service File 1915-1916, National Archives of Australia.

266 "Wounded Return Hospital Ship Karoola", *Argus*, 6 December 1915.

267 Quoted in Grant 2018, 339.

268 Quoted in Gilbert 1994, 478.

269 Bean 1941e, 532.

270 Norman Edgley, *The AIF Project*, UNSW Canberra, at www.aif.adfa.edu.au, extracted on 14 September 2020.

271 Joseph George Stewart, *The AIF Project*, UNSW Canberra, at www.aif.adfa.edu.au, extracted on 14 September 2020.

272 See Archibald Colin McPherson, Army Service File 1915-1918, National Archives of Australia.

273 Ibid.

274 Ibid.

275 William Thomas Burridge, Army Service File 1915-1917, National Archives of Australia.

276 See "Harry Duff Badmington", *The AIF Project*, UNSW Canberra, at www.aif.adfa.edu.au, extracted on 14 September 2020.

277 See "Richard Charles Badmington", *The AIF Project*, UNSW Canberra, at www.aif.adfa.edu.au, extracted on 14 September 2020.

278 See Francis Henry Quick, *The AIF Project*, UNSW Canberra, at www.aif.adfa.edu.au, extracted on 14 September 2020.

279 See Douglas Charles Hardy, Army Service File 1941-1945, National Archives of Australia and "Radio Active", The ABC Staff Journal, Sydney, Volume 11, No.5, June 17, 1957 Bibliography

About the Author

Peter Hendy has had a distinguished career both in the private sector and in government. He is an economist and company director. He has run national industry associations and been at the senior levels of the public service both in Australia and internationally, and has been Chief of Staff of the Minister for Defence. He is a former Federal Member of Parliament and a Minister of the Crown. He is the author of a number of books and has written articles for all the leading newspapers in Australia. He lives in Sydney with his family.

Index

www.ingramcontent.com/pod-product-compliance
Lightning Source LLC
LaVergne TN
LVHW020041110826
845155LV00029B/585
* 9 7 8 1 9 2 2 4 4 9 7 6 4 *